THE SHRINE AND CULT OF
MU'ĪN AL-DĪN CHISHTĪ OF AJMER

Shaykh Mu'īn al-dīn Chishtī was one of the most revered mystics of the Indian subcontinent in the thirteenth century. His tomb in Rajasthan is a centre of pilgrimage even today.

This book defines the role of Sufi mystics in Islam, and places Shaykh Mu'īn al-dīn in a historical context, disentangling the Mu'īn of history from the legendary creation of later chronicles. The author traces the reasons behind the rise of the legend and why it assumed the form it did. He also describes the history of the shrine, and the customs and hierarchy of attendants that have grown up around it in the last five hundred years.

This well written and researched classic will appeal to all visitors to Chishtī's dargah. Students and scholars of religion, Islamic studies, history, sociology, and philosophy will find it a valuable addition to their repertoire.

P.M. Currie was educated at Sherborne, Cambridge, and Oxford, where he obtained a D.Phil. A retired civil servant he has had postings in Jamaica, Washington, London, and Bonn.

*This volume is sponsored by
the Inter-Faculty Committee for South Asian Studies
University of Oxford*

Oxford University South Asian Studies Series

THE SHRINE AND CULT OF MU'ĪN AL-DĪN CHISHTĪ OF AJMER

P. M. CURRIE

OXFORD
UNIVERSITY PRESS

OXFORD
UNIVERSITY PRESS

YMCA Library Building, Jai Singh Road, New Delhi 110 001

Oxford University Press is a department of the University of Oxford.
It furthers the University's objective of excellence in research, scholarship,
and education by publishing worldwide in

Oxford New York
Auckland   Cape Town   Dar es Salaam   Hong Kong   Karachi
Kuala Lumpur   Madrid   Melbourne   Mexico City   Nairobi
New Delhi   Shanghai   Taipei   Toronto

With offices in
Argentina Austria Brazil Chile Czech Republic France Greece
Guatemala Hungary Italy Japan Poland Portugal Singapore
South Korea Switzerland Thailand Turkey Ukraine Vietnam

Oxford is a registered trade mark of Oxford University Press
in the UK and in certain other countries

Published in India
By Oxford University Press, New Delhi

First Published 1989
Oxford India Paperbacks 1992
New Edition 2006
Second impression 2007

ISBN-13: 978-0-19- 568329-5
ISBN-10: 0-19-568329-3

Printed by De Unique, New Delhi 110 018
Published by Oxford University Press
YMCA Library Building, Jai Singh Road, New Delhi 110 001

To my Father

Contents

Figures

Acknowledgements

I would like to record my gratitude to Simon Digby for his supervision and encouragement, to the many in Ajmer who assisted me, to the Oriental Institute and Exeter College, Oxford, for financial support, to Imam Muhammad Ahmad Ovaisi and Afsaneh Mashaikhi for help with the translations, and to my father for the index.

Transliteration

The system of transliteration on which the spelling is based is that of the Royal Asiatic Society.[1] For ease of reading, diacritical points and underlinings of *Ch, Gh, Kh,* and *Sh* have been omitted in the text, but a list of words with all diacritical marks which have been spelt without them in the text is given in Appendix II. Anglicized forms which have been preferred are also included in the list. For the sake of simplicity, spelling has been standardized throughout the text even in quotations from other authorities, and place names have been left in their familiar anglicized forms.

[1] *Journal of the Royal Asiatic Society,* 1924, pp. 172–6.

1

The Role of Saints in Islam

Scholars have tended to use the word 'saint' to translate a plurality of Arabic, Persian and Urdu terms. By rendering walī, murshid, shaykh, darvīsh, sufi, pīr or marabout as 'saint' the reader is led to believe that he is dealing with a single category. This obscures the considerable diversity which underlies these terms. There is a further danger that this simplistic translation glosses over the fact that saints in Christendom and 'saints' in Islam are produced by widely different cultural situations. Turner has drawn attention to this problem:

Arabic terms of marabout, darvīsh, sufi, walī cannot be translated into the Christian term of 'saint', because the history, institutions and cultural frameworks of these religions are distinctive. The centralised, complex and stringent process of canonisation is crucial to the Christian understanding of saintship. Precisely because no such centralised, ecclesiastical machinery exists in Islam, there is no official or homogenous terminology of *maraboutism* (saintship in Islam). When the western anthropologists talk about Islamic saints, they use the term as a shorthand for a diversity of roles.[1]

However, this shorthand is only justifiable if it can be demonstrated that there is a basic unity behind the diversity of types of 'saint' in Islam. The nature of this diversity, therefore, needs to be examined. This inquiry begins with a brief survey of the terminology involved in the context of Islam in the subcontinent of India. After looking at the range of this diversity, a minimal definition of 'saint' in the Muslim context will be suggested, and the reasons for the existence of saints will be explored.

Walī: This word, derived from a root which in Semitic languages expresses the idea of adherence, attachment, and nearness, means firstly: he who is close, follower, friend, relative ... . In religious

[1] B. S. Turner, *Weber and Islam*, p. 61.

2 Mu'īn al-dīn Chishtī of Ajmer

language the idea of nearness was extended also to the relations of men to God. ... From the general meaning of 'someone who is close' in Old Arabic usage the word was extended also to the protector, helper and patron, curiously enough also applied to divinely venerated beings of whom man believes that they help those who venerate them. Walī, the devout, pious man became walī equipped with the attribute of miracles, the intermediary (shāfi') between God and man.[2]

The latter meaning is not found in the Quran. In the Quran walī has several meanings:

That of a near relative whose murder demands vengeance (xvii, 59), that of friend of God (x, 63), or ally of God; it is also applied to God himself—'God is the friend of those who believe' (ii, 258). The same title was given to the Prophet and later it is one of the names of God in the Muslim rosary.[3]

However, later, in Sufi literature, walī came to mean specifically one who is close to God:

God has saints [awliyā', plural of walī] whom He has specially distinguished by His friendship and whom He has chosen to be the governors of His kingdom and has marked out to manifest His actions and has peculiarly favoured with diverse kinds of miracles (karāmat) and has purged of natural corruptions and has delivered from subjection to their lower soul and passions, so that all their thoughts are of Him and their intimacy is with Him alone.[4]

These 'friends of God' are organized into a hierarchy:

The saints have been classed in a hierarchy according to a system which is found in much the same form in different authors. There are always saints on earth; but their sanctity is not always apparent; they are not always visible. It is sufficient that their hierarchy goes on and that they are replaced on their death so that their number is always complete. 4,000 live hidden in the world and are themselves unconscious of their state. Others know one another and act together. These are in ascending order of merit: the akhyār to the number of 300; the abdāl, 40, the abrār, 7, the awtād, 4, the nukabā', 3 and the Pole, who is unique, the Qutb or Ghaws.[5]

---

[2] Goldziher, *Muslim Studies*, p. 332.
[3] Carra de Vaux, 'Walī', *Encyclopaedia of Islam*, vol. iv, Part 2, 33–4.
[4] al-Hujwīrī, *Kashf al-Mahjūb*, pp. 212–13.
[5] de Vaux, 'Walī', p. 34.

The terms pīr and murshid are used most confusingly by writers on the subject. The varying opinions on the meaning of these two words have been summarized by Mayer:

Darling distinguishes between the pīr as a healer (using this as a general term for the person who solves specific physical and moral problems) and the murshid as guide (using this term to denote the giver of general moral and spiritual exhortation and teaching).[6] ... Wilber distinguishes between the murshid as the spiritual preceptor and member of a Sufi order, and the pīr as the centre of the cult of saint worship.[7] ... And Westphal-Hellbusch remarks 'the murshids were and are holy-men, otherwise called pīr or faqīr but, in their capacity as spiritual leader, they are called murshid.'[8] On the other hand, a number of writers use the two terms synonymously when speaking of the role of spiritual guide. Titus, for example, states that 'the spiritual guide is known as the murshid, pīr or shaykh',[9] and O'Brien speaks of the necessity of having a pīr or murshid, spiritual adviser, a guide on the right path.[10] ... Again, Rose states that 'the pīr is also known as murshid, and corresponds to the shaykh of the Sufi'[11] ...

Mayer suggests that while both pīr and murshid may refer to the role of spiritual guide, murshid is not used to refer to the role of healer. This conclusion he supports with his own observations.[12] However, in my experience, this distinction is more ideal than real; in interviews a high proportion of Indo-Muslims did not recognize a difference between the two words, and regarded them as interchangeable. An explanation of this twin usage often given by those interviewed was that one was originally a Persian word and the other Arabic. There was some confusion as to which was which.

The distinctions, if any, between pīr and murshid are less important than the distinction between the two roles which they perform. As labels for these two roles the words are more

[6] Darling, *Rusticus Loquitur*, pp. 249, 302.
[7] Wilber, *Pakistan*, p. 101 and the following.
[8] Westphal-Hellbusch, *The Jat of Pakistan*, p. 33.
[9] Titus, *Islam in India and Pakistan*, p. 119.
[10] A. J. O'Brien, 'The Muhammadan Saints of the Western Panjab', *Journal of the Royal Anthropological Institute*, vol. 41 (1911), 517.
[11] H. A. Rose, *A Glossary of the Castes and Tribes of the Panjab*, vol. i, p. 522; A. C. Mayer, 'Pir and Murshid: An Aspect of Religious Leadership in W. Pakistan', *Middle Eastern Studies*, 3 (1966–7), 161–2.
[12] Mayer, 'Pir and Murshid', 162–4.

useful than as terms for two different 'types' of holy man. The confusion can be reduced by the introduction of a third term, shaykh.

The word shaykh has a variety of meanings—a venerable old man, the chief of a tribe or head of a village, a new convert to Islam. But it is also used as a title which encompasses both the roles implied by pīr and murshid, and is, therefore, more useful as both functions tend to be performed by the same person. Thus, an Indo-Muslim, when referring to his shaykh will often talk of his pīr-o murshid.

It is misleading for the terms Sufi, darvīsh, faqīr to be translated as 'saint'. They are wide-ranging in their meaning, and it is difficult, therefore, to be specific in their definition. For instance, a shaykh, murshid, or pīr might define himself as a faqīr, darvīsh or sufi but not all faqīrs, darvīshes and sufis qualify as shaykhs or murshids or pīrs. A sufi is one who tends towards the mystic life as it has developed within the framework of Islam, whereas a darvīsh or faqīr is one who is attached full-time to the religious life either as a dependant of a Sufi establishment or as an independent wandering mendicant.

This examination of the range of words usually translated as 'saint' indicates the variety of types which lie behind the use of the word in the Muslim context. This variety is further emphasized by that which is subsumed in each of these Muslim categories.

To be accepted as a great shaykh in his lifetime an individual needed to possess certain qualities: an ability to perform miracles, descent from the Prophet or his companions, connections with a prestigious Sufi *silsila*, a mastery of Islamic doctrines and Sufi texts, a tendency towards ecstasy, a reputation for eccentricity or asceticism. A shaykh could have all these qualifications, or a combination of some of them.

The possible combinations of these qualities could give rise to a shaykh who approximated to the ideal portrayed in Sufi hagiography—a man of the greatest learning and spirituality who guided his disciples along the mystical path and dispensed help and advice to all who came to his *khānqāh*. He, therefore, had two functions to perform—he acted as spiritual teacher and guide to his disciples. However, the number of individuals who were wholly dedicated to the spiritual life was few compared to those who came to the shaykh to 'exploit his spiritual powers to cure an ailment or fulfill a wish'.[13]

Since a shaykh was expected to heal both mental and bodily diseases by spiritual means, large crowds assembled in the *khānqāhs*.... People who sought the guidance of a shaykh in their perilous journey in the realm of the spirit were few; most of the visitors thronged round him for the solution of their worldly problems, through amulets, blessings or recommendations.[14]

The ideal shaykh was a physician of men's souls.

The shaykhs seldom allowed anybody to leave the *khānqāh* unsatisfied.... With their deep insight into human character they assuaged the wounds of their visitors and gave them that unshakable faith in God and moral values which sustained them in the midst of the severest tribulations of life.[15]

Moreover, the ideal shaykh personified the values of Islam. He carried the burden of rendering the transcendant Allāh relevant and accessible to the needs of everyday life and the common man.[16] He was believed to be endowed with supranormal powers, with such powers he could ameliorate the lot of his followers. He was an agent of the miraculous, to whom one could turn in difficulty. The shaykh's

prayers, and occult and thaumaturgic techniques tranquillised mind and emotions, appeasing or curing psychological as well as bodily ills.[17]

[13] M. Mujeeb, *The Indian Muslims*, p. 121.
[14] al-Hujwīrī, *Kashf al-Mahjūb*, p. 55.
[15] K. A. Nizami, 'Some Aspects of Khanqah Life in Mediaeval India', *Studia Islamica*, p. 63.
[16] Cf. Gellner, *Saints of the High Atlas*, p. 8.
[17] Spencer-Trimingham, *The Sufi Orders in Islam*, p. 131. The discussion here is confined to the ideal shaykh. The individual 'success rate' of any one shaykh is not relevant. It is the beliefs about shaykhs and their functions which are important in the present context. However, there is no reason to doubt that, as medical practitioners, they could be successful. That popular belief had a basis in reality is supported by recent research which suggests that 'faith healing' can have marked psychological and physiological effects. Much work has been carried out on the 'Placebo Effect', whereby the prescription of a chemically inert medicine results in a successful cure. Since a placebo is inert, the beneficial effect must lie in its symbolic power. But such

However, the fact that spiritual prestige could be inherited through ties of lineal descent meant that a type of shaykh very different from this ideal could flourish. This is particularly evident in the religious life of rural areas where almost every village has its hereditary shaykh.

The landlord has tenants, the pīr murīds (disciples). The landlord lived on his rents, the pīr on his offerings. ... There is almost nothing to be said for the ordinary pīr. He is even more of a parasite (than the landlord) and exploits the peasants' ignorance of the next world as systematically as any money-lender his ignorance of this. ... These men, indeed, are spiritual quacks who forget that many of the early pīrs, from whom they claim descent and derive authority, were true physicians—healers of the soul and quickeners of the spirit.[18]

An individual may be revered as saintly in Islam solely because of his insanity or eccentricity.

There is ... a class of holy men and women that is recruited from idiots and madmen. Derangement of the mind is in any case attributed to supernatural influence. ... Harmless lunatics are venerated as saints, whose reason is in heaven while the body is on earth. They are not held responsible for any absurdities they commit.[19]

Extreme asceticism is also a sufficient qualification for sanctity. Indo-Muslim hagiography is replete with stories of

---

a symbol can prove instrumentally effective and cause substantial physiological change. 'The most likely supposition is that it (the placebo) gains its potency through being a tangible symbol of the physician's role as healer. In our society, the physician validates his power by prescribing medication, just as the shaman in a primitive tribe may validate his by ... spitting out a bit of blood-stained down at the proper moment.' (J. D. Frank, *Persuasion and Healing*, p. 66). Thus, the amulets which Muslim shaykhs distributed to alleviate suffering were a kind of placebo. There was a shared set of beliefs between shaykh and 'patient' and therefore a confidence in the treatment. As well as possible physiological improvement there would also be psychological gain. 'The ideology and ritual supply the patient with a conceptual framework for organising his chaotic, mysterious, and vague distress and give him a plan of action, helping to regain a sense of direction and mastery to resolve his inner conflicts.' (Frank, *Persuasion and Healing*, p. 63.) Lévi-Strauss makes a similar point in *Structural Anthropology*, p. 198.

[18] Darling, *Rusticus Loquitur*, pp. 336-7. Cf Burton, *History of Sindh*, pp. 204-7, and Manucci, *Memoirs of the Mughal Court*, pp. 21-2; both gave similar, but rather more colourful, descriptions of the degeneracy of hereditary shaykhs.

[19] Westermarck, *Pagan Survivals in Muhammadan Civilisation*, p. 93.

individuals who live in caves or the jungle, spurning the company of all save Allāh.[20] Such holy men are not only encountered in the literature, they are still to be met with in the contemporary Indo-Muslim world.

Others may derive their sanctity from millenarian ambition. For example, Saiyid Muhammad Mahdī, who lived between 1443 and 1504, is still believed by his followers to have been the last Imām, the promised Mahdī.[21]

A major distinction between types of shaykh is that between *ba-shar'* and *be-shar'*. The former attempted to minimize their differences from the ulama' and sought to abide by the sharī'a. In contrast were the *be-shar'* darvīshes who were deliberately antinomian. The *qalandars* are an example of this type:

The way of life and recorded behaviour of the *qalandars* and associated orders are those of militant protest-groups of an extremist nature, not only rejecting the assumptions regarding what constitutes a good life current in the Indo-Muslim community but also acting in public in a manner intended to provoke opposition. Their garb was a deliberately bizarre and outrageous uniform. Their *samā'*, or musical parties, ... placed strong insistence on the practice of *Nazar ilā'l-murd*, gazing at good-looking boys. ... They not only resorted to drugs of the hashish family, but could be seen to do so in the most provocative circumstances, scattering it over the *sajjāda* (prayer-carpet) of a great Shaykh. In many of the instances recording the arrival of *qalandar* bands or of individual *qalandars* at Sufi *khānqāhs*, their behaviour is of a calculated impropriety, designed to question the atmosphere of reverence which surrounded the presiding Sufi Shaykh. ... Demands for accommodation and alms were made in an aggressive and threatening manner, with resorts to violence if their demands were not met. ... There can be little doubt that the strength and attraction of the movement lay in its extreme antinomianism or repudiation of the received values of society.[22]

So far only those who have been recognized for their sanctity during their own lifetime have been mentioned. A second

[20] See also Mu'īn al-dīn Chishtī, *Anīs al-Arwāh*, pp. 5–6; Muhammad Gesūdarāz, *Jawāmi' al-Kilm*, p. 213; Muhammad Ghawsī Shattārī, *Gulzār-i Abrār*, p. 219; Rukn al-dīn Quddusī, *Lata'if-i Quddusī*, pp. 18–19.

[21] Sir Richard Carnac Temple, 'A General View of the Indian Muslim Saints', Chapter 7, pp. 1–12 (MS in BSOAS Library); Elliot and Dowson, *The History of India as Told by its Own Historians*, vol. 4, pp. 501–3.

[22] Digby, 'Qalandars and Related Groups' (Unpublished paper), pp. 24–5.

category of saint involves those who are sanctified after their death. Hasluck recognized that 'It is possible for a dead man to become a saint posthumously, if certain phenomena considered characteristic of the resting place of saints, in particular luminous appearances, occur at his tomb.'[23] However, it is not only miracles which prompt this kind of posthumous vogue. Martyrdom is another qualification for posthumous sanctity, a *shahīd* being considered especially holy because of the status of jihad (holy war) in Islam.[24]

The hereditary nature of spirituality means that an individual may need to explain and legitimize his spiritual authority by attributing it in part to inheritance from a former darvīsh. Thus, a darvīsh may be upgraded in the spiritual hierarchy after his death to validate the claims of a later shaykh or his followers.[25]

A third major category of 'saint' includes those who can have little claim to an earthly existence, but who are nevertheless at the centre of lively cults.

All over India buildings, which are called tombs or shrines, and old structures of varying description, with a forgotten history, have one or more attendants, who make a sort of living out of them. They are, of course, definitely assigned by their caretakers to some holy personage, not now traceable. Specimens of this class are the *naugazas* ... who are quite innumerable ... More often than not the *naugaza* is nothing more than a tomb or shrine or even only a mound—in one case the *naugaza* tomb is a disused milestone—that has acquired sanctity by legend.[26]...

The *naugaza* and his like introduce us to a class of saint that has a name but no personality that can be ascertained. He may indeed be merely a peg on whi͙   ͙ hang a proverb, an aphorism, a story or a legend—a being '   ' in as a reality by the people, but not traceable as such c   ·ation.[27]

[23] F. W. Hasluck, *Christianity and Islam under the Sultans*, pp. 255–6.
[24] The class of *shahīd* has come to include many isolated tombs of European army officers, who died in India and are revered as if they had been Muslim martyrs. See Editorial Notebook, *Bengal Past and Present* (July–September, 1928), 61. Temple, *Indian Muslim Saints*, Chapter 9, pp. 3, 15.
[25] An example of this elevation is furnished by the posthumous career of Mu'īn al-dīn Chishtī. See below, pp. 66–96.
[26] Temple, 'Indian Muslim Saints', Introduction, p. 28.
[27] Ibid., Chapter 11, p. 1. Numerous examples are then cited.

Muslim substitutes for Hindu gods, heroes, and sacred springs, trees and mountains, provide a further category of 'saint'. An example is the shrine of Zinda Pīr in the valley of the Shori river in the Lund country, which

stands behind a hot sulphur spring which is efficacious in cases of skin disease and lameness. As the name implies the spring is believed to be frequented by an immortal and invisible saint.[28]

Here is a case of a pre-Islamic cult associated with a holy spring being transformed into a Muslim saint-cult. In a similar way, the Muslim saint, Sakhī Sarwar, has been identified with 'the benevolent fertilizing earth-god of the Hindu'.[29] The shrine of Shāh Shams al-dīn Daryaī provides another instance of the same process and here, remarkably, Hindus have managed to retain the position of guardians of the tomb. A story is told which links the cult of Shams al-dīn Daryaī with the worship of a former tree-spirit:

Some years after the death of Daryaī some carpenters felled a *Siras* tree which grew close to his tomb and began to cut it into several pieces to use in a building. Suddenly a terrible voice drew their attention, the earth began to tremble and the trunk of the tree raised itself up at the same time. The workmen ran away frightened and the tree did not delay in becoming green.[30]

Gugga Pīr occupies a similarly ambivalent position. Temple has examined the traditions associated with him and concludes that he was originally 'Gugga, the Rajput gūrū and defender of Hinduism', who became 'Gūrū Gugga, the Zinda Pīr and Muslim saint' and that 'the legends about him were twisted round to meet the new conditions.'[31]

Khizr is a mythical figure in Islam who is often found to take over the shape of former Hindu gods and spirits and become the object of an originally 'pagan' cult.

It is now generally recognized that the conquered nations who were converted to Islam managed to carry with them into the new religion

[28] *Gazetteer of the Dera Ghazi Khan District, Panjab*, p. 55.
[29] Temple, 'Indian Muslim Saints', Chapter 28, p. 8b.
[30] J. H. Garcin de Tassy, *Mémoires sur les Particularités de la Religion Musulmane dans l'Inde*, pp. 92, ff.
[31] Temple, 'Indian Muslim Saints', Chapter 28, p. 8b.

many of their former doctrines. In a similar way Khizr became the depository of all kinds of ancient myths and popular rites current in lands occupied by Islam.[32]

He appears, for instance, in India as a substitute for the Hindu gods of the water and is particularly revered by sailors and fishermen. In Sind the Hindu cult of the Indus, hypostasized in the figure of Uderolāl, has been transformed into the cult of Khizr. Likewise, the fishermen of the Panjab worship Khizr instead of the Indus and elsewhere he is found as the Muslim substitute for Ganga, the mother.[33] Such examples of Hindu gods or spirits changing their names and becoming Muslim saints could be multiplied almost indefinitely.[34]

These examples reveal the diversity of the idea of 'sainthood' in Indian Islam. But it needs to be considered whether, beneath this diversity, there are any common characteristics which could justify talking of 'saints' as if this was an intelligible, single concept in the Muslim context.

Several attempts have been made to do this in the past. Thus, Nicholson identified ecstasy as the necessary qualification of sainthood:

Neither deep learning in divinity, nor devotion to good works, nor asceticism, nor moral purity makes the Muhammadan a saint; he may have all or none of these things, but the only indispensable qualification is that of ecstasy or rapture which is the outward sign of 'passing-away' from the phenomenal self. Anyone thus enraptured is a walī, and when such persons are recognized through their power of working miracles, they are venerated as saints.[35]

This is clearly not always the case. Some 'saints' have explicitly pronounced against miracles, and there is seldom any sign of the 'passing-away' of hereditary pīrs, who, though devoid of

---

[32] I. Friedlander, 'Khizr', *Encyclopaedia of Religion and Ethics*, vol. 7, 695.

[33] G. E. L. Carter, 'Religion in Sind', *Indian Antiquary*, Vol. XLVI and D. Ibbetson, *Outlines of Panjab Ethnography*, para. 219.

[34] For a similar observation but in a different context, see E. Westermarck, *Ritual and Belief in Morocco*, vol. 1, p. 91. For the tenacity of Hindu cults in a Muslim guise see, among other things, Y. Husain, *L'Inde Mystique au Moyen Âge*, p. 17 and J. Wise, 'The Muhammadans of Eastern Bengal', *Journal of the Asiatic Society of Bengal*, vol. 63 (1894), 34.

[35] R. A. Nicholson, *The Mystics of Islam*, p. 123.

The Role of Saints in Islam   11

any spiritual qualities, are still greatly reverenced. Indeed, it is difficult to understand how the apocryphal inhabitants of nine-yard tombs (*naugazas*) or holy springs could be 'enraptured'. Turner suggests 'a necessary but not sufficient condition for Islamic saintship is descent from an established holy founder and ultimately from the Prophet.'[36] This, too, is misleading. Such descent claims may well improve the status of an individual but there are many 'saints' with no such claims even if their followers soon provide them.[37]

O'Brien made another attempt to provide this elusive, necessary condition of Muslim sainthood. 'It is not essential that saints should be of known piety. They are approved because of their magical powers and not for their spiritual quality.'[38] Temple agrees with this:

It does not matter who your pīr or saintly guardian is or what his personal character, as long as you can rely on his magical power to help you in distress and look after you generally.[39]

Thus, an individual is a 'saint' if he is believed to be able to provide for human needs through supernatural intervention. However, this definition would still exclude some 'saints'. The definition must make room for the 4,000 walī 'who are concealed and do not know one another and are not aware of the excellence of their state, but in all circumstances are hidden from themselves and from mankind.'[40] By definition such 'saints' have no followers and none of the magical powers that O'Brien and Temple maintain are a vital element of saintship.

These attempts to provide the essential, necessary qualification for 'sainthood' all deal with the consequences of sainthood, rather than its cause. That which unites walī, pīr, shaykh and murshid into a single category is more fundamental; it is their relationship with Allāh. They are close to Allāh and special recipients of *baraka*.

[36] Turner, *Weber and Islam*, p. 65.
[37] C. Shackle, *Some Problems of Islamic Sociology in S.E. Asia*, p. 79.
[38] O'Brien, 'Saints of the Western Panjab', p. 509.
[39] Temple, 'Indian Muslim Saints', Chapter 27, p. 4.
[40] al-Hujwīrī, *Kashf al-Mahjūb*, p. 213.

Baraka can be translated by 'beneficent force, of divine origin, which causes superabundance in the physical sphere, and prosperity and happiness in the psychic order'.[41]

A saint is a 'person who has *baraka* in an extraordinary degree'.[42] He receives this *baraka* because of his position of peculiar proximity to Allāh. The attributes of saints, such as have been listed above, are signs that the individual possesses *baraka*. The purpose of the saint cult is to mobilize the *baraka* embodied in the saint for either esoteric or mundane purposes.[43]

There is, however, a certain circularity in this attempted definition of a 'saint' in Islam. An individual is a saint because he has certain qualities; but these qualities are the consequence of his being a saint. To escape the circle the idea of *baraka* may be invoked. *Baraka* is a gift from Allāh. But this does not break the circle for the observer who is detached from the belief system. In theory Allāh chooses all those whom he wishes to use as his intermediaries by his gift of *baraka*. In reality the choice is made by the people.[44]

The essence of Muslim sainthood to the believer is derived from the particular relationship of proximity between Allāh and the saint. The saint is believed to translate this relationship into action in the phenomenal world. In the case of pīr, murshid, and shaykh (and the walī who is recognized by his fellowmen) this will take the form of spiritual and material aid to their followers. The hidden walī, while not apparently capable of this, are used by Allāh as 'the governors of the universe ... through the blessing of their advent the rain falls from heaven, and through the purity of their lives the plants spring up from the earth and through their spiritual influence the Muslim gains victories over the unbelievers.'[45]

---

[41] G. S. Colin, 'Barakat', *Enc. of Islam* (new ed.), p. 1032. Cf. D. F. Eickelman, *Moroccan Islam, Tradition and Society in a Pilgrimage Centre*, p. 160.
[42] Westermarck, *Ritual and Belief*, p. 120; cf. Turner, *Weber and Islam*, p. 65.
[43] Cf. C. Geertz, *Islam Observed*, pp. 50–1; Eickelman, *Moroccan Islam*, p. 158.
[44] This is clearly not possible for the hidden walī who are elected by Allāh but for the unbelieving observer these do not exist. See E. Gellner, *Saints of the High Atlas*, p. 151; Eickelman, *Moroccan Islam*, p. 180.
[45] al-Hujwīrī, *Kashf al-Mahjūb*, p. 213.

Thus sainthood in Islam is essentially a function of a relationship—the relationship of the saint to Allāh in the eyes of the believer, and the relationship of the saint to his followers in the eyes of the observer—rather than any particular quality of the saint's personality or spirituality. The accepted signs of this relationship (eccentricity, asceticism, descent, learning, spiritual discipline, expertise in ecstatic techniques, etc.), where visible, are sufficiently all-embracing and elastic not to disqualify any individual on the grounds of his personality, and where they are absent they can soon be supplied.[46] This relative unimportance of the saint as an individual with peculiar qualifications is underlined by an observation of O'Brien:

> Though every peasant must have a pīr, few take trouble over the selection of any particular one. In places, for instance, they are chosen by writing the names of several on scraps of paper and taking the first that happens to sink in the water into which they are thrown.[47]

There is a similarly casual approach in the choice of which tomb should be at the centre of a saint cult. It may be a disused milestone, the last resting place of a European army officer, the grave of a nine-yard giant, or the mausoleum of an outstanding Sufi shaykh. They all share in being symbols of the continuing process of divine grace at work in this world. It is a special relationship, not any external characteristic, which is the basic qualification of sainthood in Islam and which enables all saints to act as intermediaries between the believer and Allāh and symbolize his continued interest in the phenomenal world.

It is this underlying unity of a shared relationship which justifies the use of the one word 'saint' to signify in shorthand the diversity of terms and types which have been discussed above.

However, the very existence of such 'saints' in Islam demands explanation; the veneration of saints is clearly opposed by the word of Allāh as revealed through his Prophet in the Quran.

In ancient Islam an insurmountable barrier divides an infinite and unapproachable Godhead from weak and finite humanity. ... No

---

[46] See below, pp. 88–96.
[47] O'Brien, *Saints of the Western Panjab*, pp. 510–11.

human perfection can participate in the realm of infinite perfections. ... There is no creature which, owing to its perfection, deserves even a shadow of the veneration due to God; there is no cult conceivable which is directed towards an object other than Allāh, no call for help, no recourse in misfortune is thinkable, except to Allāh.[48]

The Quran polemicizes against those others who 'worship their rabbis and their masters, and the Messiah, the son of Mary, as gods beside Allāh; though they were ordered to serve one God only. There is no God but Him.'[49]

According to the Quran these 'gods beside Allāh' were powerless. They could

never create a single fly though they combine to do this, and if a fly carried away a speck of dust from them they could never retrieve it.[50]

Even Muhammad was regarded as an ordinary mortal:

The fact of election to the office of prophet is not due to the perfection of the individual concerned, nor can such perfection be acquired by spiritual endeavour; the prophet's appointment is merely an arbitrary action of God. ... The prophet is no more perfect than any other man, but as human as everybody else, and only God's arbitrary grace makes an unworthy person the interpreter of His will.[51]

It is significant that Muhammad's enemies were constantly demanding of him displays of supernatural powers and transcendental knowledge. For example, 'They solemnly swear by Allāh that if a sign be given them they would believe in it.'[52] Or again, 'The unbelievers ask, "Why has no sign been given him by his Lord?" Say: "Allāh alone has knowledge of what is hidden." '[53] Such signs were consistently denied them, but, in spite of these denials, his supporters tended to credit him with such supranormal gifts. They could not understand how the last and greatest of the prophets could not be equipped with the powers which any sage or fortune-teller of the contemporary Arab world could boast.[54]

[48] I. Goldziher, *Muslim Studies*, vol. 2, pp. 255–6.
[49] Quran, 9 : 31.   [50] Ibid., 22 : 73.
[51] Goldziher, *Muslim Studies*, vol. 2, p. 257.
[52] Quran, 6 : 109.   [53] Ibid., 10 : 20.
[54] Goldziher, *Muslim Studies*, vol. 2, p. 260.

Contact with the Christian Church, as it grew closer after conquest, brought about a rivalry between religious heroes. It was inconceivable that the central figure of Islam should have been without that supernatural power which, especially to the Christians of the day, seemed so important and so convincing a characteristic of the Chosen of the Lord.[55]

So, in spite of himself, 'It did not take long before a thousand miracles of the Prophet could be listed.'[56] Thus was the gap between the divine and the human bridged. The way was now free to equip human beings with supernatural gifts, and so the saints with their claims to veneration and invocation appear.[57]

Muhammad had not been able to obliterate altogether earlier pagan beliefs. With the defeat of the ancient gods and masters of their old traditions, Muslim converts tended to create mediators between themselves and the omnipotent and transcendant Allāh. The cult of the saints satisfies, within a monotheistic religion, a polytheistic need to fill the enormous gap between men and God; a need which 'originated on the soil of the old pantheon.'[58]

While the life and work of Muhammad closed the cycle of prophecy, Allāh did not leave men wholly without guidance. There was the revealed law, and the ulama' to guard and interpret it. Other mechanisms soon developed to help fill the lacuna that divided man from Allāh; for the Shī'as there was the Imām and for the Sufis the possibility of a direct communion with God. The common man soon came to believe that such Sufi divines could act as intermediaries between themselves and Allāh. In the words of al-Hujwīrī:

God has caused the prophetic evidence to remain down to the present day, and has made the saints the means whereby it is manifested, in order that the signs of the Truth and the proof of Muhammad's veracity may continue to be clearly seen.[59]

The veneration of saints was soon established as a major characteristic of Muslim life. The scholars were left to seek

[55] Von Grunebaum, *Muhammadan Festivals*, p. 68.
[56] Goldziher, *Muslim Studies*, vol. 2, p. 262.   [57] Ibid.
[58] K. Hose, *Handbuch des Protestantischen Polemik*, quoted Goldziher, *Muslim Studies*, vol. 2, p. 259.
[59] al-Hujwīrī, *Kashf al-Mahjūb*, p. 21.

theological justification for this development which contradicted the original principles of Islam. This was possible because
Islam is endowed with a certain degree of flexibility through
the operation of *ijmāʿ*:

Ijmāʿ leaves the door open to the entry of new formulae and opinions,
combatted at first as dangerous innovations (*bida*). Then, as resistance
dies down, they are partially admitted by the orthodox schools and
finally confirmed by *ijmāʿ*, from which they obtain at least a sort of
passport, a *tolerari potest*. We may instance the cult of the Prophet,
the festival ordained in his honour ... the belief in miracles ... the
existence and intercession of the saints ... the veneration of their
tombs.[60]

Hadīs were soon manufactured to support this cult of saints.
For instance, Allāh is made to say: 'He who appears hostile
against a walī, on him I declare war.'[61] The theologians were
not long in forming a scholarly rationale to substantiate such
hadīs.[62]

After centuries of mystical experimentation mysticism came to
embrace a Logos doctrine which, without impairing the divine Unity,
provided a philosophical basis for the practical devotion to saints and
the Prophet which had formed in response to people's need.[63]

Ibn al-ʿArabī developed the doctrine of the pre-existent
Muhammad al-Haqīqat al-Muhammadiyya who became incarnate in Adam, the prophets and the *aqtāb*, each of whom is
insān al-kāmil (the Perfect Man).[64]

The need for direct knowledge of the Word of God brings *Haqīqat
al-Muhammadiyya*, the Logos, in every epoch to take on the form of
one known as *Qutb Zamanihī* (the Axis of His Age), who manifests
himself only to a few chosen mystics.[65]

In this theological scheme the saint is the living symbol of the
qutb. The disciple should, therefore, become absorbed into his

[60] H. Lammens, *Islam, Beliefs and Institutions*, p. 95.
[61] Quoted Goldziher, *Muslim Studies*, vol. 2, p. 336.
[62] Some sects, notably the *Ahmadiyya* (see C. Padwick, *Muslim Devotions*,
p. 237) and the *Mutazillites* (see al-Hujwīrī, *Kashf al-Mahjūb*, p. 215) have
always been hostile to the idea of saints in Islam.
[63] Spencer-Trimingham, *The Sufi Orders of Islam*, p. 161.
[64] ʿAfifi, *The Mystical Philosophy of Ibn al-ʿArabī*, pp. 66–92.
[65] Spencer-Trimingham, *The Sufi Orders of Islam*, p. 163.

shaykh, and in that way he 'is spiritually introduced to the Prophet'.[66] It is worth noting here the close link with Shī'ism. The *qutb* correlates with the Shī'ite idea of the Imām.[67]

Some of the Sufi teachings about the primordial light of Muhammad and the theories of saintship correspond very closely in their hierarchical structures to Shī'ite theories.[68]

Some would go so far as to agree that 'the *Qutb* and the Imām are two expressions possessing the same meaning and referring to the same person.'[69] Al-Tabataba'i makes the same point:

Sanctity resulting from the initiation into the spiritual path, which Sufis consider as the perfection of man, is a state which, according to Shī'ite belief, is possessed in its fullness by the Imām and through the radiance of his being can be attained by his true followers.[70]

The parallelism of Shī'ism and Sufism is significant for it implies that, despite their divergent techniques, there was a gulf in the stark, rigid monotheism preached by Muhammad which needed to be bridged.

The Sufis and Shī'is preserve the spiritual sense of the divine revelation.[71] Both provide man with a way to God and bridge the gap between them. The following quotation helps to illustrate why there was this need for intermediaries:

I discussed more than once with this officer the necessity of having a pīr or murshid, a spiritual adviser, a guide to the right path, etc., and pointed out that if the Deity was All-Knowing, All-Powerful, and Omni-Present, He could have no need for any intermediaries. After arguing for some time, he hit on an idea which he thought would appeal to me. 'Sahib', he said, 'you are the Deputy Commissioner, the Head of the District, and all local affairs are in your hands. In order to know everything and to superintend everything, you have to be very busy. I am fairly high among your subordinates, but even I cannot invade your rooms at any moment. I have to go to the doorkeepers, and they lead me to your presence if you are at liberty.'[72]

[66] Ibid.
[67] A. Schimmel, *Mystical Dimensions of Islam*, p. 83.
[68] Ibid.
[69] Saiyid Haydar 'Alī, quoted S. H. Nasr, *Sufi Essays*, p. 111.
[70] al-Tabataba'i, *Shī'ite Islam*, p. 114.
[71] Spencer-Trimingham, *The Sufi Orders of Islam*, p. 133.
[72] O'Brien, *Saints of the Western Panjab*, p. 517.

As time elapsed, the presence and life of Muhammad became increasingly remote. The popular imagination required more immediate and accessible substitutes, and these substitutes were the saints.

The concept of sinlessness and infallibility, which the scholastics had come to attribute to Muhammad, began to be attributed, though to a lesser degree, to the saints. The Traditions of the saints assumed an importance almost as great as the Prophetic Traditions, and because of the simplicity of their form and content, and the more familiar background of time and space in which they were produced, they soon achieved great popularity.[73]

Orthodoxy had come to accept the idea of prophetic intercession; this aspect of the prophetic function was also passed on to the saints. As the cult of the Prophet developed and passed from popular belief into respectable doctrine, reverence for the places associated with him increased.[74] The beginnings of the veneration of sacred places are found in the earliest practices of Islam. The cult of the Kaʿba was in part inspired by the need to render pagan ceremonies acceptable to the new order.

'The further we move on in time the more richly blossoms the reverence towards holy memorial places.'[75] Tradition has it that 'Allāh forbade the soil to consume the bodies of prophets buried in it.'[76] This belief was extended to include the bodies of saints and martyrs. Their tombs were, therefore, intrinsically worth visiting for they continued to survive there. The idea of pilgrimage was not alien to Islam with its prescriptive hajj, and Goldziher notices how there was

an endeavour to attribute the privileges of the sanctuary at Mecca to other sacred places. This probably sprang partly from practical needs … it was desired to provide the poorer sections of the population in

[73] N. Hasan, *Chishti and Suhrawardi Movements in Mediaeval India*, p. 23.

[74] H. Delehaye, *The Legends of the Saints*, p. 28: 'The people as a whole is attracted by the material side of things, its thoughts and feelings are all associated with objects of sense … and so great men live less in the people's memory than in the stones, rocks, and buildings with which their names have become associated.'

[75] Goldziher, *Muslim Studies*, vol. 2, pp. 279–80.

[76] Quoted ibid., p. 286.

outlying parts of the Muslim world with some substitute for this important religious function.[77]

Gesūdarāz of Gulbarga

was told in one of his reveries that when, for good reason, people were unable to make the pilgrimage to Mecca, a visit once in their lives to his mausoleum would convey the same merit.[78]

Gradually beliefs and practices associated with the Prophet were transferred to the saints, until the saints became almost substitutes for the Prophet. Hence, traditions such as 'The shaykh in his group is like the Prophet in his country';[79] or 'The shaykh in the midst of his murīds, is as Muhammad in the midst of his companions.'[80]

This background of a developing interest in, and acceptance of saint-cults in Islam is an essential basis of any detailed study of Mu'īn al-dīn. Only against such a background does the emergence of this historically shadowy figure become intelligible.

---

[77] Ibid., p. 288.
[78] Sharif, J., *Islam in India*, p. 210.
[79] Quoted Schimmel, *Mystical Dimensions*, p. 237.
[80] Shihāb al-dīn 'Umar Suhrawardī, *Awārif al-Ma'ārif*, p. 19.

2

The Quest for the
Mu'īn al-dīn Chishtī of History

The purpose of this chapter is to disentangle the Mu'īn al-dīn of history from the Mu'īn al-dīn of faith and legend. There has so far been little scholarly success in de-mystifying the Mu'in al Din legend.[1]

Unfortunately, there are no reliable histories which refer to Mu'īn al-dīn. The three contemporary historians do not mention him.[2] There remains the mystic literature which consists of four different genres: *malfūzāt*—the collected conversations and discourses of Sufi shaykhs; *maktūbāt*—the collected correspondence of the shaykh; mystical treatises and poems written by the shaykh; and *tazkirāt*—compilations of anecdotes about the shaykh.

All such literary types are well-represented in the bibliography of Mu'īn al-dīn. The four categories will be considered below in turn.

Malfūzāt. Mu'īn al-dīn is alleged to have recorded the conversations of his murshid, Shaykh 'Usmān Hārwanī, in a volume entitled *Anīs al-Arwāh*. The conversations of Mu'īn al-dīn are said to have been committed to writing by his khalīfa, Shaykh

[1] K. A. Nizami, 'Khwāja Mu'īn al-dīn Hasan Chishtī', *Encyclopaedia of Islam*, New edition, vol. 2, pp. 49, 50, contains biographical comments on Mu'īn al-dīn's career but these must be treated with care. The three sources that are drawn on—the *Siyar al-Awliyā'*, the *Siyar al-Arifīn*, and *Akhbār al-Akhyār*—are not reliable. In some cases they contradict each other and in others they draw on apocryphal works.

[2] Minhāj al-Sirāj Jūzjānī, *Tabaqat-i Nasirī*; Fakhr-i Mudabbir, *Adab al-Muluk*; Sadr al-dīn Hasan Nizami, *Tāj l-Ma'sir*; K. A. Nizami, *Some Aspects of Religion and Politics in Thirteenth Century India*, p. 181.

Qutb al-dīn Bakhtyār Ūshī, in the *Dalīl al-ʿĀrifīn*. However, both internal and external evidence show that both these works are fabrications. The pervasive element of the miraculous need not be relied on alone to establish that both works are apocryphal. There are abundant errors of fact. In an article on the 'Mystic Records of the Sultanate Period', M. Habib has drawn attention to many of these, some of which are cited below.[3]

In the *Anīs al-Arwāh* 'the anonymous fabricator gives himself completely away by making Shaykh ʿUsmān refer to Ahmad Maʿshūq, a mystic, who according to Shaykh Nizām al-dīn Awliyā', flourished in the succeeding century, and by making Shaykh ʿUsmān quote from the *Mashāriq al-Anwār*, which was written at least a generation after his death.'[4]

The following statement appears in the second *majlis* of the *Dalīl al-ʿĀrifīn*:

Once I was at Bukhara among the externalist scholars. I heard the following anecdote from them: 'Once the Prophet saw a man saying his prayer and not bowing and prostrating himself as in the proper Muslim prayer. The Prophet stood there and when the man had finished his prayer, the Prophet asked, "How many years is it since you have been praying like this?" "Prophet of Allāh," he replied, "it is about forty years since I have been praying like this." The Prophet's eyes filled with tears. "You have said no proper prayers during these forty years. Had you died (during this period) you would not have died according to my traditions (sunnat)." '[5]

The traditions of Muslim prayer were not forty years old at the time of Muhammad's death. It is unlikely that Muʿīn al-dīn would have made such a gross mistake.

Habib gives another example:

The *Jāmiʿ al-Hikāyāt* of ʿAwfī was completed about the year 630 AH (AD1232–3). Nevertheless, Shaykh Muʿīn al-dīn, while still at

---

[3] 'Mystic Records of the Sultanate Period', *Mediaeval Indian Quarterly* (October, 1950), iii, 1–42. This article was a landmark in the study of early Indo-Muslim religious literature. It is the only authoritative attempt to sort out the fabricated from the genuine works. All subsequent historians owe a great debt to this pioneering work. His comments are cited frequently in this section although it will emerge that his conclusions cannot always be trusted and that he did not go far enough in his job of·sifting the authentic from the fabricated.

[4] M. Habib, 'Mystic Records', p. 20.   [5] Ibid., p. 21.

Baghdad—that is before 1192 AD for certain—is made to say in *Majlis* No. V: 'I have read your *Jāmiʿ al-Hikāyāt* ...'[6]

The date of the *Jāmiʿ al-Hikāyāt* means that it was being written while Muʿīn al-dīn was dying. AD 1192 was the approximate date of Muʿīn al-dīn's arrival in India, and he did not return to Baghdad. Muʿīn al-dīn's itinerary is further confused when he is made to say while still at Baghdad, 'I was at Multan ʾ[in India] once.'[7]

The external evidence which confirms that the *Anīs al-Arwāh* and the *Dalīl al-ʿĀrifīn* are fabrications is provided, in the first instance, by the *Fawāʾid al-Fuʾād*. Of the origins and accuracy of this work, Habib writes:

On Sunday, 3 *Shaʿbān*, 707 AH (AD Jan.1307), the poet, Amīr Hasan Sijzī, called on Shaykh Nizām al-dīn Awliyā at Ghiyaspur, and on returning home decided to write a summary of what he had heard from the shaykh that day and to make a similar record of all succeeding meetings or *majlis*. After he had made some progress, he informed the shaykh of what he was doing. The great shaykh blessed the enterprise. He told Amīr Hasan that when living in the *Jamāʿat Khāna* of Shaykh Farīd, he also had made a record of his master's conversations and that the manuscript he had prepared was still with him. But whereas the great shaykh's record of his master's teachings was merely a memoranda [*sic*] for personal use, Amīr Hasan's work was, from the very beginning, planned for publication. As he proceeded with the work, the pages were revised by Shaykh Nizām al-dīn, who filled up the lacunae (*bayāz*), which Amīr Hasan had left wherever he had been unable to follow the shaykh's conversation. The work, completed in five thin volumes, was brought up to 19 *Shaʿbān*, 722 AH (AD 1322). Accurate manuscripts of this book have always been available.

Amīr Hasan proved to be an excellent and accurate recorder. He avoided the futile ornamentations, figures of speech and other artificialities of language which were so dear to the Persian prose writers of those days and concentrated his effort on preserving, so far as was possible, all the characteristics of the great master's technique. The style of the work is simple, direct and lucid: its chief excellence lies in its accuracy. The *Fawāʾid al-Fuʾād* was an immediate and lasting success. ... For the research scholar of the present day, the *Fawāʾid al-Fuʾād* has a great historical value: it is a standard work concerning

---

[6] Ibid., p. 22.
[7] Ibid.

the life and the teachings of the Chishtī mystics with reference to which the accuracy and genuineness of all other works can be judged.[8]

However, there is no mention of either the *Anīs al-Arwāh* or the *Dalīl al-ʻĀrifīn* in the *Fawāʼid al-Fuʼād*. This is inconceivable if either book was genuine. The existence of the *Anīs al-Arwāh* at the time of the *Khair al-Majālis*, the conversations of Naṣīr al-dīn, Khalīfa of Niẓām al-dīn Awliyāʼ, recorded by Hamīd Qalandar, is witnessed by the following passage where Naṣīr al-dīn rejects any claim to its authenticity, or the authenticity of any *malfūzāt* of any Chishtī shaykh prior to Niẓām al-dīn:

A friend represented after this: 'There is a difficulty in the *malfūz* of Shaykh ʻUsmān Hārūnī. It is this. He says, "He who kills two cows commits one murder, and he who kills four cows commits two murders. He who kills four goats, commits one murder and he who kills twenty goats, commits two murders." '

'First, 'Shaykh Naṣīr al-dīn replied, 'the word is not Hārūnī but Hārwanī. Hārwan is a village and Khwāja ʻUsmān used to live in it. It has been said about him and people like him, "Men live in villages." Many shaykhs and men of God are to be found in villages.'

Then he added: 'These *malfūz* are not his. I have also come across this manuscript; there are many statements in it that are not worthy of his conversations.'

Then he added: 'Shaykh Niẓām al-dīn Awliyāʼ has said, "I have written no book, because neither Shaykh al-Islām Farīd al-dīn, not Shaykh al-Islām Qutb al-dīn, not the Chishtī saints, nor any of the preceding shaykhs of my order has written any book." '

I represented: 'It is stated in the *Fawāʼid al-Fuʼād* that someone came to Shaykh Niẓām al-dīn Awliyāʼ and said that he had heard a man declare that he had seen a book written by the great shaykh and that the shaykh replied, 'I have written no book and my masters (also) have written no book'

The shaykh said: 'Yes, Shaykh Niẓām al-dīn has written no book.'

I asked again, 'These manuscripts that have appeared in these days—the *malfūzāt* of Shaykh Qutb al-dīn and the *malfūzāt* of Shaykh ʻUsmān Hārwanī—did they not exist in the time of Shaykh Niẓām al-dīn Awliyāʼ?'

Shaykh Naṣīr al-dīn replied: 'They did not; otherwise the great Shaykh would have ordered and they would have been found.'[9]

[8] Ibid., pp. 2–3.
[9] *Majlis* No. XI of the *Khair al-Majālis* by Hamīd Qalandar, ed. K. A. Nizami, p. 52. Quoted M. Habib, 'Mystic Records', pp. 15–16.

The evidence, both internal and external, is conclusive; that both the *Anīs al-Arwāh* and the *Dalīl al-'Ārifīn* are fabrications. The above passage from the *Khair al-Majālis* helps to establish the approximate dates of the compilation of these apocryphal *malfūzāt*. The *Anīs al-Arwāh* must have been written between the time of Nizām al-dīn's death and the writing of the *Khair al-Majālis* (i.e., between *c.* AD 1324 and 1355). The *Dalīl al-'Ārifīn* must have been written some time after the *Khair al-Majālis* but before the *Siyar al-Awliyā'* which draws on it extensively (i.e., between *c.* AD 1355 and 1385).

Maktūbāt. Texts of letters believed to have been written by Mu'īn al-dīn are frequently encountered in the later hagiographies.[10] That none of the early hagiographers used these suggests that even they were suspicious of the authenticity of the letters or that the letters had not yet been written.

Mystical treatises and diwan. M. Habib has considered the authenticity of the *diwan*:

None of our genuine works have referred to any poetical compositions or *diwans* of the Chishtī Shaykhs. But the *Miftāh al-'Āshiqīn* in *majlis* No. II makes Shaykh Mu'īn al-dīn Ajmērī recite a *ghazal* of Shaykh al-Islām Khwāja Qutb al-dīn, while in *majlis* No. VII Muhibbullah (the supposed author) is made to recite a *ghazal* of Shaykh al-Islām Khwāja Mu'īn al-dīn. Later on complete *diwans* attributed to these shaykhs appeared. They have now been printed along with a *diwan* attributed to Shaykh Muhiy al-dīn 'Abd al-Qādir Jīlānī.

It is impossible on the basis of internal evidence only to come to any conclusion about the authenticity of these *diwans*. There are naturally no historical references in them and it would not be reasonable to look into them for any consistent system of thought as in the *malfūzāt*. But the external evidence we get is sufficient. Indian scholars in general have never admitted the authenticity of these *diwans* and in this they have been doubtless right. But regard for public opinion has prevented them from making a public declaration that these *diwans* are forgeries. Now it is quite likely that the Chishtī mystics, like the

---

[10] See also the Persian Text of the 'Letter of Khwāja Mu'īn al-dīn Chishtī addressed to Khwāja Qutb al-dīn', ed. Ghulām Ahmad Sanbhalī, and the two twentieth-century English hagiographies of Mu'īn al-dīn: W. D. Begg, *The Holy Biography of Hasrat Khwaja Mu'inuddin Chishti*, pp. 105–10; and Z. H. Sharib, *Khwaja Gharib Nawaz*, pp. 142–7.

great shaykh, occasionally composed a quatrain or a few lines. All educated Musalmans of the middle ages did so. But had Shaykh Qutb al-dīn or Shaykh Mu'īn al-dīn left complete *diwans* behind them, the mystic circles of Shaykh Farīd, Shaykh Nizām al-dīn Awliyā' and Shaykh Nasīr al-dīn Chirāgh would have preserved them as their most cherished treasures. But their complete silence in the matter definitely proves that no such *diwans* existed in their days. The number of verses quoted in our genuine texts is remarkably large, but no verse of the first two shaykhs of the Chishtī *silsila* finds a place among them. Even Amīr Khurd, who cannot write five prose sentences without quoting a verse, has no verse to quote from the Chishtī mystics. The reason is obvious. They had left no 'poetical remains' behind them.[11]

Mu'īn al-dīn is also alleged to have written the *Ganj al-Asrār*, a treatise he is supposed to have composed at the instance of 'Usmān Hārwanī for the use of Sultān Iltutmish. Some ascribe other religious works to Mu'īn al-dīn.[12] All such ascriptions may be rejected, again on the basis of the testimonies of Shaykh Nizām al-dīn and Shaykh Nasīr al-dīn. Furthermore, there is no mention in the early hagiographies of 'Usmān Hārwanī visiting Delhi and nowhere do they refer to any religious treatise written by Mu'īn al-dīn.

Tazkirāt. Table 2.1 lists some of the more important *Tazkirāt* which mention Mu'īn al-dīn Chishtī in chronological order.[13]

TABLE 2.1

Important Tazkirāt *containing References to Mu'īn al-dīn Chishtī*

1388	Amīr Khurd	*Siyar al-Awliyā'*
1536	Jamālī	*Siyar al-'Ārifīn*
1605	'Abd al-Samad	*Akhbār al-Asfiyā*
1613	Muhd. Ghausī Shattarī	*Gulzār-i Abrār*
1623	'Ali Asghar Chishtī	*Jawāhir-i Farīdī*
1634	'Alī Akbar Husain Ardistanī	*Majma'al-Awliyā'*
1640	Sultān Dārā Shikoh	*Safīnat al-Awliyā'*
1641	Jahān Āra Begum	*Mu'nis al-Arwāh*
1641	'Abd al-Haqq Dihlawī	*Akhbār al-Akhyār*

[11] M. Habib, 'Mystic Records', pp. 36–7. K. A. Nizami states that the apocryphal *Diwan* of Mu'īn al-dīn Chishtī are really the work of Maulana Mu'īn Haravi, *Religion and Politics*, p. 182, n. 3, d.

[12] e.g. Z. H. Sharib, *Khwaja Gharib Nawaz*, pp. 102–3.

[13] The date of the hagiographies cannot always be established with certainty. The date given is the latest possible date of composition.

1647	Allāh Diyā Chishtī	*Siyar al-Aqtāb*
1654	'Abd al-Rahman Chishtī	*Mirāt al-Asrār*
1682	Ghulām Mu'īn al-dīn	*Ma'ārif al-Wilāyat*
1865	Muhd. Ghulām Sarwar	*Khazīnat al-Asfiyā*
1879	Bābū Lal	*Waqā'i Shāh Mu'īn al-dīn Chishtī*
1881	Madār Bakhsh Mukhtār	*Tuhfa-i Ajmer*
1888	Muhd. Akbar Jahān (called Shiguftah)	*Tuhfa-i Mu'īnīya*
1893	Muhd. Mushtāq Ahmad Murādabādī	*Mazar-i 'Irfān*
1894	Imām al-dīn Hasan Khān	*Mu'īn al-Awliyā'*
1897	Muhd. Hāfiz Allāh Chishtī	*Barī Sawānih-i 'Umrī*
1898	Muhd. Mazhar al-Hādī Hakīm	*Fazā'il-i Khwāja*
1903	Muhd. Akbar Jahān	*Ta'rīkh-i Khwāja-i-Ajmēr*
1904	'Alī Zafar	*Zafar al-Islām*
n/d	Qurban 'Alī	*Hasht Bahisht*
1914	Najm al-dīn	*Munākib al-Habīb*
1949	'Abd al-Rahīman Sabāh al-dīn	*Bazm-i Sūfiyya*
1955	Muhd. Fārūqī	*Ta'rīkh al-Awliyā'*
1960	W. D. Begg	*The Holy Biography of Mu'inuddin Chishti*
1961	Z. H. Sharib	*Khwaja Gharib Nawaz*

The sources relevant to the quest to establish an authentic life of Mu'īn al-dīn can now be summarized. The *malfūzāt*, *maktūbāt*, the religious treatises and *diwans* ascribed to Mu'īn al-dīn are all fabrications. Contemporary historians do not mention Mu'īn al-dīn. The genuine *malfūzāt*, which are closest to him in time, say very little about him. The *tazkirāt* are all removed from him by at least 150 years, but it is on these that we are forced to depend.

Since the completion of the first of these *tazkirāt*, the *Siyar al-Awliyā'*, legendary accretions to the historical facts about Mu'īn al-dīn have continued to grow. The notice of Mu'īn al-dīn in the *Siyar al-Awliyā'* is brief. The first detailed account of his life appears in the *Siyar al-'Ārifīn*, which was completed in *c.* AD 1536. Jamālī was the last of the hagiographers who was in any position to collect reliable traditions regarding Mu'īn al-dīn's life. He belonged to the Suhrawardī order and, true to its traditions, he travelled extensively throughout the Muslim world.[14]

The traditions which he heard he set down in the *Siyar*

[14] M. Habib, 'Mystic Records', p. 10.

al-ʿĀrifīn when he returned to India.[15] It is reasonable to assume that after Jamālī the historical sources, such as they were, had been exhausted. If more detail was required the only source of supply was the imagination of the hagiographers, and the pious inventions of devotees and descendants. Any details which appear after Jamālī about Muʿīn al-dīn's life are more likely to be contributions to legend than to history.[16]

Before the earliest hagiographies which mention Muʿīn al-dīn are commented upon in detail, the relevant parts of their texts are presented below in an English translation.[17]

Siyar al-Awliyāʾ

42 It is stated that Shaykh al-Islām Muʿīn al-dīn Hasan Sijzī said that once on his travels with Khwāja ʿUsmān Hārwanī, they arrived at the Tigris River to find there was no boat.[18] Khwāja ʿUsmān Hārwanī told Muʿīn al-dīn to close his eyes. When Muʿīn al-dīn reopened them he beheld that they were both standing on the other side of the river. He asked ʿUsmān Hārwanī how this had happened. ʿUsmān Hārwanī replied that he had simply recited the *Sūra Fātiha* five times.

It is stated that one day a miserable old man came to Muʿīn al-dīn. Muʿīn al-dīn inquired after the reason for the old man's misery. The old man replied that more than forty years earlier he had lost his son and still did not know whether he was dead or

---

[15] The claims to historicity of such traditions will be discussed below. See pp. 39–56.

[16] The *Akhbār al-Akhyār* (1641) is generally regarded as being an unusually reliable source of information on the Indo-Muslim mystics (see M. Habib, 'Mystic Records', p. 11; and Nizami, *Religion and Politics*, p. 182). However a close examination of the text reveals that this high opinion of its historicity cannot be justified. For example, ʿAbd al-Haqq quotes wholesale from the apocryphal *Dalīl al-Ārifīn*. He supplies three items of information that are not in either the *Siyar al-ʿAwliya* or the *Siyar al-Ārifīn*: an inscription appearing on the forehead of the dead saint; Muʿīn al-dīn marrying a second time; and him dying on 6 Rajab 633 A.H. These traditions make their first appearance c. 400 years after Muʿīn al-dīn's death and therefore have slight claim to historicity.

[17] Where it does not disturb the meaning of the original extensive honorifics have been omitted in the translation. Numbers in the left-hand margin refer to page numbers in the original text.

[18] The name *Sijzī* indicates Muʿīn al-dīn's connection with the province of Sijistān, or Seistān. *Sijzī* is often misspelt *Sanjarī* in the hagiographies.

alive. The old man had come to Mu'īn al-dīn believing that if the
saint prayed for his son, he would once again see him. The saint
meditated for a while and then asked the crowd assembled around
him to pray. The saint prayed too and afterwards instructed the
old man to return home. When the old man arrived there, the
people gathered around him congratulating him on the return of
his son. Then the old man saw his son and his son kissed his feet.
The old man asked where his son had been all these years. He
replied that the *dev* had carried him away and incarcerated him on
an island. That very day he had seen a darvīsh resembling his
father who approached and called out to him. He put his hands on
his chains which straight away fell from him. The darvīsh instructed him to put his feet on the darvīsh's feet and close his eyes.
When the son did this, in an instant he found himself at the door
of his home.

It is also said by Mu'īn al-dīn Sijzī that a disciple of 'Usmān
Hārwanī was living in his neighbourhood. When the disciple
died, Mu'īn al-dīn went with the funeral procession, but when
the rest of the people returned from burying him, Mu'īn al-dīn sat
on the grave for a while. Mu'īn al-dīn saw the angel of punishment
come to the disciple. Shortly afterwards 'Usmān Hārwanī also
appeared and told the angel not to punish him as he was a disciple,
to which the angel replied that this disciple had acted contrary to
'Usmān Hārwanī. 'Usmān Hārwanī countered, saying that while
the disciple had doubtless been against him, he was still connected
as a disciple to his teacher. Then Allāh was heard ordering the
angel to leave 'Usmān Hārwanī's disciple saying, 'I forgive him
for the sake of 'Usmān Hārwanī.'

Shaykh of Shaykhs, in truth the origin of all, the pole-star of
the blessings of Allāh, the symbol of goodness, the inheritor of all
the prophets, the vice-regent of the Holy Prophet in India, Mu'īn
al-Haqq, al-Shar', al-Dīn, Khwāja Mu'īn Hasan Sijzī—May
Blessings be on his grave—who had all the merits of a great
shaykh, famous in the highest rank for his many miracles, was the
khalīfa of 'Usmān Hārwanī.

43   It has been stated that he said: 'After receiving the blessing of
becoming the disciple of 'Usmān Hārwanī I spent the next twenty
years in his service. Never for a second or a minute did I spend
time on my own comfort rather than in his service during all those
twenty years. I carried his bedding whether at home or on journeys.
When he realized my determination and devotion he blessed me
according to his own position.'

It is stated that Shaykh al-Islām Mu'īn al-dīn said that the sign
of the recognition of Allāh is the running away from the business

of this world and quietness in contemplation. He added that we see the Love, the Lover and the Beloved emerge like charmed snakes from their baskets. In other words, in the Oneness of God we see everything. He added, 'While pilgrims physically circumambulate the Ka'ba, the *'ārif*, wishing to see Allāh, circumambulate His throne and the veils of His light. For ages I circumambulated the Ka'ba, but now the Ka'ba circumambulates me.'

He also said that a murīd reaches the stage of *faqr* only when he has removed himself from the phenomenal world. One of his disciples asked him when the disciple can be regarded as firm in the Way. He answered: 'When the recording angel of evil has been out of work for twenty years.'

He also said that the sign of the love of God is the obedience of the disciple and the absence of fear of being cast from the Way. The sign of misfortune is that after sinning he should wish to be loved.

He added that on the Day of Judgement, Allāh will order the angels to bring hell out of the mouths of snakes. Then will hell burn so furiously that the entire universe will be consumed in an instant. If someone wishes to protect himself from this conflagration he must worship Allāh. There is no better way than this. He was asked what was meant by this kind of worship: 'To listen to the plight of the oppressed, to help the needy and to fill the stomachs of the hungry.' The man who does these three things may consider himself a friend of Allāh. First he should have generosity like a river; secondly, kindness like the sun and, thirdly, humility like the earth. The man who is blessed is the man who is generous. The man who is respected is the man who is clean. The man who removes the burden of others is the real *mutawaqil*. To be firm in the Way depends on two things: to respect the service of Allāh and to pay homage to Allāh.

Hazrat Sultān al-Mashā'ikh says that when Hazrat Shaykh Mu'īn al-dīn came to Ajmer it was the capital city of Rāi Pithaurā.[19]
44 Mu'īn al-dīn settled down there and Pithaurā and his entourage strongly objected to this. When they witnessed the miracles and might of the Shaykh they were not able to breathe. One of his disciples was an employee of Rāi Pithaurā who began to make trouble for him. The disciple approached Mu'īn al-dīn for help. The Shaykh interceded on his behalf but Pithaurā refused to listen and said, 'This man tells of the Unseen.' When Mu'īn al-dīn heard of

---

[19] For information on Pithaurā see G. Sharma, *Early Chauhan Dynasties*, pp. 72–90.

this he said, 'We have caught Rāi Pithaurā alive and have given him to the army of Islam.' Accordingly in those days Sultān Muʿizz al-dīn came with his army from Ghazni and fought with Pithaurā who fell alive into the hands of the Sultān.

I, the author, believe in my heart that there is no higher thing or greater miracle than the fact that those pious men, who became the disciples of this King of Religion, helped the servants of Allāh, ignored the pride of this world and thought the hereafter to be their real home. Until the Day of Judgement the proclamation of the greatness of this King of Religion will ring in every corner of the heavens and in the ears of all the angels. And people will achieve the Place of Truth through his love.

The other miracle is that before his arrival the whole of Hindustan was submerged by unbelief and idol-worship. Every haughty man in Hind pronounced himself to be Almighty God and considered himself as the partner of God. All the people of India used to prostrate themselves before stones, idols, trees, animals, cows and cow-dung. Because of the darkness of unbelief over this land their hearts were locked and hardened.

[A couplet follows.] All India was ignorant of the orders of religion and law. All were ignorant of Allāh and His Prophet. None had seen the Kaʿba. None had heard of the Greatness of Allāh.

Because of his coming, the Sun of real believers, the helper of religion, Muʿīn al-dīn, the darkness of unbelief in this land was illumined by the light of Islam.

[Another couplet follows contrasting the new situation with the old.] Because of his Sword, instead of idols and temples in the land of unbelief now there are mosques, *mihrāb* and *mimbar*. In the land where there were the sayings of the idol-worshippers, there is the sound of 'Allāhu Akbar'.

The descendants of those who were converted to Islam in this land will live until the Day of Judgement; so too will those who bring others into the fold of Islam by the sword of Islam. Until the Day of Judgement these converts will be in the debt of Shaykh al-Islām Muʿīn al-dīn Hasan Sijzī and these people will be drawing closer to Almighty Allāh because of the auspicious devotion of Muʿīn al-dīn.

[Two further anecdotes involving Muʿīn al-dīn occur in the section of the *Siyar al-Awliyāʾ* on Shaykh Qutb al-dīn Bakhtyār Kākī.]

50 Nizām al-dīn [Awliyāʾ] said that when Shaykh Muʿīn al-dīn came from Ajmer to Delhi, Shaykh Najm al-dīn Sughrā was Shaykh al-Islām of Delhi. There was a bond of friendship between them, so Muʿīn al-dīn went to meet Najm al-dīn Sughrā. He saw

that a platform was being built by the house of Najm al-dīn. He approached closer and said, 'Perhaps the pride of becoming Shaykh al-Islām has overcome you.' Shaykh Najm al-dīn replied, 'I am still just as devoted to you but you have placed a murīd in this city who does not understand the implications of my position as Shaykh al-Islām.' Mu'īn al-dīn smiled and said, 'Do not worry. I will take Bābā Qutb al-dīn away with me.'

In those days the reputation of Qutb al-dīn in Delhi had reached the greatest heights. The whole population of the city had turned towards him. When Shaykh Mu'īn al-dīn returned to his house he said, 'Bābā Bakhtyār, you have become so well-known that people are complaining of you. Come and stay with me in Ajmer. I will serve you properly.' Shaykh Qutb al-dīn submitted, 'I have not the impertinence to sit before my Lord or even to stand before him.'

51   Then he went with his Shaykh [Mu'īn al-dīn] towards Ajmer. This caused a stir throughout Delhi. The populace of the city, including Sultān Shams al-dīn, set out after them. As Shaykh Qutb al-dīn passed, people took up the dust he had trodden on and displayed signs of worry and distress. When Mu'īn al-dīn saw this he said, 'Bābā Bakhtyār, make this your place because the people are so sorely distressed at your departing. I do not wish to cause so much misery and heartbreak. Go, I have left the city under your protection.'...

65   Shaykh Mu'īn al-dīn and Shaykh Qutb al-dīn were together in the same cell. Shaykh Mu'īn al-dīn said to Shaykh Qutb al-dīn, 'O Bakhtyār, how much longer will you burn that young man [Shaykh Farīd al-dīn] up with spiritual exercises? You must reward him with something.' Shaykh Qutb al-dīn answered, 'What power do I have in front of you?' Mu'īn al-dīn announced, 'This is your murīd.'

Then he stood up and suggested that they both gave him their blessings. So Mu'īn al-dīn stood on the right and Qutb al-dīn on the left with Shaykh Farīd al-dīn between them, and whatever blessings they had received they bestowed on him.

The two saints have bestowed the two worlds on you.
You have received kingship from these kings of the age.
The realms of both this and the other world belong to you.
The entire creation in fact has been made over to you.

Siyar al-'Ārifīn

5   Khwāja Mu'īn al-dīn, the beloved of Allāh—May the blessings of Allāh be on his grave—was well-known among the distinguished

mashā'ikhs of the world, renowned in the field of piety, endowed with attributes of Allāh, and in his *halqa* were all the *aqtāb* and *aghās* of Hindustān. His saintly father was Khwāja Ghiyās al-dīn, who was in the highest state of wisdom and piety. When he died and left the physical world for the Unseen, Mu'īn al-dīn was in his fifteenth year. He inherited a garden and a water-mill. Once, when he was sitting in contemplation, a *majzūb* named Ibrāhīm Qundūzī suddenly passed by the garden. When Mu'īn al-dīn saw the darvīsh, Ibrāhīm Qundūzī, had come under the trees, he came to him and kissed his hands and feet and sat him down under the trees and offered him a bunch of grapes and himself sat down respectfully. He [Qundūzī] took a morsel from under his arm and chewed it between his teeth and took it out of his mouth and put it with his own hand into the mouth of Mu'īn al-dīn. Through eating that morsel a light was kindled within him.

So he became wholeheartedly disillusioned with his property and house and after two or three days sold all his property and chattels and distributed [the proceeds] among the darvīshes. He set off travelling. For a time he lived in Samarqand and Bukhara and learnt the whole of the Quran by heart and gained external knowledge. From there he left for Iraq. When he arrived at Hārwan in Nishapur he found the holy Shaykh of Shaykhs, the *Ghaws* of the world, 'Usmān Hārwanī—may the blessings of Allāh be on his grave. Mu'īn al-dīn remained in his service for 2½ years busying himself in study and spiritual striving and exercise. When he completed his task the holy 'Usmān bestowed the cloak of *khilāfat* on him.

Mu'īn al-dīn asked for leave to go to Baghdad. He came to the town of Sijz and at that time the great Shaykh Najm al-dīn lived there.[20] He found him and remained in his company for 2½ months. From there he came to the town of Jīl and found Shaykh Muhiy al-dīn 'Abd al-Qādir Jīlī. This saint was at that time living in the town of Jīl. ... In that place Mu'īn al-dīn found Shaykh Muhiy al-dīn 'Abd al-Qādir and remained in his company for 57 days and received many kinds of spiritual benefits and inner peace from him. Even now there is preserved the sacred cell of Mu'īn al-dīn in that place. It is well-known and has been repaired. This darvīsh [the author] had the honour of visiting this holy cell and prayed a supererogatory prayer there.

[20] The chief town of the province of Sijistān, or Seistān, was Zaranj. According to G. LeStrange (*Lands of the Eastern Caliphate*, pp. 21–2, 335) this was often known as Sijistān, or Madīnat-Sijistān. So Sijz in this context probably refers to Zaranj, the capital of Sijistān.

After meeting Muhiy al-dīn 'Abd al-Qādir, Mu'īn al-dīn came to Baghdad where he encountered Shaykh Ziyā' al-dīn, the pīr of Shihāb al-dīn. For a time he enjoyed his company. At that time Shaykh Awhad al-dīn Kirmānī was in Baghdad in the early days of his discipleship. It is recounted by Shaykh Husām al-dīn Chelebi, the great khalīfa of the author of the *masnawi*, Maulānā Jalāl al-dīn, that Shaykh Awhad al-dīn Kirmānī was given the cloak of *khilāfat* by Shaykh Mu'īn al-dīn and also that Shaykh Shihāb al-dīn 'Umar reached the state of the Perfect Man. It is also narrated by Shaykh Husām al-dīn Chelebi that Mu'īn al-dīn came from Baghdad to Hamadan and met Shaykh Yūsuf Hamadānī and from there he set out for Tabrīz where he found Shaykh Abū Sa'īd
7 Tabrīzī who was the pīr of Shaykh Jalāl al-dīn Tabrīzī. He was a great shaykh—solitary, courageous and trusting in God.

It is told by Sultān al-Awliyā, Shaykh Nizām al-dīn Muhammad Badāvanī, that Saiyid Abū Sa'īd Tabrīzī was the perfect disciple and man of God just like Shaykh Jalāl al-dīn Tabrīzī. Also it is related by Shaykh Farīd, who heard of it from his own pīr, Qutb al-dīn Bakhtyār Ūshī, that Mu'īn al-dīn Sijzī was in such a strange state of austerity and spiritual striving that after seven days he broke his fast with only a charred cake of bread weighing five *misqāl* and wetted with water. It is also told by Nizām al-dīn Muhammad Bukhārī that the clothes of that saint were two pieces of cloth, which were patched. He used to pick up pieces of material and whenever his garment was torn he used to patch it with whatever he found.

When he arrived at Isfahan from Ush, he asked for Shaykh Mahmūd Isfahānī, who was one of the great shaykhs. At that time Qutb al-dīn Ahmad bin Musa Ūshī from Ush, a town in Transoxiana, wanted to become the murīd of Shaykh Mahmud ...
[The story of the inheritance of the patched garment follows.]

It has been heard that Mu'īn al-dīn received the *khirqa* [of *khilāfat*] from Shaykh 'Usmān Hārwanī when he was 52 years old. He was greatly esteemed for his spiritual devotion and was a pīr who had no ties. He used to travel alone and wherever he went he used to stay in the graveyard and every day he used to finish reciting the holy Quran twice. Whenever he gained a little fame or if anyone recognized him he used to leave that place so no one
8 would know him. 'Usmān Hārwanī often used to say, 'My Mu'īn al-dīn is the Beloved of Allāh and I am proud that he is my disciple.' Shaykh 'Usmān loved him greatly. But at that time Mu'īn al-dīn took leave of him and left for Baghdad. ...
[A story of 'Usmān Hārwanī converting a group of fire-worshippers follows.]

9   Mu'īn al-dīn came from Tabriz towards Mihna and Khirqan in the year Shaykh 'Abd al-Hasan Khirqānī died. Shaykh 'Abd al-Khair was in Mihna and welcomed Mu'īn al-dīn who stayed in that area for two years. He then went to Astarabad. Afterwards he met Shaykh Nasīr al-dīn Astarabādī, who was one of the most powerful shaykhs and perfect in spirit. He was 107 years old ... Mu'īn al-dīn came from Astarabad to Herat and was in that area for a while. He was on the move all day and every day. He did not feel like settling down and generally slept at the mausoleum of Shaykh 'Abdullah Ansarī. There was only one darvīsh accompanying him. He usually said his *'Ishā* prayer. Constantly he was travelling. When he became famous in that area and all the people realized his power, he came to Sabzawar where there was a ruler
10   called Muhammad Yādgār, who was nasty, dirty and notorious in heresy. He tried to kill anyone with the name of Abu Bakr, 'Umar or 'Usmān. Near the city there was a garden with a little pool. He had constructed a building there and every time he went there he used to drink, and engaged in all manner of evil pursuits.

       Shaykh Mu'īn al-dīn went to that garden on his arrival at Sabzawar and performed his ablutions in the pool, prayed and started to recite the Quran. Muhammad Yādgār was going to the garden that day, and the darvīsh who was with Mu'īn al-dīn told him that the ruler's servants had just arrived in the garden, that the ruler was following, and that it would be better for Mu'īn al-dīn to leave the garden since the ruler was a violent man. Mu'īn al-dīn did not take in what he had been told. He was sitting in the shade of a pine tree near the pool.

       At that moment the ruler's servants arrived and spread the ruler's rugs around the pool. However much they tried to get rid of the shaykh they were unsuccessful. The ruler arrived. Mu'īn al-dīn did not move. When the ruler saw the shaykh he started trembling. His countenance changed and all his entourage were also impressed by the shaykh. The ruler tremblingly threw down his saddlebag and approached with his hands joined in front of him. Mu'īn al-dīn gave him a sharp look and the ruler was overcome and fainted. Seeing this his entourage all put their heads to the ground. Mu'īn al-dīn told his darvīsh to fetch some water from the pool and put it on the face of the ruler. The darvīsh did exactly as he was told and shortly afterwards Muhammad Yādgār regained his senses and put his head on the ground. Mu'īn al-dīn asked him, 'Have you repented?' He answered, 'Yes'. When the shaykh asked him if he had given up all evil thoughts, he answered, 'Yes, completely.' Mu'īn al-dīn told him to make his ablutions and repent. He did so and started to follow the shaykh. He became his murīd and all his entourage did likewise.

It is said that on the day when Muhammad Yādgār became a follower of Mu'īn al-dīn he put all his property and belongings in 11 front of the shaykh. The shaykh told him to satisfy all his enemies and restore all that he had extorted by force to its rightful owners so that Allāh would accept his repentance and give him His mercy. Muhammad Yādgār did as he was told. He freed all his slaves, both male and female, and gave [things] to them. He had two wives. He divorced both and became a complete follower with absolute faith in the shaykh. He himself became one of the lions of Truth. This story comes from Maulānā Muhammad Najafī who was one of the famous people of Sabzawar, renowned for his righteousness and godliness. When the author was passing from Herat to Sabzawar he heard the story from the said maulānā.

Mu'īn al-dīn went from Sabzawar to Hisar and Muhammad Yādgār went with him. He appointed Muhammad Yādgār to be his [representative] in Hisar, so that is where he [Muhammad Yādgār] is buried. From there Mu'īn al-dīn came to Balkh to see Shaykh Ahmad Khizr, and stayed there for a few months. Maulānā Ziyā' al-dīn Hakīm Balkhī was also there. He did not believe in Sufism, and usually told his pupils that Sufism is a kind of feverish delirium and is not countenanced by the sane. He had no belief at all in it and had nothing except curses to say for the Sufis. He had a small village, school and garden near Balkh. He spent most of his time there. He used to leave civilization and go hunting in the wilderness. Once the saint was passing through the place where Hakīm Ziyā' al-dīn used to hunt, when he [Mu'īn al-dīn] caught a fowl, and intended to roast it and eat what he had found. He was sitting by a tree and told his servant to start a fire and prepare the kebabs. He was making two genuflexions when Maulānā Ziyā' al-dīn Hakīm passed by and saw the darvīsh praying and his servant making a kebab. After all he had heard about the pure-spirited one he could not resist going to see him. So he greeted him and sat down. The servant of Mu'īn al-dīn brought the kebabs. 12 The saint said the *Bismillāh*, took a piece of the bird and put it in front of Maulānā Ziyā' al-dīn Hakīm. He began to eat another piece himself. As soon as Maulānā Ziyā' al-dīn ate his piece of kebab, he suddenly had a strong feeling within and the inner darkness left him and was replaced by the secrets of the enlightened ones. Then the saint took a piece which he had chewed and put it into the mouth of the *hakīm*. The *hakīm* regained his senses. Having seen the light of truth, he threw out all his books on philosophy, divorced himself from all property and worldly matters, and

became a murīd of Mu'īn al-dīn. All his pupils started to follow
the shaykh and Mu'īn al-dīn chose Ziyā' al-dīn to be his representative there.

Mu'īn al-dīn went to Ghazni and was received by 'Abd al-
Wahid, the pīr of Shaykh Nizām al-dīn 'Abd al-Muwayyid. Then
he went to Lahore where he met Shaykh Husain Zanjānī. At that
time Sultān Mu'īzz al-dīn Muhammad Sām captured Delhi and
left Sultān Qutb al-dīn Aibak, his slave, as the ruler while he
himself returned to Ghazni. On the way he died. Mu'īn al-dīn
took leave of Shaykh Husain Zanjānī and went to Delhi. When he
arrived there he rested for a few months. His blessed room was in
the place where the grave of Shaykh Rashīd Makkī is nowadays,
and part of the remains of the mosque and minaret is still standing.
When the crowds of both high and low estate which came to him
became too much, he set out from Delhi towards the region of
Ajmer.

13   In spite of the fact that this area had been illuminated by Islam,
there were still wretched unbelievers in control at the distance of
one *farsang*. Sultān Qutb al-dīn Aibak appointed Saiyid Husain
Mashhadī as the local governor. ... Most of the notorious
unbelievers of that area were impressed by Mu'īn al-dīn and
became believers. Those who were not converted nevertheless
sent much *nazr* and *futūh*, and still these unbelievers come to his
shrine every year and give money in large quantities and do what
they can in the way of service there.

It is said that Mu'īn al-dīn visited Delhi during the reign of
Sultān Shams al-dīn Iltutmish and the details of these visits are
recorded by Qutb al-dīn Bakhtyār. ... [The story of one of these
visits is recounted by Jamālī in his section on Qutb al-dīn. It is,
however, included here since it fits into the narrative at this stage
of Mu'īn al-dīn's life.]

21   It is said that at this time Mu'īn al-dīn came [to Delhi]. This was
very important to Qutb al-dīn who wanted to tell Sultān Iltutmish
of the visit. However, Mu'īn al-dīn told him not to, saying, 'I
have come here to see you, and do not wish to be bothered by
other people. I shall only stay for two or three days and do not
want to be pestered by a crowd of the lowly and great.' In spite of
this all the mashā'ikh came to see him and had the pleasure of
conversing with him. But, although Qutb al-dīn and Shaykh
al-Islām Najm al-dīn Sughrā had been very close when they were
in Khurasan, Najm al-dīn was jealous of Qutb al-dīn and did not
visit them. On the second or third day, Mu'īn al-dīn went to see
Shaykh Najm al-dīn in his house. Najm al-dīn did not go out to
greet him. He was supervising some workmen who were installing

a new seating platform. Muʿīn al-dīn was vexed by this behaviour and asked what was wrong with Najm al-dīn. 'Is it the pride of becoming the Shaykh al-Islām that has gone to your head?' On hearing this Najm al-dīn was very upset and apologised, saying, 'I am still the same earthly person who used to follow in your footsteps. You have made one of your murīds Shaykh al-Islām and all the mashāʾikh of the city are aware of my position, but this does not make any important difference.' Muʿīn al-dīn smiled having heard this and said to Najm al-dīn, 'I am going to take Qutb al-dīn back to Ajmer with me.' The Shaykh al-Islām asked him to stay to have something to eat, but Muʿīn al-dīn did not accept the invitation.

It is said that Farīd al-dīn was in the service of Qutb al-dīn and was able to kiss the feet of Muʿīn al-dīn. Muʿīn al-dīn often used to say, 'Qutb al-dīn, you have caught a noble falcon which will not build its nest except in the tree of Heaven! Farīd al-dīn is a lamp which will illuminate the company of darvīshes. A few days later Muʿīn al-dīn left for Ajmer and Qutb al-dīn accompanied him. When they left Delhi everyone was in mourning and great pain so that wherever they went people picked up the soil as *tabarruk*. When Muʿīn al-dīn witnessed this he instructed Qutb al-dīn to stay in Delhi since the people were so upset, 'I do not wish to break so many hearts. Stay in the city. This city should be under your care.'

It is heard that Shams al-dīn, when he heard they were going, ran after them and when he reached Muʿīn al-dīn, he asked if Qutb al-dīn could stay. All this petitioning made Muʿīn al-dīn accept and Qutb al-dīn returned to the city. ... [Details of the other khalīfas of Muʿīn al-dīn now follow.]

14   It is related by Shaykh Nizām al-dīn that a Hindu lived in the area of Ajmer. Muʿīn al-dīn used to say that this man was saintly. People were surprised that Muʿīn al-dīn could call a non-believer a god-like saint. But in the end this Hindu became a Muslim ... .

16   It is said that Muʿīn al-dīn had children in old age and that his first child was born when he arrived back from his visit to Delhi. It is said that Saiyid Wajīh al-dīn Muhammad Mashhadī, who was the governor of that region, had a daughter with all the necessary virtues. She was old enough but he could not find a suitable match. One night he had a dream in which the Prophet came to him and told him to marry her to Shaykh Muʿīn al-dīn. Saiyid Wajīh al-dīn knew of the shaykh's status and told him of his dream. The shaykh said that he was reaching the end of his life but, since this was the wish of the holy Prophet, he would obey. He married her and they had children. He lived for another seven years and died when he was 97 years old on Monday, 6 Rajab.

The Reliability of the Siyar al-Awliyāʾ *and*
Siyar al-ʿĀrifīn

The brevity of the section on Muʿīn al-dīn in the *Siyar al-Awliyāʾ* demands consideration. Amīr Khurd was well-placed to know all the traditions about Muʿīn al-dīn that were current in north India at the time. He had become a disciple of Nizām al-dīn Awliyāʾ as a child. 'He was too young to receive any instruction from the great shaykh himself but he had grown up in the shaykh's circle and had sat at the feet of his leading khalīfas and disciples.'[21] He later entered government service and was posted to the Deccan. On his return to Delhi he presented himself at the khānqāh of Shaykh Nasīr al-dīn. 'His mind now comparatively at peace, Amīr Khurd sat down to write a history of the Chishtī *silsila* in India. ... He had considerable qualifications for such a task. His father had given him a sound education in Arabic and Persian. He had access to the private papers of Shaykh Nizām al-dīn Awliyāʾ. He had, in his earlier days, associated with a large number of the great shaykh's disciples. His parents, as well as his uncles, had a considerable stock of old memories which they had passed on to him.'[22]

However, having set out to write the history of the Chishtīs in India, Amīr Khurd gives very little information on the Chishtī shaykh who first came to live in the subcontinent—Muʿīn al-dīn. This implies either lack of information and/or lack of interest.

The negative evidence of the genuine *malfūzāt* must be invoked here. The silence of Nizām al-dīn and Nasīr al-dīn in an age when memories of events and men of the past were preserved almost exclusively in the form of oral traditions suggests that they did not consider Muʿīn al-dīn to be a shaykh of particular merit or importance. There must also have been a lack of information about him; given the habit of Chishtī shaykhs establishing authority for their actions and teachings by quoting the precedents of earlier representatives of the *silsila*, if any anecdotes about Muʿīn al-dīn had come to the ears of Nizām al-dīn or Nasīr al-dīn they would surely have reproduced them in their recorded *majlis*.

[21] M. Habib, 'Mystic Records', p. 6.   [22] Ibid., p. 7.

Amīr Khurd's narrative, slight though it is, needs to be read with caution for two reasons. First, because Amīr Khurd, unlike Amīr Hasan and Hamīd Qalandar, who took down the conversations of Nizām al-dīn and Nasīr al-dīn, 'was subject to no internal or external checks. As a result his work, though informative and quite indispensable, is not such a safe guide. The miraculous element begins to appear.'[23]

Secondly, much of the detail of Muʿīn al-dīn's life, and all the sayings which appear in the *Siyar al-Awliyā'* have been taken by Amīr Khurd from the fabricated *malfūzāt*.[24]

Neither can the expanded narrative of Jamālī be accepted without question. The claims to historicity of the traditions Jamālī heard during his travels are dubious. Habib properly asks:

What reliance can we place on oral tradition that is over 2½ to 3 centuries old? ... Now did any unwritten traditions about the two Chishtī shaykhs ('Usmān Hārwanī and Muʿīn al-dīn) really survive in these countries, or was it Persian courtesy that gave the Indian visitor information without which he would have been deeply disappointed?[25]

The Authenticity of the *Siyar al-Awliyā'* and the *Siyar al-ʿĀrifīn*

The texts of the *Siyar al-Awliyā'* and the *Siyar al-ʿĀrifīn* will be examined in the light of each of four main considerations in turn.

1. The historian cannot accept the miraculous or fantastic as authentic aspects of the shaykh's life.[26]

2. Contradictions between the two sources will suggest that one or both are inaccurate.

3. Where reliable external sources contradict the *tazkirāt*, credence should be given to the former.

[23] Ibid.
[24] For M. Habib's statement to the contrary, see Ibid., p. 22, note 3.
[25] Ibid., pp. 10–11.
[26] This is perhaps open to argument, and devotees of Muʿīn al-dīn would not all accept this proposition. However the fourth criterion can be applied to the miracle-stories with similar results. Displays of miraculous powers were not countenanced by the Chishtī shaykhs of the twelfth and thirteenth century. See below, pp. 60–1.

4. Doubts as to the reliability of the *tazkirāt* must be raised
where there are dissimilarities between what is known about
the Chishtī *silsila*, and particular anecdotes and teachings recorded in the *tazkirāt*.

Unacceptability of the Miraculous

Once the miraculous has been taken out of the *Siyar al-Awliyā'*
there is very little left.[27] The following anecdotes must be dis-
carded as legendary on the basis of the first criterion: the
crossing of the Tigris; the discovery of the lost son; Mu'īn al-dīn
at the grave of a fellow murīd; Mu'īn al-dīn as a cause of Sultān
Shihāb al-dīn's invasion of India and capture of Rāi Pithaurā.
The *Siyar al-'Ārifīn* is less pervaded by miracle stories. The
anecdotes of Mu'īn al-dīn's meetings with Ibrāhīm Qundūzī,
Muhammad Yādgār and Ziyā' al-dīn Hakīm need not be rejected simply because of the miraculous nature of the conversions to
the mystic path. These are the only instances of the intrusion of
the miraculous into Jamālī's account of Mu'īn al-dīn.

Contradictions between Siyar al-Awliyā' and Siyar al-'Ārifīn

Doubt is raised where Jamālī contradicts or conflicts with Amīr
Khurd. Thus, while Amīr Khurd says that Mu'īn al-dīn remained in the service of his pīr, 'Usmān Hārwanī, for twenty
years, Jamālī says that it was for two and a half years. The
longer period Amīr Khurd borrows from the apocryphal *Dalīl
al-'Ārifīn*.[28] Jamālī's version seems the more probable.

Another contradiction appears in their different accounts of
Mu'īn al-dīn's arrival in Ajmer. The *Siyar al-Awliyā'* states that
Mu'īn al-dīn arrived in Ajmer during the reign of Pithaurā,
whereas Jamālī says that 'This area had already been illuminated
by Islam' and that Ajmer was under the local government of
Saiyid Husain Mashhadī. He adds, 'There were still wretched
unbelievers in control at the distance of one *farsang*.'[29]

[27] The morphology of the miracle-stories is examined below. See pp.
91–5.
[28] *Dalīl al-'Ārifīn*, pp. 4–5.
[29] *Siyar al-Awliyā'*, pp. 43–4; *Siyar al-'Ārifīn*, p. 13.

The historians Badāyūnī and ʿAbd al-Fazl both support Jamālī's version—that Muʿīn al-dīn arrived either at the time of the successful invasion of India or after it, but not before.[30] These three sources, therefore, contradict the tradition retailed by Amīr Khurd, and later by ʿAbd al-Haqq in the *Akhbār al-Akhyār*, which derived from Nizām al-dīn Awliyāʾ.[31] It is not certain which tradition is correct but Jamālī had more reason to distort the truth here than Amīr Khurd. His rejection of the *Siyar al-Awliyāʾ*'s version may arise from his desire to associate the Suhrawardī *silsila*, to which he himself belonged, with the earlier glories of the city and kingdom of Delhi; the fact that he ignores the tradition of Muʿīn al-dīn's arrival before the victory of the Ghorids may be a deliberate attempt to play down the connection between the Chishtīs and the triumph of Islam in Hindustan.[32]

The differences may be resolved by an attempt at harmonizing the two versions. Digby suggests that either ʿMuʿīn al-dīn did in fact visit Ajmer before the successful invasion, was driven out by Prithvī Rāja's hostility to the Musalmans, [after which] he returned with the invading armies, when any wrongs he had suffered were avenged by the capture and execution of Prithvī Rāja,'[33] or 'that Muʿīn al-dīn's conflict with the "wretched unbelievers" ' was 'projected backwards by legend into a great conflict with Rāi Pithaurā.'[34] But this is speculation and at this distance in time it is not possible to establish which of these possibilities is the more accurate.

Contradictions between External Sources and Tazkirāt

External sources suggest that there is no sound evidence behind Jamālī's list of the shaykhs whom Muʿīn al-dīn is alleged to have met. For example, the *Fawāʾid al-Fuʾād* mentions that Husain

[30] *Muntakhab al-Tawārīkh*, vol. I, p. 70; *Āʾīn-i Akbarī*, vol. 3, pp. 361–2.

[31] The *Tabaqāt-i Nāsirī* is sometimes used to support this version. See vol. 1, p. 465. However, the Muʿīn al-dīn Ūshī mentioned in this passage is not connected with Muʿīn al-dīn of Ajmer. The latter is not known to have been to Ush or to have had any personal connection with that town. It was his khalīfa, Qutb al-dīn who came from Ush, hence his name Qutb al-dīn Ūshī.

[32] Digby, *Crosscurrents*, I, pp. 16–17.   [33] Ibid., p. 17

[34] Ibid., p. 16.

Zanjanī died AH 460/1070 which means that Mu'īn al-dīn could never have met Husain Zanjanī.[35] According to the *Nafahāt al-Uns*, Shaykh Yūsuf Hamadānī died in 1140.[36] The earliest date of Mu'īn al-dīn given in any of the hagiographies is 1135. The *a priori* impossibility of these two meetings casts doubt on the reliability of Jamālī's other descriptions of Mu'īn al-dīn's encounters with notable shaykhs during his travels. No external evidence to confirm these alleged meetings has been found. However, the possibility of the meeting with 'Abd al-Qādir Jīlānī is somewhat substantiated by Jamālī reporting that he was shown the cell where Mu'īn al-dīn stayed on this occasion. The other alleged encounters may be classified as improbable, but not impossible.

There are only three other aspects of the story that are open to the external checks of the genuine *malfūzāt*. The *Surūr al-Sudūr* by Hamīd al-dīn Savālī provides confirmation of Mu'īn al-dīn's going to Delhi. It is, however, not clear whether Hamīd al-dīn is referring to Mu'īn al-dīn travelling through Delhi on his way to Ajmer, or to a subsequent visit to Delhi from Ajmer.[37]

Jamālī is wrong when he quotes Nizām al-dīn Awliyā' as saying that Mu'īn al-dīn used to call a Hindu, who lived near Ajmēr, a man of God. Jamālī is here misquoting from the *Fawā'id al-Fu'ād* where Nizām al-dīn 'told a story of Khwāja Hamīd al-dīn Savālī, who time and again used to say of a Hindu man, "This is a walī of Allāh." '[38] Jamālī has substituted Mu'īn al-dīn for Hamīd al-dīn. The attribution of this remark to Mu'īn al-dīn must, therefore, be rejected. The genuine *malfūzāt* confirm the fact that Mu'īn al-dīn was the principal khalīfa of 'Usmān Hārwanī, and that Qutb al-dīn was the principal khalīfa of Mu'īn al-dīn.[39] Nizām al-dīn states that Hamīd al-dīn was a disciple of Mu'īn al-dīn.[40]

---

[35] Nicholson's introduction to *Kashf al-Mahjūb*, p. xl. See also Sabah al-dīn 'Abd al-Rahman, 'Critical Study of the Dates of Birth and Death of Mu'īn al-dīn Chishtī', *Indo-Iranica*, vol. 17, 32.

[36] *Nafahāt al-Uns*, pp. 337–9.

[37] K. A. Nizami, *Religion and Politics*, p. 181, note 2.

[38] *Fawā'id al-Fu'ād*, p. 118.   [39] *Khair al-Majālis*, p. 8.

[40] *Fawā'id al-Fu'ād*, p. 346.

By the time Amīr Khurd wrote his *Siyar al-Awliyā'* both the apocryphal *malfūzāt, Anīs al-Arwāh* and *Dalīl al-'Ārifīn*, were in circulation. Even though it has been established that they were not genuine, whatever biographical references they contain cannot be ignored. It is possible, but not probable, that they may contribute something to the story of Mu'īn al-dīn's life by either confirming or contradicting the accounts of the early hagiographers. In the absence of any more reliable sources, attention must be turned to the early fabricated works.

Biographical References to Mu'īn al-dīn in the
Anīs al-Arwāh

Mu'īn al-dīn Hasan Sijzī narrates that there was a fellow-murīd of his living in his area. 'When he died the people came back from his burial, but I stayed at his grave. I was busy in contemplation when I saw two angels of torment come to him and want to punish him. The saintly pīr and murshid ['Usmān Hārwanī] came towards them and said sternly, "Do not punish him. He is my murīd." They went away according to his order. After a short while they returned and said, "Hazrat, it is a commandment of Allāh that, although he was your murīd, he was still far away from your Way [*Tarīqa*]." He said to them, "That may have been the situation but he was nevertheless closely associated with me. It is my responsibility to help him." While this conversation was going on the angels were ordered, "Go back! Do not punish him. We have forgiven him because he is so dear to the saint." '[41]

This anecdote, reproduced by Amīr Khurd in his *Siyar al-Awliyā'*, has already been rejected. The next relevant reference concerns Mu'īn al-dīn's initiation as a disciple of 'Usmān Hārwanī.

This one, who prays for all Muslims, the faqīr, the humble, the weakest of all the slaves of Allāh, Mu'īn al-dīn Hasan Sijzī, was blessed in the city of Baghdad in the mosque of Khwāja Junaid Baghdādī with meeting and kissing the feet of Hazrat Khwāja 'Usmān Hārwanī. There were many great shaykhs present with my murshid at that time. As soon as I had kissed the holy ground, he said to me, 'Say two *raka'ts* of prayer.' I did as he said.[42]

Some editions of the *Anīs al-Arwāh* then continue thus:

[41] *Anīs al-Arwāh*, p. 4.   [42] Ibid., p. 5.

'Sit with your face towards the Ka'ba.' I sat down as ordered. 'Recite the *Sura-i Baqar.*' I recited it. 'Repeat the words, *Subhān Allāh* [Holy God] twenty times.' I repeated them. Khwāja 'Usmān then got up and turning his face towards the sky, took my hands in his own. 'Come,' he said, 'I will take you to Almighty God.' With these words he took a [pair of] scissors in his blessed hands and cut off my hair. He placed his cap over my head and gave me his woollen dress. 'Sit down.' I sat down. 'Recite the *Sura-i Ikhlās* one thousand times.' I recited it. 'The tradition of the *silsila* now requires a night and day of prayer,' he said, 'Go and keep this night and day alive with your devotions.' I passed a night and day in prayer according to the order of my master.

When the next day dawned I again presented myself before the khwāja. 'Sit down,' he said. I sat down. 'Raise your eyes.' I looked towards the sky. 'What do you see?' he asked. 'I see up to the Great Throne (*'Arsh-i A'zam*),' I replied. 'Look below.' I turned my eyes towards the ground. 'What do you see?' he asked. 'I see down to the depths of the Earth,' I replied. Then he said, 'Sit down and recite the *Sura-i Ikhlās* one thousand times.' I recited it. 'Raise up your eyes again,' he said. I did so. 'How far do you see now?' 'Till the curtain of the Highest,' I replied. 'Open your eyes and look in front,' he said. I did so. He placed two of his fingers before me. 'What do you see?' he asked. 'I see eighteen thousand spheres [*'Ālam*],' I replied. 'Go,' he said, 'your work is accomplished.' A brick was lying before him. 'Pick it up,' he said. I picked it up and found that it was a handful of gold coins. 'Take them to the darwīshes and distribute them in charity.' When I had returned, he said, 'Remain with me for a few days.' I replied, 'Your order is Supreme, I will stay.'[43]

None of the *tazkirāt* dispute the fact that Mu'īn al-dīn became the disciple of 'Usmān Hārwanī. But no credence need be given to the *Anīs al-Arwāh* account of how Mu'īn al-dīn was initiated into discipleship. Shaykh Nasīr al-dīn testifies that Mu'īn al-dīn would never have written in this way. Moreover, the author appears to have got the location wrong. Jamālī says that it was 'in the town of Hārwan, in the area of Nishapur' that Mu'īn al-dīn met his future murshid and became his disciple.[44]

According to the *Anīs al-Arwāh*, Mu'īn al-dīn and 'Usmān

[43] *Anīs al-Arwāh*, quoted M. Habib, 'Mystic Records', pp. 17–18.
[44] *Siyar al-Ārifīn*, p. 5.

Hārwanī then left Baghdad and travelled to Mecca and
Medina:

He [ʿUsmān Hārwanī] took me under the *navidān* [aqueduct] of
the Kaʿba and prayed for this faqīr [Muʿīn al-dīn]. A voice replied,
'We have accepted Muʿīn al-dīn Sijzī.' He left then and went to
holy Medina. I was also with him. When we reached the holy tomb
of the prophet of Allāh, he said to me, 'Make *Salām*.' I obeyed and
a voice issued from the tomb, '*Wa ʿalaikum al-salām*, O pole-
star of the shaykhs.' On hearing this he said, 'You have achieved
Perfection.'[45]

This anecdote must be a fabrication for ʿAmīr Khurd tells us on
good authority that none of the Chishtī shaykhs performed the
hajj pilgrimage.[46] The narrative in the *Anīs al-Arwāh* continues
thus:

Afterwards he left and came to a city in Badakhshan. He met a great
saint who was a descendant of Khwāja Junaid Baghdādī. He was 140
years old. He was greatly absorbed in Allāh. He was lame in one
foot. That foot had been cut off from its root. We were surprised at
seeing this. When asked the reason for cutting off one foot, he said, 'I
have been a recluse for a long time in this cell. I never put even one
foot out of this cell through physical desire. But one day it happened
that through physical desire I did put this severed foot outside, and
putting the second one out, I intended to depart. Then an angel said,
'O Pretender! you have forgotten your vow.' Hearing this voice I
was warned and was ashamed of breaking my covenant. A knife was
lying beside me. I took it from its sheath at once and cut off the foot
which I had placed outside and threw it away. Forty years have
passed since that incident. I have felt surprise every day since, and
will be ashamed to show my face among the darvīshes on the day of
judgement.'
    After listening to this we left that place and came to Bukhara and
met there imāms, high dignitaries and shaykhs. All of them were so
praiseworthy that we cannot express it in words.
    In that way for ten years I was a traveller in the company of Hazrat
ʿUsmān. After that we again came to Baghdad and stayed there for a
few days. Then we started to travel again. We travelled for the next
ten years. I used to walk with the luggage of my saintly pīr and
murshid on my head.

45 *Anīs al-Arwāh*, p. 5.
46 M. Habib, 'Mystic Records', p. 19.

Afterwards we came to Baghdad again and 'Usmān Hārwanī went into retreat. He said to me, 'I want to become a recluse. I shall not come out of the cell for a few days. Once a day it is essential for you to come to me so I can give you spiritual stimulation so that after me these teachings will be in your hands as a memorial of me to you.' After saying this he went into retirement. I, in accordance with his order, went to him every day. Whatever I heard from his sacred tongue I put into writing so these countless benefits might be collected... .[47]

It is possible that Mu'īn al-dīn visited Badakhshan and Bukhara at some time, but it is only likely that he went there with 'Usmān Hārwanī if his discipleship lasted for the twenty years mentioned both by the author of the *Anīs al-Arwāh* and the *Siyar al-Awliyā'*. It has already been argued that Mu'īn al-dīn was a disciple for only two and a half years—the period mentioned by Jamālī. If this is correct, these anecdotes are almost certainly inaccurate.[48] The sentence, 'I used to walk with the luggage of my saintly pīr and murshid on my head' is echoed by Amīr Khurd who probably borrows it from this source. The *majālis* of 'Usmān Hārwanī have already been shown to be fabricated. The last part of the quotation from the *Anīs al-Arwāh* is too obviously a device to create a situation in which Mu'īn al-dīn can be made to record the spurious teachings of his murshid to have any substance.

After the final *majlis* the following words are put into 'Usmān Hārwanī's mouth:

'All the teachings which came during these conversations are for your [Mu'īn al-dīn's] benefit. It is essential that you act in accordance with all that I have said so you will not be ashamed on the Day of Judgement.' After that he said, 'The true murīd and khalīfa is he who considers whatever he hears from his pīr and acts wholeheartedly upon it.' When he finished saying this, he gave the prayer-rug (*musallā*), cloak (*khirqa*) and staff (*'asā*) to this well-wisher

[47] *Anīs al-Arwāh*, pp. 5–6.
[48] The anecdote of the ascetic in Badakhshan is not rejected because of any improbability of his cutting off one foot. Acts of self-mutilation are not uncommon in the Sufi world; but this is perhaps a little too extreme to be probable.

[Mu'īn al-dīn]. Then he said, 'These *amānat* [things given and committed to the trust of a particular person] reached me from the *khwājagān* of Chisht. I have given them to you and have put them into your custody. It is essential that when you see a true Muslim to follow you after [your death] you should give them to him.' When he finished saying this, I put my head on the soil. He took me up lovingly and embraced me. This well-wisher [Mu'īn al-dīn] left him.[49]

If this anecdote were true it would undoubtedly have been recorded by Amīr Khurd in the *Siyar al-Awliyā'*, or by Nizām al-dīn in the *Fawā'id al-Fu'ād*. The *amānat* of the *silsila* had by that time assumed considerable importance as symbols of the continuity of the traditions of the Chishtī order and of the authority of their temporary custodians. As it is, there are no contemporary references to this incident. Amīr Khurd, who was familiar with the apocryphal *Anīs al-Arwāh*, must have had good reason to reject it. So there is no evidence to accept this tradition as authentic.

A similar argument suggests that the anecdote in the *Siyar al-Awliyā'*, and its elaboration in the *Siyar al-'Ārifīn*, of both Mu'īn al-dīn and Qutb al-dīn giving their blessing to Farīd al-dīn, is apocryphal.[50] A story which so conveniently illustrates the continuity of the *silsila* would doubtless have appealed to Nizām al-dīn and Nasīr al-dīn and have appeared in their recorded *majālis*. The fact that they do not use the anecdote suggests that this incident never, in fact, occurred. However, the evidence for this is not conclusive.

There is nothing inherently improbable about the remaining Delhi anecdote in which Mu'īn al-dīn meets Qutb al-dīn and the Shaykh al-Islām, Najm al-dīn Sughrā.[51] While this incident does serve the obvious didactic purpose of demonstrating the popularity of the Chishtī shaykhs despite their humility and lack of involvement with the state, there are no external grounds for rejecting the anecdote.

---

[49] *Anīs al-Arwāh*, p. 35.
[50] *Siyar al-Awliyā'*, p. 65; *Siyar al-'Ārifīn*, p. 21.
[51] *Siyar al-Awliyā'*, p. 21; *Siyar al-'Ārifīn*, pp. 50–1.

Biographical References to Mu'īn al-dīn in the Dalīl al-'Ārifīn

The first such reference concerns the initiation of Qutb al-dīn Bakhtyār into the discipleship of Mu'īn al-dīn:

On Wednesday 5th *Rajab*, 613 AH he [Mu'īn al-dīn] came to the mosque of 'Abd al-Lais Samarqandī in the city of Baghdad and I [Qutb al-dīn] had the *bay'āt* of Hazrat Khwāja Bozorg. He bestowed on me the four-cornered cap.[52] He graciously accepted me into the company of his *halqa* (mystic circle). That day Shaykh Shihāb al-dīn 'Umar Suhrawardī, Shaykh Tāj al-dīn Muhammad Isfahanī and many other great Sufis were present in the sacred *majlis*. ... He faced me and said, 'When I came into the presence of 'Usmān Hārwanī, I served him for twenty years. I never counted the days turning into nights or the nights turning into days. Day and night I used to be present in his service with my hands joined together before me [in respect]. When he went somewhere I accompanied him, walking with his luggage on my head. When he saw my dedication he opened the door of his bounty and generosity.[53]

The first problem here is the date; by AH 613/1216–17 Mu'īn al-dīn had arrived in India. Alternative editions of the *Dalīl al-'Ārifīn* give the date AH 514/1120–1 to this *majlis*. This is equally absurd as the earliest date in any of the literature of Mu'īn al-dīn's birth is 1135.[54] Mu'īn al-dīn's account of his discipleship given here fits in with the references in the *Anīs al-Arwāh* and the *Siyar al-Awliyā'*. This multiple attestation is no argument for its authenticity. The account given by Jamālī of the length of Mu'īn al-dīn's discipleship has already been given preference.

In the sixth *majlis* of the *Dalīl al-'Ārifīn*, Mu'īn al-dīn says:

We and many other sufis were sitting in the presence of 'Usmān Hārwanī. An ancient and scrawny man appeared. He ['Usmān] had respect for him, stood up to greet him, and made him sit on the

---

[52] The four-cornered cap was a symbol of the Chishtī's renunciation of *a*) this world, *b*) everything in the hereafter except for God, *c*) food and sleep except the essential minimum, and *d*) the desires of the self.

[53] *Dalīl al-'Ārifīn*, pp. 4–5.

[54] Neither the *Siyar al-Awliyā'* nor the *Siyar al-'Ārifīn* give the years of Mu'īn al-dīn's birth or death.

cushion beside him. The old man said, 'Thirty years have passed now since I lost my young boy. I do not know whether he is alive or dead. God knows if he lives or if he has died. I searched for him but could not find him. Now I have come to you to ask for your supplication. Please kindly pray for me.' On hearing this, Hazrat Khwāja became quiet for a while. He meditated and then said, 'Let us pray before Allāh for his son.' He prayed and said to the old man, 'Go back and you will find your son at the door of your house.' The old man left the assembly and returned after a short while with his boy. He presented him at the feet of the khwāja and said, 'When I returned home I was on the road when the people of my neighbourhood came and told me the happy news, "Congratulations to you, the boy has come." Now I have brought my boy into your presence.' He ['Usmān Hārwanī] asked the boy, 'Where have you been for these thirty years?' The boy answered, 'In the prison of *devs* for thirty years. But a short while ago a saint similar to you, in fact exactly like you, freed me saying, "Close your eyes." I closed my eyes. When I opened them I was back in my home.' He wanted to say more but 'Usmān Hārwanī gestured him to be quiet. The young man was silent. The old man and the young boy became murīds of 'Usmān Hārwanī and said, 'May the name of Allāh be glorified that such people, although having such power, keep themselves concealed.'[55]

This anecdote appears in the *Siyar al-Awliyā'* but there the miracle is performed by Mu'īn al-dīn himself, not by 'Usmān Hārwanī.[56] This suggests that the *Siyar al-Awliyā'* is a later work than either the *Anīs al-Arwāh* or the *Dalīl al-'Ārifīn*. Shaykh Nasīr al-dīn's comment on the apocryphal *malfūzāt* of 'Usmān Hārwanī shows that the *Anīs al-Arwāh* had already been written, but he does not mention the *malfūzāt* of Mu'īn al-dīn beyond the implication that no genuine work existed. The forms in which this anecdote appears in the *Dalīl al-'Ārifīn* and the *Siyar al-Awliyā'* suggest that it was Amīr Khurd who borrowed from the *Dalīl al-'Ārifīn* and not the other way round. The anonymous compiler of the *malfūzāt* of Mu'īn al-dīn would have used every available resource to increase the prestige of Mu'īn al-dīn; this would not have involved ascribing a miracle to Mu'īn al-dīn's pīr which Amīr Khurd had previously ascribed to Mu'īn al-dīn. The change of ascription only makes sense if the *Siyar al-Awliyā'* is the later work.

---

[55] *Dalīl al-'Ārifīn*, pp. 27–8.   [56] *Siyar al-Awliyā'*, p. 42.

So the belief that Amīr Khurd did not use the apocryphal works is unfounded. The length of Mu'īn al-dīn's discipleship, the miracle of the lost son, Mu'īn al-dīn at the grave of a fellow murid, the sayings of Mu'īn al-dīn—all these items Amīr Khurd has borrowed from the fabricated *malfūzāt* for the *Siyar al-Awliyā'*.[57]

In the ninth *majlis* of the *Dalīl al-'Ārifīn* it is written:

I [Mu'īn al-dīn], Khwāja 'Usmān Hārwanī, and Shaykh Awhad al-dīn Kirmānī were travelling together to Medina. We reached the city of Damascus. ... Subsequently the conversation turned to the subject of darvīshes exhibiting their miraculous powers. Khwāja 'Usmān Hārwanī put his hand beneath the prayer-rug, took out some gold coins and gave them to a darvīsh to bring some sweetmeats for the assembled company. Then, Shaykh Awhad al-dīn Kirmānī put his hand on a nearby stick which by God's grace was turned to gold. I out of respect for my murshid did nothing. 'Usmān Hārwanī turned to me saying, 'Why do you do nothing?' At this, I produced four round loaves from my pocket and gave them to a hungry darvīsh. The darvīsh and Muhammad 'Ārif remarked, 'A darvīsh who does not have such power does not merit the title darvīsh.'[58]

Since the miraculous is unacceptable as evidence for the historian, this anecdote can be rejected without further question. Moreover, the reference to a journey to Medina is of itself sufficient to condemn the reliability of this anecdote.[59]

The author of the *Dalīl al-'Ārifīn* subscribes to the idea that Mu'īn al-dīn arrived in India before the final Muslim conquest:

When he [Mu'īn al-dīn] finished telling of these things, his eyes filled with tears and he said, 'Now shall I travel to the place where I shall be buried.' After saying this, he took his leave of everyone. Then he said to me, 'You will come with me.' I, and many other darvīshes, accompanied Hazrat Khwāja. We journeyed for two months before we arrived at Ajmer where we settled down. At that time Ajmer was the habitation of Hindus. There were no Musalmans there. But after our arrival so many became Muslims that we could not count them....[60]

57 M. Habib, 'Mystic Records', p. 22, note 3.
58 *Dalīl al-'Ārifīn*, pp. 43–5.   59 See above, p. 45.
60 *Dalīl al-'Ārifīn*, pp. 55–6.

He also supplies a scene set in the Jama Mosque at Ajmer, in which the *tabarrukāt* which Mu'in al-dīn had received from 'Usmān Hārwanī are handed over to Qutb al-dīn, who is sent to Delhi:

> After stating these things he [Mu'in al-din] wept and said, 'O darvīshes, they have brought me here to be buried. Now, within a few days, I shall leave this world for ever.' Shaykh 'Alī Sijzī, his scribe, was present there. He said to him, 'Prepare a mandate in the name of Shaykh Qutb al-dīn Bakhtyār that he should go to Delhi. I have bestowed on him the khilāfat and *sajjāda* of the *khwājagān* of Chisht.' After that he said to me [Qutb al-dīn], 'Delhi is your place.' Then, when the *misāl* was finished, he gave it to me. I thanked him and with his pious hands he put his turban on my head and bestowed upon me the staff of 'Usmān Hārwanī, his Quran for recitation, and his prayer-rug, and said, 'This is the *amānat* of the Holy Prophet of Allāh entrusted to me by the *khwājagān* of Chisht, I have given it to you.'[61]

This is the first mention of such a ceremony. The *Siyar al-Awliyā* makes no reference to the *tabarrukāt* and its transmission from Mu'in al-dīn to Qutb al-dīn.[62] The *Siyar al-'Ārifīn* merely refers to the *khirqā*, and special prayer-rug, staff and sandals that reached Qutb al-dīn from Mu'in al-dīn.[63] There are no details. Had there been any reliable traditions, Nizām al-dīn, Nasīr al-dīn or Jamālī would have related them. The anecdote, in the form it takes in the *Dalīl al-'Ārifīn*, is stereotyped and unconvincing. The final words of Mu'in al-dīn are suspiciously close to those of 'Usmān Hārwanī in the final *majlis* of the *Anīs al-Arwāh*. Furthermore, the whole incident is almost word for word the same as the account of Shaykh Bāyazīd Bistamī's death in the *Tazkirāt al-Awliyā'*.[64]

There are numerous other references to places and people in the *Dalīl al-'Ārifīn*, but these are too obviously devices to provide a context for a particular saying, or a setting for a particular *majlis*, to be acceptable as biography.

---

[61] Ibid., p. 56.

[62] There are variations in the different texts of the *Siyar al-Awliyā'* here. The edition which Habib uses reproduces this anecdote from the *Dalīl al-'Ārifīn* in full.

[63] *Siyar al-'Ārifīn*, p. 30.   [64] M. Habib, 'Mystic Records', p. 22, note 3.

All the references which have any claim to being accurate biography have now been analysed, but no apocryphal work does anything to fill out the picture of the Mu'īn al-dīn of history. The only significant point that emerges from the examination of the *Anīs al-Arwāh* and the *Dalīl al-'Ārifīn* is the extent to which Amīr Khurd borrowed from these apocryphal works. This says little for the overall accuracy of the *Siyar al-Awliyā'*.

Dissimilarities between Established Traditions of the Chishtī and Hagiographical Material on Mu'īn al-dīn

There are few specific instances of contradictions between the hagiographies and the more reliable sources.[65]

As mentioned earlier, Nizām al-dīn Awliyā' used to recall how Hamīd al-dīn called a local Hindu a 'walī of God'.[66] This raises the whole question of the attitudes of the early Chishtī shaykhs towards non-Muslims. Jamālī states that Mu'īn al-dīn converted most of the unbelievers around Ajmer.[67] Amīr Khurd emphasizes how the coming of Mu'īn al-dīn to India removed the cloud of unbelief.[68] In the *Dalīl al-'Ārifīn* Qutb al-dīn is made to say, 'when we arrived there [in Ajmer] so many people became Muslims that we could not count them.'[69] These statements do not necessarily imply that Mu'īn al-dīn was an evangelist and actively involved in conversion, although that is how later hagiographers have represented him.[70]

In fact, it is clear that the attitude of the early Chishtīs (about whom there are reliable records), to non-believers was one of tolerance. The tolerance of Hamīd al-dīn Savālī is witnessed by his remark from the *Fawā'id al-Fu'ād*. Nizām al-dīn repeats this statement with evident approval. The poet Amīr Khusrau, a disciple of Nizām al-dīn, expresses religious tolerance and the need for mutual respect between religions:

[65] These relatively reliable sources are more useful in building up a general picture of the practices and life-style of early Chishtīs in India. See below, pp. 56–65.

[66] *Fawā'id al-Fu'ād*, p. 118. In the *Siyar al-'Ārifīn* (p. 14) this remark is wrongly attributed to Mu'in al-dīn.

[67] *Siyar al-'Ārifīn*, p. 13.

[68] *Siyar al-Awliyā'*, p. 44.

[69] *Dalīl al-'Ārifīn*, p. 56.

[70] See below, pp. 93–4.

O those who sneer at the idolatry of the Hindu
Learn also from him how worship is done
Though the Hindu is not faithful like me
He often believes in the same things as I do.[71]

It is also known that Nizām al-dīn's murshid, Farīd al-dīn, welcomed Hindu Jōgīs to his *khānqāh*.[72]

In the light of these reliable traditions, Jamālī's statement that 'those who were not converted nevertheless sent much *nazr* and *futūh*' to Mu'īn al-dīn, seems more probable than the idea of wholesale conversion to Islam which later hagiographers imply. Jamālī continues by saying that 'still these unbelievers come to his shrine' (at the time of Jamālī's visit to Ajmer). Scholars who have mentioned the situation of the early Chishtī shaykhs in India agree that they were not unacceptable to non-Muslims:

The existence of recluses living apart from their fellows was familiar in India, and Sufis were thus a part of an established tradition. It is not surprising therefore that the Sufi pīrs were as much revered by the Hindus as were the Hindu Gūrūs and ascetics, all of them being regarded by the Hindus as being of the same mould.[73]

Furthermore, the Chishtīs were prepared to be flexible in the outward forms of their religious observance:

The popularity and success of the Chishtī saints in India was [because] they adopted many Hindu customs and ceremonials in the initial stages of the development of their *silsila* in India. The practice of bowing before the shaykh, shaving the head of new entrants to the mystic circle, audition parties (*samā'*) and the *chillā-i ma'kūs* [the inverted *chillā*] had close resemblances to Hindu and Buddhist practices and consequently the appeal of the Chishtī *silsila* in the non-Muslim environment.[74]

The attraction of the shaykh lay elsewhere than in the alleged miraculous power which later hagiographers deploy in the interest of conversion stories. There were Hindu Jōgīs in plenty who could boast similar expertise.[75]

---

[71] Quoted Nizami, p. 262.
[72] K. A. Nizami, *The Life and Times of Shaykh Farīd Ganj-i-Shakar*, p. 105.
[73] Thapar, *History of India*, p. 30.
[74] Nizami, *Religion and Politics*, pp. 178–9.
[75] Hence the development of a particular class of anecdotes in the hagio-

For the lower Hindu castes acceptance of Islam means an escape from the degraded stature they had in Hindu society to at least theoretical equality with the ruling community; it also meant in pre-Mughal India better chances of state appointments.[76]

Arnhold agrees that 'it is this absence of class prejudice which constitutes the real strength of Islam in India, and enables it to win so many converts from Hinduism.'[77] Nizamī emphasizes the same point:

The unassuming ways of the mystics, their broad human sympathies, the classless atmosphere of their *khānqāhs* attracted these despised sections of Indian society to their fold. Here they found an entirely different social order; all discriminations and distinctions which Hindu society had imposed on them were meaningless in the *khānqāhs* ... the *khānqāh* thus became the spearhead of Muslim culture.[78]

So both the early sources and later scholars agree in hinting at the tolerance of the first Chishtī shaykhs in India. These Sufis were not evangelists: religious tolerance emerges as one of the principles governing the attitudes of the Chishtī *silsila*.

The parts of the life of Mu'īn al-dīn, as told by the earliest hagiographers, Amīr Khurd and Jamālī, which pass the test of authenticity, are: Mu'īn al-dīn was the son of Ghiyās al-dīn. His father died when he was fifteen years old. He was known as Mu'īn al-dīn Sijzī (often misspelt Sanjarī) indicating that he lived in Sijistān, though it is not certain where he was born. He met a darvīsh, Ibrāhīm Qundūzī, who greatly impressed the young man. He sold his property and went to Balkh and Samarqand to be educated. He met 'Usmān Hārwanī and became his disciple. He stayed with his murshid for two and a half years. He left his murshid and travelled around the Muslim world. It is not certain where he went or whom he met. He avoided becoming well-known in any one place by keeping on the move. He received the *khirqā* of khilāfat from his murshid,

---

graphies—miraculous combats between Jōgīs and Sufis.

[76] Ahmad, *Studies of Islam in the Indian Environment*, p. 82.

[77] Arnhold, *The Preaching of Islam*, p. 291.

[78] K. A. Nizami, 'Some Aspects of *Khānqāh* Life in Medieval India', *Studia Islamica*, vol. 8, 64.

'Usmān Hārwanī. He converted Muhammad Yādgār and Hakīm Ziyā' al-dīn of Balkh to the Sufi way. He travelled to India at the time of Shihāb al-dīn Ghorī's conquest of India. It is not known exactly when Mu'īn al-dīn arrived at Ajmer, before, during or after the final conquest. However, it is certain that he had to contend with a certain amount of opposition from unbelievers. He established himself at Ajmer and won the respect of both believers and non-believers. His two principal disciples were Qutb al-dīn Bakhtyār Ūshī and Hamīd al-dīn Savālī. He travelled to Delhi, stayed with Qutb al-dīn and met the Shaykh al-Islām. In his old age he married the daughter of Wajīh al-dīn Muhammad Mashhadī, brother of the first Muslim governor of Ajmer. He and his wife had children. He died seven years after his marriage, on 6th Rajab, at the age of 97. The years of his birth and death are not recorded.

The only items of Mu'īn al-dīn's biography for which there is evidence in sources more reliable than the hagiographies are:his being the principal khalīfa of 'Usmān Hārwanī; his travelling to Delhi; the discipleship of Hamīd al-dīn Savālī, and his conversation with him; and Qutb al-dīn Bakhtyār Ūshī being his principal khalīfa. The nature of the sources from which the remaining conclusions are drawn means that they cannot be anything more than possibilities, or, at the most, probabilities.

There are two ways by which the background to the picture of the life of Mu'īn al-dīn can be drawn in further detail; the first is an examination of his teachings recorded in the *Siyar al-Awliyā'*, and the second is an examination of the earliest reliable sources, which, while they do not deal with Mu'īn al-dīn himself, give an idea of the traditions of the Sufi order which he represented.

The Teachings of Mu'īn al-dīn

All the teachings of Mu'īn al-dīn which are recorded in the *Siyar al-Awliyā'* are taken from the fabricated *Dalīl al-'Ārifīn*.[79]

[79] As already discussed (p. 39 above), this contradicts Habib's assertion that Amīr Khurd did not borrow from the apocryphal works. 'Mystic Records', p. 22, note 3.

Amīr Khurd has evidently sifted through the *majālis* of this apocryphal *malfūz*, and borrowed the passages that struck him as being least objectionable and most in accord with Chishtī precepts. Thus, he avoided including passages such as the following two, which later hagiographers saw fit to borrow:

An *'ārif* is he who receives from the Unseen tens of thousands of manifestations of God every moment, to whom ecstasy comes in an instant, who with one stride reaches beyond the *arsh* and with another returns to his own place. The perfect *'ārif* has a special eye so he can see whatsoever is written [for the future].[80]

There is the rank of *'ārif*. When they reach this status, they can see the whole universe and all that is therein between their two fingers. The *'ārif* is he to whom whatsover he wants comes, and whatever he asks is heard.[81]

There is no evidence to support the authenticity of any of the sayings of Mu'īn al-dīn in the *Dalīl al-'Ārifīn*. If any of his utterances were still remembered at the time of the composition of the *Dalīl al-'Ārifīn*, it is highly probable that there would be references to them either in the *Fawā'id al-Fu'ād*, or the *Khair al-Majālis*. However, there are no such references, and therefore no reason to accept even Amīr Khurd's selection of Mu'īn al-dīn's teachings as authentic. In the absence of any source for his teachings other than the apocryphal *malfūzāt*, and the hagiographies which have borrowed from them, the impossibility of reconstructing his teaching must be admitted.

Traditions of the Early Chishtīs in India from the Reliable Sources

The sources that are generally reliable are the *malfūzāt* of Hamīd al-dīn Savālī (*Surūr al-Sudūr*), Nizām al-dīn Awliyā' (*Fawā'id al-Fu'ād*) and Nasīr al-dīn Chirāgh-i Delhī, khalīfa of Nizām al-dīn Awliyā' (*Khair al-Majālis*). Certain general points about the life of the Chishtī shaykhs in thirteenth-century India may also be established by reference to the *Awārif al-Ma'ārif* of Shihāb al-dīn 'Umar Suhrawardī and the *Kashf al-Mahjūb* of al-Hujwīrī. Both were widely read and regarded

---

[80] *Dalīl al-'Ārifīn*, quoted *Siyar al-Aqtāb*, p. 139.
[81] *Dalīl al-'Ārifīn*, quoted *Akhbār al-Akhyār*, p. 50.

as handbooks on the theory and practice of Sufism in India. All these sources can be used to obtain information about the shaykhs who followed Muʿīn al-dīn. Of these the closest was Hamīd al-dīn Savālī. The *Surūr al-Sudūr* records his conversations and was compiled by his grandson on the basis of personal memoranda some time after his death.[82] There are, however, only two extant copies of this work and neither was accessible, so we are forced to rely on quotations from this source wherever they occur.[83]

Because of the different circumstances in which Muʿīn al-dīn and the later Chishtī shaykhs lived, the details of Chishtī life in the latter part of the thirteenth and early fourteenth centuries cannot safely be held to apply to the lifetime of Muʿīn al-dīn. However, certain general principles which governed the life of the Chishtī shaykhs emerge from an examination of these later *malfūzāt*, the *Awārif al-Maʿārif* and the *Kashf al-Mahjūb* which they used as their guides.

In the *Fawāʾid al-Fuʾād*, Nizām al-dīn Awliyāʾ tells the following story of Hamīd al-dīn Savālī:

When he [Hamīd al-dīn] repented and received the *khirqā*, his former companions and associates came to him and said, 'Once more let us pursue our pleasure.' Hamīd al-dīn replied, 'This will never happen.' Again they tried to persuade him. Hamīd al-dīn again replied, 'This will never happen.' They pressed him further but he said to them, 'Go and sit in a corner, for I have tied up my pyjama-cord so tight that I shall not even open it for the houris on the morrow of the Resurrection.'[84]

At this point the *Siyar al-ʿĀrifīn* takes up the story:

After becoming the disciple of Muʿīn al-dīn, he [Hamīd al-dīn] divorced his wife, gave all his money and property to the poor and started to cultivate himself the ten *jarib* of land which he owned by the river. He grew his own food. He was content and no longer interested in the things of this world. He wore tattered clothes. He did not accept gifts. He only ate once a week ...[85]

The *Fawāʾid al-Fuʾād* has a second reference to the life of Hamīd al-dīn. Nizām al-dīn told his audience that

---

[82] Nizami, *Religion and Politics*, p. 270
[83] The two manuscripts are in the dargāh of Hamīd al-dīn at Nagaur, and the private collection of K. A. Nizami.
[84] *Fawāʾid al-Fuʾād*, p. 346.   [85] *Siyar al-ʿĀrifīn*, pp. 13–14.

In the district of Nagaur, there lived a great saint called Hamīd al-dīn Savālī. Some people asked him, 'Why are the names of some Sufis forgotten when they pass away, while the names of others reach the ends of the world? Why is there this difference?' He [Hamīd al-dīn] replied, 'The names of those who have striven to publicise themselves in this life are forgotten after their death. But the names of those who concealed themselves are known throughout the world after their death.'[86]

The two remaining *malfūzāt*, *Fawā'id al-Fu'ād* and *Khair al-Majālis*, are far removed from Mu'īn al-dīn both in time and in circumstance. The political and material status of Nizām al-dīn Awliyā' and his contemporary Sufi shaykhs were very different from those of Mu'īn al-dīn three generations earlier. In the Delhi of Nizām al-dīn, Sufis were no longer living on the fringes of society and respectability. Both Baranī and Amīr Khusrau testify to the central importance of Nizām al-dīn in the social and religious life of late thirteenth-century northern India.[87] Nasīr al-dīn managed to hold the spiritual empire of the Chishtī order together for thirty years after Nizām al-dīn's death, but with his own death the whole edifice collapsed.[88]

Suhrawardī lays down fifteen rules to govern the behaviour of the shaykh, and fifteen for that of his murīds.[89] The murīds must submit themselves to the authority of the shaykh, who in turn, must dedicate himself to assist in the progress of his murīds along the Sufi way (*tarīqat*):

The spiritual director so teaches that he makes the servants of God to be loved by His servants and makes the servants of God to be loved by Him. He leads the novices along the road of purification, and when the soul is purified, the mirror of the heart is polished and there is reflected in it the splendour of the Divine Glory, and there shines within it the radiance of the Divine Beauty, and the insight is rapt away to the contemplation of the splendour of the Eternal Majesty and the vision of the Everlasting Perfection. Then the servant cannot

[86] *Fawā'id al-Fu'ād*, p. 3.

[87] Baranī, *Ta'rīkh-i Fīrūzshāhī*, pp. 343–7. For Amīr Khusrau's admiration of Nizam al-dīn Awliyā' see also an English translation of one of his poems in M. Mujeeb, *The Indian Muslims*, p. 175.

[88] For the difficulties with which Nasīr al-dīn had to contend see *Khair al-Majālis*, pp. xix, lv, lxv, and Mujeeb, *Indian Muslims*, pp. 160–1.

[89] *'Awārif al-Ma'ārif*, p. 113.

but love his Lord and that is the fruit of purification. The mirror of
the heart also, when it is polished, reflects this world and all it
contains, and the world to come and all its treasures, and to the inner
sight is revealed the reality of the two worlds. Then the servant
attains to the Two Abodes and he desires what is abiding and
renounces what is transient. It is the work of the spiritual director to
help towards this purification.[90]

Success on the mystic path depends on purity of motive:

The Sufi shaykhs observe the following rule when a novice joins them
with the purpose of renouncing the world: They subject him to
spiritual discipline for the space of three years. If he fulfils the
requirements of this discipline, well and good; otherwise they declare
that he cannot be admitted to the Path (*tarīqat*). The first year is
devoted to the service of the people, the second year to the service of
God, and the third year to watching over his own heart. He can serve
the people only when he places himself in the rank of servants and all
other people in the rank of masters, i.e. he must regard all, without
any discrimination, as being better than himself, and must consider it
his duty to serve all alike; not in such a way as to deem himself
superior to those whom he serves, for this is a manifest perdition and
evident fraud, and is one of the infectious cankers of the age. And he
can serve God Almighty only when he cuts off all his selfish interests
relating either to this world or to the next, and worships God
absolutely for His sake alone inasmuch as whoever worships God
absolutely for anything's sake worships himself and not God. And he
can watch over his heart, so that in the presence of intimacy [with
God] he preserves his heart from the assaults of heedlessness. When
these three qualifications are possessed by the novice, he may wear
the *muraqqa'* as a true mystic, not merely as an imitator of others.[91]

To ensure the attainment of 'the fruits of purification' the
discipline of the daily life of a *khānqāh* was severe. The *'Awārif
al-Ma'ārif* prescribes a rigid timetable of compulsory prayer,
devotions and recitations of the Quran. There are occasional
breaks allowed when 'if he have an important worldly matter,
in it he [the murīd] engageth.' But, 'if God shall have given him
the bounty of leisure, he should regard as booty the being
engaged in worship of God.'[92]

    [90] Ibid., quoted in M. Smith, *Readings from the Mystics of Islam*, No.
99.
    [91] *Kashf al-Mahjūb*, pp. 54–5.   [92] *'Awārif al-Ma'ārif*, p. 113.

Khilvat (retirement) was held to be essential for progress to
be made along the spiritual path:[93]

Retreat is like a smith's forge in which, by the fire of austerity, the
desire becomes fused, purified, delicate and gleaming like a mirror
and in it appeareth the form of the Invisible. For every morning of the
retreat, a veil should be lifted and the retreatant finds himself drawing
nearer to God, so that in forty mornings, the fortyfold veil should be
lifted and the purified human nature should return from a land that is
far-off to the land of proximity, and the vision of the splendour of
Eternity without beginning should be made certain for it and manifested to it.[94]

. The Chishtī shaykhs believed in the possibility of miracles,
and this was in keeping with the established cosmology of the
time:

You must know that miracles may be vouchsafed to a saint so long as
he does not infringe the obligations of religious law. Both parties of
the orthodox Muslims agree on this point, nor is it intellectually
impossible, because such miracles are a species of that which is
predestined by God, and their manifestation does not contradict any
principle of the religious law, nor, on the other hand, is it repugnant
to the mind to conceive them as a genus.[95]

It was (and is) a general belief in Islam that Allāh intervenes
in a miraculous way in the affairs of man through inspired
intermediaries. But the early Chishtī shaykhs did not insist that
miracles were of primary importance, although as Mujeeb
remarks, 'In a society where the miraculous was a part of
established belief, the Sufi could not, even if he wanted to,
assert that spiritual attainment had nothing to do with supernatural powers.'[96] In fact, Nizām al-dīn Awliyā' said that,
kashf—things revealed to a Sufi—and *karāmat* (miracles) are
obstacles in the path because 'there are a hundred stages in the
path of Sufism and *karāmat* is no more than the seventeenth.

[93] The conventional duration of *khilvat* was forty days. For the significance
and frequency of the number 'forty' in Islam see *'Awārif al-Ma'ārif*, p. 41;
and F. W. Hasluck, *Christianity and Islam under the Sultans*, vol. 2,
pp. 392–6.
[94] *'Awārif al-Ma'ārif*, quoted M. Smith, Reading no. 98.
[95] *Kashf al-Mahjūb*, p. 218.
[96] Mujeeb, *The Indian Muslims*, p. 119.

Anyone who stops at this stage fails to attain the remaining eighty-three.[97] Far from flaunting his miraculous powers, the shaykh was required to conceal them: 'Allāh has made it obligatory on the saints to hide their miracles.' He goes on to say that 'the performance of miracles is no achievement. A Musalman should be helpless in the path of truth.'[98]

The life of Nizām al-dīn Awliyā', as it is revealed in the *Fawā'id al-Fu'ād* and *Siyar al-Awliyā'*, closely conforms to the model given by the *Kashf al-Mahjūb* and the *'Awārif al-Ma'ārif*.[99] Unlike some of his Suhrawardī contemporaries, Nizām al-dīn avoided all involvement with the state. He ordered that it was not permitted for a darvīsh to accept any grant, stipend or favour from any Sultan or official.[100] That Nizām al-dīn's murshid, Shaykh Farīd, was of the same opinion is witnessed by the following anecdote which occurs in both the *Fawā'id al-Fu'ād* and the *Khair al-Majālis*: Shaykh Badr al-dīn, a fellow disciple of Qutb al-dīn, accepted an offer from the court Treasury to build him a *khānqāh*. He was later charged with embezzlement. This was regarded as punishment from on high: Shaykh Farīd al-dīn remarked on hearing this—'He who does not follow the principles of his master is confounded with such troubles and worries that his heart gets no peace.'[101]

Since acceptance of government endowments and grants was

---

[97] *Fawā'id al-Fu'ād*, quoted Mujeeb, p. 119.

[98] *Fawā'id al-Fu'ād*, quoted Nizami, *Religion and Politics*, p. 284. See also A. Schimmel, *The Mystical Dimensions of Islam*, p. 212: 'The aversion of the spiritually advanced mystics for the kind of miracle-mongering that constituted part of the activities of the "shop-keeper *shaykhs*" and pseudo-mystics has found its crudest expression in an alleged *hadīs*: "Miracles are the menstruation of men." This saying, which seems to belong to the Indian or at least eastern part of the Muslim world, indicates that miracles come between man and God. Just as the husband avoids intercourse with his wife during the days of her impurity, so God denies mystical union to those who perform miracles.'

[99] It is known, for instance, that Nizām al-dīn studied the *'Awārif al-Ma'ārif* with his pīr, Farīd al-dīn. (*Fawā'id al-Fu'ad*, quoted K. A. Nizami, *The Life and Times of Shaykh Farīd*, p. 75.) For a sketch of the daily routine of Shaykh Nizām al-dīn, see Nizami, *Religion and Politics*, pp. 206–7.

[100] *Fawā'id al-Fu'ād*, quoted Nizami, *Religion and Politics*, p. 246. See also *Jawami 'al-Kilm*, p. 213; *Siyar al-Awliyā'*, pp. 286–7; and *Khair al-Majālis*, pp. 89, 279.

[101] Quoted Nizami, *Shaykh Farīd*, p. 35.

prohibited, the Chishtī *khānqāhs* relied on *futūh* (unsolicited charity) to meet its necessary expenses:

A man should not ask for anything with his tongue, nor should he think in his heart that it would be good that a particular individual gave him something. But if without any request or desire on his part a thing comes to him it is lawful.[102]

It was also permitted for the Chishtī shaykhs to cultivate wasteland (*zamīn-i ihyā*) as is witnessed by the biographical note quoted from the *Surūr al-Sudūr* on Hamīd al-dīn Savālī in the *Siyar al-'Ārifīn*.[103]

Any surplus at the *khānqāh* was distributed to visitors and those in need. Shaykh Nizām al-dīn Awliyā' advised his nephew: 'Whatever comes to thee keep it not but spend it.'[104] The Chishtīs quoted the following *hadīs* in favour of their policy of a kitchen open to all comers: 'If someone visits a living man and gets nothing from him to eat, it is as if he had visited the dead.'[105]

The major characteristic of the Chishtī *silsila* that has not been considered so far is their fondness of *samā'*. Of the four Sufi orders popular in the Indian subcontinent, the Chishtīs were alone in consistently seeking ecstatic inspiration in music. The use of *samā'* has always been controversial in Islam. The doctors who elaborated the laws of the schools generally pronounced against it.[106] They held that it was more likely to lead to sensuality than to spirituality. However, the Chishtīs insisted that *samā'* was consonant with Muslim law, even though they were not insensitive to its dangers.

Suhrawardī lists the dangers of *samā'* but approves its practice if performed under the correct circumstances. He laid down strict rules to prevent the *samā'* harming the spiritually immature and to guard against the hypocrisy of affected ecstasy.[107] He then continues:

---

[102] *Fawā'id al-Fu'ād*, quoted Nizami, 'Some Aspects of Khānqāh Life in Medieval India', *Studia Islamica*, vol. 8, 60.   [103] See above, p. 57.

[104] *Siyar al-Awliyā'*, quoted Nizami, 'Early Indo-Muslim Mystics and their Attitudes towards the State', *Islamic Culture*, vol. 23, 15.

[105] *Fawā'id al-Fu'ād*, quoted Nizami, *Religion and Politics*, pp. 205–6. For a detailed discussion of *Futūh* and its distribution through the Langar Khāna in Chishtī *Khānqāhs*, see Chapter 10 of *Siyar al-Awliyā'*.

[106] Robson, *Tracts on Listening to Music*, p. 2.

[107] *'Awārif al-Ma'ārif*, pp. 223–32.

Music does not give rise, in the heart, to anything which is not already there; so he whose inner self is attached to anything else than God is stirred by music to sensual desire, but the one who is inwardly attached to the love of God is moved by hearing music to do His will. … The common folk listen to music according to nature, and the novices listen with desire and awe, while the listening of the saints brings them a vision of the Divine gifts and graces, and these are gnostics to whom listening means contemplation. But, finally, there is the listening of the spiritually perfect to whom, through music, God reveals Himself unveiled.[108]

al-Hujwīrī warns that 'it is more desirable that beginners should not be allowed to attend musical concerts, lest their natures become depraved.' But as a safeguard he issues the following instructions:

It is necessary that a spiritual director should be present during the performance, and that the place should be cleared of common people, and that the singer should be a respectable person, and that the heart should be emptied of wordly thoughts, and that the disposition should not be inclined to amusement, and that every artificial effort (*takalluf*) should be put aside. You must not exceed the proper bounds until audition manifests its power, and when it has become powerful you must not repel it but must follow it as it requires: if it agitates, you must be agitated, and if it calms, you must be calm; you must be able to distinguish a strong natural impulse from the ardour of ecstasy. The auditor must have enough perception to be capable of receiving the Divine influence and of doing justice to it. When its might is manifested on his heart he must not endeavour to repel it, and when its force is broken he must not endeavour to attract it.[109]

On the question of the legality of the *samā'* Nizām al-dīn Awliyā' said, *samā'* is itself neither lawful nor unlawful. Indeed it is said that a certain saint was asked, "What is *samā'*?" He answered, "First tell me, who is the listener?" '[110]

An anecdote from the *Nafahāt al-Uns* gives an idea of the origins of *samā'* in the Chishtī *silsila*. The story concerns the

---

[108] Ibid., quoted Smith, Reading no. 100.
[109] *Kashf al-Mahjūb*, p. 419.
[110] Introduction to ninth section of *Siyar al-Awliyā'* where Amīr Khurd quotes a similar set of rules for *samā'* established by Nizām al-dīn Awliyā'. For the legality and effects of *samā'* depending on the status of the listener, cf. the following verse quoted Nicholson, *Mystics of Islam*, p. 65:

When an anchorite goes into a tavern, the tavern becomes his cell.
But when the wine-bibber goes into a cell, that cell becomes his tavern.

conflict and reconciliation of Qutb al-dīn Maudud, a representative of the *silsila* resident at Chisht, and Ahmad-i Jām, an outsider who came to Herat in order to gain spiritual ascendancy over it.[111] Qutb al-dīn and his followers regarded this as an aggressive attempt to annex a part of the territory over which they held *wilāyat*. So Qutb al-dīn, with 2,000 armed followers, went forth from Chisht to oppose him. Ahmad-i Jām proved in every way too strong for the shaykh, overcoming the inconvenience of a torrential rainstorm which Qutb al-dīn raised against him, and not being caught out when the disciples of Qutb al-dīn proposed to raise up a curse to strike him down when he was off his guard during the afternoon siesta. Qutb al-dīn's disciple said:

> We have decided among ourselves that the best course is that we should despatch a spy so that at the time when the shaykh retires to his siesta and there is no-one waiting on him, some of us should come to you, and start a *samāʿ* and induce an ecstatic state and in the course of it throw a thing upon him.[112]

However, Ahmad-i Jām is not caught out and a reconciliation follows. Digby suggests that this anecdote of Qutb al-dīn exposes one of the origins of the *Chishtī samāʿ* as being a shamanistic dance.[113] The anecdote also shows that *samāʿ* was practised by the Chishtīs well before the time when Muʿīn al-dīn introduced the order into India.

That Muʿīn al-dīn may have practised *samāʿ* can perhaps be inferred from the *Khair al-Majālis*. The legality of the use of musical instruments in the *samāʿ* is being discussed. Nasīr al-dīn thinks that there should be no instruments but only singing and clapping. Some manuscripts then include a remark by Hamīd Qalandar who observes that Muʿīn al-dīn is said to approve of *samāʿ* with musical instruments. The assembled company then agree that this information derives from the apocryphal *malfūzāt* which are condemned as unreliable, but the fact that Muʿīn al-dīn enjoyed *samāʿ* is not disputed.[114]

---

[111] *Nafahāt al-Uns*, p. 328. Qutb al-dīn Mawdud was the khalīfa of the khalīfa of ʿUsmān Hārwanī.

[112] *Nafahāt al-Uns*, p. 328.   [113] Digby, *Crosscurrents*, I, p. 4.

[114] *Khair al-Majālis*, p. 286.

This brief survey of the reliable sources which are closest to Mu'īn al-dīn suggests that nine principles governed the lives of the early Chishtīs in India. These were

Obedience of the murīd to the murshid.

Renunciation of the concerns of the material world.

Independence from the state.

Approval of *samā'*.

Strenuous personal routine of prayers and devotions.

Dependence on either cultivation of waste-land, or unsolicited offerings.

Disapproval of displays of miraculous powers.

Service to others in the form of *a*) teaching and guidance; *b*) distribution of surplus food and wealth.

Tolerance and respect for other religions.

It is probable that Mu'īn al-dīn conformed, at least in some degree, to these principles. But this must remain no more than a probability. The possibility of his having been a 'non-conformist' cannot be ignored.

3

The Legend of
Mu'īn al-dīn Chishtī

The historical facts, probabilities and possibilities of the life of
Mu'īn al-dīn have been extracted from the traditions about his
career recorded in the earliest sources. Although the parts of
his life which can be established with any degree of probability
are meagre, a substantial legend developed around these very
few facts. In this chapter we will examine why this legend
developed at all, and why it assumed the particular form it did.

The first full treatment of the legend is found in the *Siyar
al-Aqtāb* which was compiled in the mid-seventeenth century.
The way in which the legend had evolved by then can best be
perceived by extensive translation of the text:[1]

> 100   Mu'īn al-dīn Hasan al-Husainī al-Sijzī Chishtī was well
>   known for his miracles and asceticism and was endowed with all
>   the merits of Perfection. He had high status and was a great
> 101   healer. He was a Saiyid by true descent. There is no doubt about
>   his genealogy. He wore the cloak of poverty (*faqr*) and disciple-
>   ship from Imām al-Awliyā' 'Usmān Hārwanī. Through his
>   coming to Hindustan the way (*tarīqa*) of Islam was established
>   there. He destroyed the darkness of unbelief and *shirk* which
>   had prevailed there since time immemorial through revealing
>   clear reasons and arguments. For this reason Mu'īn al-dīn is
>   called *nabī al-Hind* (the prophet of India). For seventy years his
>   Ablution was not broken without him washing before prayer.
>   On whomsoever his propitious glance fell, that man was
>   immediately brought to Allāh. Whenever a sinner came into his
>   illuminated presence, he immediately repented. Mu'īn al-dīn

[1] Notes indicating the sources which the author of the *Siyar al-Aqtāb* has
used in his compilation are indicated in footnotes to the translation. The
teachings of Mu'īn al-dīn which the author has culled from the apocryphal
malfūzāt are omitted.

was continually in a state of contemplation. He had a hidden eye and during prayer he opened it and on whomsoever his glance fell, that man became a perfect saint. Whoever remained in his presence for three days became a man of miracles. He knew the whole Quran by heart and was a man of *samā'*. Every day he used to recite the whole Quran and every night he used to recite the whole Quran. Each time he finished reading the Quran a voice came from the Unseen world saying 'O Mu'īn al-dīn, your recitation has been accepted.' He always used to listen to *samā'* and neither any of the 'Ulamā' nor any of the *fuqahā* of his time objected to his *samā'*. He always used to fast during the day and pray during the night. He used to say his dawn (*fajr*) prayer with the Ablution of the night (*isha*) prayer.[2] Every evening he used to break his fast with one *misqāl* weight of dried bread dipped in water. He used to wear a patched cloth. When it was torn he used to mend it with a piece of clean material.

If I tried to write in this compilation of all the events and circumstances concerning the saint which have been written in the biographical books of great *mashā'ikh* and the *tazkirāt* of great saints it would never end. The events of the life of the saint are brighter than the moon and stars. So I have extracted some of these events and made use of only a few authentic sources.

It is related that the saint comes originally from a Saiyid family of Sijzistan. His holy father, Ghiyās al-dīn Hasan al-Husainī, was extremely pious and righteous. The birth place of the saint is in Isfahan. But he was brought up in Khurasan. When he reached the age of fifteen, his holy father died and his garden became the sole means of livelihood. He used to pray
102 constantly in the garden. One day a *majzūb* named Ibrāhīm Qundūzī passed by the garden. Mu'īn al-dīn knew of him and ran to greet him and kissed his hands. He brought him into the garden and offered him a bunch of grapes. The perfect *majzūb* took a morsel out from under his arm and put it in the pious mouth of Mu'īn al-dīn. Mu'īn al-dīn ate it and at that time the zeal of love and devotion to Allāh was born in his heart.[3]

He withdrew from worldly affairs, and the world and its business lost its attraction for him because of his pious heart. Whatever he possessed he distributed among the poor. He himself turned to Khurasan and there busied himself in acquiring knowledge. He learnt the Quran by heart. From there he reached Samarqand, but in that place also his heart was not satisfied.

[2] In other words, he did nothing impure, nor did he sleep between the two prayers.
[3] *Siyar al-'Ārifīn*, p. 5.

So he turned towards Iraq and from there went to Araby. Thence he came to the town of Hārwan and after that he arrived at Baghdad where he had the blessing of kissing the feet of 'Usmān Hārwanī. In those days there always used to be great saints present at the *mahfil* of 'Usmān Hārwanī. 'Usmān Hārwanī used to shower his unlimited beneficence on those saints.[4]

Thus the order came, 'O Mu'īn al-dīn, renew your ablutions and pray two prayers (*dogāna*).' Mu'īn al-dīn did as he was told. Then he said, 'Sit facing the Ka'ba.' He sat down. 'Usmān Hārwanī said, 'Recite the *Sūra Baqr*.' He recited it. Then 'Usmān Hārwanī said, 'Now recite *Darūd sharīf* once.' He recited it. 'Usmān Hārwanī turned his face up towards the sky and took the hand of Mu'īn al-dīn and said, 'Mu'īn al-dīn, I have made you reach Allāh and I have made you acceptable to Him.' Then 'Usmān Hārwanī took scissors to his pious head and bestowed on him the four-cornered cap and a special woollen garment and said, 'Meditate for one night and a day and recite the *Sūra Ikhlās* one thousand times.' Mu'īn al-dīn acted accordingly. Then 'Usmān Hārwanī said, 'Mu'īn al-dīn, lift your head up high.' He lifted his head. 'Usmān Hārwanī asked, 'What can you see?' He answered, 'I see everything from the '*arsh* (heavenly throne) to the bowels of the earth.' Then 'Usmān Hārwanī ordered, 'Recite the *Sūra Ikhlās* another thousand times.' He recited it again. 'Usmān said, 'Lift up your head.' He did so. 'Usmān asked, 'What can you see?' He replied, 'I see up to the Veils of Greatness.' 'Usmān said, 'Look in front of you.' He looked. 'Usmān said, 'Do it again.' He looked again. 'Usmān asked, 'What can you see?' He replied, 'I see a thousand worlds.' 'Usmān said, Mu'īn al-dīn, your task has been completed.'

103   A brick lay in front of him. 'Usmān said, 'Pick it up.' He picked it up and the brick became gold. 'Usmān told him to distribute it among the darvīshes which he duly did.[5] After that he remained in the service of his pīr for twenty years. He was with him at home and on journeys. Wherever they travelled he carried 'Usmān Hārwanī's bedding. He performed great service until he had achieved what was required.[6]

It is related of the time when Mu'īn al-dīn went to Mecca with his pīr that, when his holy pīr was standing under the canopy of the Ka'ba and supplicating on behalf of Mu'īn al-dīn, a voice came, 'Mu'īn al-dīn is My friend. I have accepted him and have

---

[4] Ibid.   [5] Cf. *Anīs al-Arwāh*, p. 5.
[6] *Siyar al-Awliyā'*, p. 43.

exalted him.' After their stay in that place, they went to the tomb of the holy Prophet. 'Usmān Hārwanī said, 'O Mu'īn al-dīn, make your *salām*.' He made his *salām* and a voice came, '*Wa'alaikum al-salām*, O pole-star of all the saints.'[7] Then they came to Baghdad and his holy pīr became a *mu'takif* (one who is continually at prayer in a mosque).[8] Accordingly he allowed Mu'īn al-dīn to go travelling and bestowed on him the blessing which he had received from the *khwājagān* (of Chisht).[9] His pīr often used to say, 'My Mu'īn al-dīn is the Beloved of Allāh. I am proud of his being my murīd and of his murīds. This is my complete glory.'[10]

It is related that Mu'īn al-dīn had a great taste for *samā'* and when he listened to *samā'* he became ecstatic (*bekhud*). Everyone in the service of Mu'īn al-dīn became people of the *samā'* as did most of the important 'ulamā' and great saints. Qutb al-dīn Bakhtyār Ūshī says that, 'Shaykh Shihāb al-dīn Suhrawardī, Shaykh Muhammad Kirmānī, Shaykh Muhammad Isfahānī, Burhan al-dīn Chishtī, Maulānā Baha al-dīn Bukharī, Maulānā Muhammad Baghdādī, the great Khwāja of Sijz, Shaykh Saif al-dīn Majuzī, Shaykh Muhammad b. Muhammad Isfahānī, Shaykh Jalāl al-dīn Tabrīzī, Shaykh Ahad al-dīn Kirmānī, Shaykh Ahmad Wahid, Shaykh Burhan al-dīn Ghaznavī, Khwāja Sulaiman, 'Abd al-Rahman and other great shaykhs of Baghdad and of the surrounding areas often used to attend the *samā'* of Mu'īn al-dīn. They used to come to kiss his feet and to get spiritual benefit. They had all kinds of different beliefs and they used to be included in the *halqa*.'

It is related that one day Mu'īn al-dīn was busy in the *haram* of the Ka'ba when he heard a voice, 'O Mu'īn al-dīn, I am pleased with you and have accepted you. Ask for whatever you desire and I shall give it to you.' Mu'īn al-dīn replied, 'O Allāh, accept those murīds who follow me and who will be descended from me.' The order came, 'O Mu'īn al-dīn, you, all your murīds and all the murīds who will be descended from you until the Day of Judgement, I accept all of them.' After that Mu'īn al-dīn often used to say, 'Whoever is my murīd, and whoever is the murīd of my murīds and whoever is descended from me until the Day of Judgement, Mu'īn al-dīn will not step into Paradise until all my murīds have entered.'

Praise be to Allāh that the unworthy writer of these words, who has no virtues, is one of the murīds of the saint. It is not impossible that I shall be accepted with the blessing of Allāh.

104

[7] *Anīs al-Arwāh*, p. 5.   [8] Ibid., p. 6.
[9] Ibid., p. 35.   [10] *Siyar al-'Ārifīn*, p. 8.

It is related that in the kitchen of Mu'īn al-dīn so many meals were cooked every day that all the impoverished people of the whole city could eat their fill. The servant in charge of this used to go every day before the saint for the expenses. He used to stand with his hands joined in respect. Mu'īn al-dīn used to take a corner of his prayer rug aside and reveal sufficient treasure. He used to tell the servant to take enough gold from this treasure to cover the kitchen expenses for that day. The servant used to do so and would cook the food and distribute it among the faqīrs.

It is related that there were seven people from Mughan near Baghdad who worshipped so assiduously that they would eat only one mouthful every six months.[11] Because of this most of the people were their devotees. One day all seven of them came to meet Mu'īn al-dīn. When his glance fell on them they were immediately under his spell; their countenances turned yellow and they started trembling. They fell at Mu'īn al-dīn's feet. The saint said, 'O you unreligious ones, you are not ashamed before Allāh that you do not worship him.' They replied, 'O saintly one, we worship fire because of fear in the hope that tomorrow it should not burn us.' The saint said, 'O foolish ones, you cannot rid yourselves of the burning of fire until you worship Allāh.' They replied, 'O Mu'īn al-dīn, pray to Allāh that this fire will not burn you and then we will believe in the God of the skies.' Mu'īn al-dīn said, 'By the order of Allāh, the fire of his palm cannot burn Mu'īn al-dīn.' A fire was burning there at that time. The saint put his fingers and hands into the fire and said, 'O fire, you must accept the hand of Mu'īn al-dīn in peace.' The fire became cold. Meanwhile, a voice came from the Hidden World (*Ghā'ib*), 'All the people present should realize that fire has no power to burn the hands of my friend.' The group from Mughan, on seeing the greatness and enlightened reason of the saint, immediately became believers and became Muslims with sincere hearts. They went into the service of Mu'īn al-dīn and in a short time became perfect saints. All ardent unbelievers who saw the blessed face of Mu'īn al-dīn became Muslims. So at that time no unbelievers lived in Baghdad.

It is related that Mu'īn al-dīn met Muhiy al-dīn Shāh 'Abd al-Qādir Jīlānī twice. The first time 'Abd al-Qādir Jīlānī saw him, he prayed for him and said, 'This man will be the leader of

[11] 'Mughān, Mughkān or Mukān is the name of the great swampy plain which stretches from the base of Mount Sablān to the east coast of the Caspian sea.' The capital of Mughān used to be a city of the same name, 'the position of which is difficult to fix'. See G. LeStrange, *Lands of the Eastern Caliphate*, p. 175.

the shaykhs of his time. Very many people will reach their (spiritual) destination through his (spiritual) wealth.' The second time they met was when Muʿīn al-dīn came to Jīlān, a small town situated under the mountain of Jūdī, where ʿAbd al-Qādir Jīlānī was living. ʿAbd al-Qādir Jīlānī made that place pleasant; he bought it with permitted (*halāl*) wealth and made it habitable for his descendants. It is situated near Baghdad. Muʿīn al-dīn arrived there and met ʿAbd al-Qādir Jīlānī. They sat together and became busy with *kalma* and *kalam*. After a while Muʿīn al-dīn said, 'O Hazrat, say something about the words of Allāh.' ʿAbd al-Qādir Jīlānī replied, 'The word of Allāh should be discussed

108 in a secluded place.' Muʿīn al-dīn said, 'There are two reasons for me not to go into a secluded place. The first is lest my pīr should hear of it and that it should grieve his heart and cause the destruction of my spiritual achievements. It is my belief that there is no-one superior in perfection to the pīr and I also do not think that there is any defect in my pīr. More than that I do not consider my pīr as being separate from Allāh. I include him among the most Perfect of this age. So how can it be justified for me to do this lest it interfere with him? Moreover to retire into a secluded place is not a great work; if the group of people know the *kalma* of Truth then there is no harm in going into retreat, but if they do not how can they learn what Hazrat has said? 'ʿAbd al-Qādir Jīlānī was silenced by this tale of Muʿīn al-dīn and did not reply. After that Muʿīn al-dīn left the service of ʿAbd al-Qādir Jīlānī.

Muʿīn al-dīn stayed in the city of Jīlān for a few months and he constructed a cell [*hujra*] in the place where he lived. He went into retreat and made *chillā*. They say that his cell in Jīlān is still in existence there. The people have repaired it ...[12]

Details concerning ʿAbd al-Qādir Jīlānī follow.

122   It is said that the ruler ordered an innocent man to be hanged. His mother came to Muʿīn al-dīn Chishtī. At the time she arrived, Muʿīn al-dīn was doing his ablutions. She began to cry and said, 'O Hazrat, listen to my complaint for Allāh's sake. The ruler of the city has ordered my son to be hanged for a murder he never committed.' Muʿīn al-dīn asked her to repeat her story. When

123   he decided she was telling the truth, he picked up his staff [*ʿasa*] and started walking. Sufis, servants, and a large crowd from the city followed him. Everyone was saying to themselves, 'Let us see why Muʿīn al-dīn has become so preoccupied. What will

[12] Cf. *Siyar al-ʿĀrifīn*, p. 6.

come of this?' At last Mu'īn al-dīn came near to the body of the murdered man. He stood still and fixed his gaze on the corpse for a long time and was quiet. The body was not in one piece. His severed head came to the hands of Mu'īn al-dīn who put it back onto the body. He pointed his staff at the body and said, 'O oppressed one, if you have been murdered without justification by the order of Allāh you will come back to life.' As soon as that was done, the murdered man moved, got up and lived. He looked like someone waiting for an order. He bowed low at the feet of Mu'īn al-dīn and stayed there for a while. Then he raised himself up and went home with his mother. From there Mu'īn al-dīn returned to his *khānqāh* and said, 'That man will have access to Allāh such that if he asks something of Allāh, Allāh will grant his request. If someone does not have such access, he cannot call himself a darvīsh.'

Now we are going to relate the details of Mu'īn al-dīn's arrival in Hindustan and the events of Rājā of Ajmer, Shādī Dev, and Ajaipāl and of the preaching of Islam in this land through the blessing of Mu'īn al-dīn so that people will know of his Perfection, Greatness and *wilāyat*.[13]

It is told that when the shaykh had received the favours of his pīr and he decided to travel, he was 52 years old. Everywhere he went he usually lived in cemeteries, and wherever his reputation spread he delayed no longer, but secretly departed from there when no one was aware of it.[14] After some time he came to the House of the Ka'ba, and stayed some days there, and then went to Medina the Radiant, and performed the pilgrimage to the holy tomb of the Prophet Muhammad, and stayed for a while there, until, one day from the inside of the pure and blessed tomb a cry came: 'Send for Mu'īn al-dīn.' The servants of the tomb called out the name and from several places heard the reply, ' I am here for thee.' They said, 'Which Mu'īn al-dīn do you want? In this dargāh there are several persons present called Mu'īn al-dīn Chishtī.' The servant came forward and told what he had been ordered, and at that moment a strange ecstasy came over the Khwāja which cannot be described. Weeping and crying out and invoking blessings, he came to the door of the tomb and stood there. The voice cried: 'Enter O polestar of shaykhs.' Lost to himself and intoxicated, the Khwāja went in, and was dignified by the sight of the world adorning beauty of that Presence, and he saw that Presence speak to him.

124

[13] The translation of the *Siyar al-Aqtāb*, pp. 123–33 was prepared by Simon Digby for his unpublished paper 'Encounters with Jogīs in Indian Sufi Hagiography' and is reproduced here with his kind permission.
[14] Cf. *Siyar al-'Ārifīn*, p. 8.

'Mu'īn al-dīn, you are the essence of my faith; but you must go to Hindustan. There there is a place called Ajmer, to which one of my sons (descendants) went for a holy war, and now he has become a martyr, and the place has passed again into the hands of the infidels. By the grace of your footsteps there once more shall Islām be made manifest, and the Kāfirs be punished by God's wrath.'

Then the Prophet—upon him be Blessings and peace—gave a pomegranate into the hands of the Khwāja, and said, 'Look into this, so that you may see and know where you have to go.' At his command the Khwāja looked into the pomegranate, and saw all that there is between the East and the West, and he looked well at Ajmer and its hills. He humbly offered prayers and sought for help from that dargāh which is the envy of the heavens; then he set out for Hindustan.

He took with him on his journey forty men, and after a while they reached Hindustan. They came the whole way, even though the Rājā of Ajmer, informed by astrologers of keen under-standing, had written with great earnestness to various places, that if a darvīsh with such a countenance should pass by that way, he should be killed. But the Khwāja and his forty com-panions travelled openly and none had any power over him, till he reached the grace-giving land of Ajmer, where he stayed outside the city beneath a tree. There was an open space there, where the camels of the Rājā of Ajmer—who was known as Mahārājā—used to sit. Suddenly the camel-driver came and saw the band of darvīshes sitting there. He said, 'O faqīrs, this place is not yours, for here the camels of Mahārājā sit.'

125   No-one said a word to him, and then he came forward with violence, until his representations displeased the Khwāja, and he got up from there, and said: 'Even though I get up, your camels shall remain seated.'

He said this and set out from there and came to the banks of the lake of Ana Sagar, which was a delightful place, and pleased him.[15] He sat down there and became occupied with his devotions.

When the camels had come and sat down in the other place, the following morning, however much the camel-driver shouted at them and tried to make them get up, they would not do so.

To continue, when the Khwāja had taken up residence at the Ana Sagar, a man said to him, 'Sir, this is the very place where Mir Saiyid Husain Khing-Sawār[16]—God's mercy upon him—

[15] Ana Sagar—a lake adjacent to Ajmer.
[16] Khing means a grey horse, and sawār means a horse rider. 'It appears that the Syed was a servant of Shihāb al-dīn Ghorī, and that at the time when he returned from the conquest of India, he made him shiqqdār of Ajmer.

at the time when he had come and conquered the country and was living in it, chose to dwell.'

The Khwāja said: 'Praise be to God, may He be exalted, for I have gained possession of the property of my brother.'

Although at that time there were very many temples of idols around the lake, when the Khwāja saw them, he said: 'If God and His Prophet so will, it will not be long before I raze to the ground these idol-temples.'

It is said that among those temples there was one temple to reverence which the Rājā and all the infidels used to come, and lands had been assigned to provide for its expenditure. When the Khwāja had settled there, every day his servants bought a cow, brought it there and slaughtered it and ate it, until the infidels got news of this, and curled up upon themselves, and were consumed with rage, and said: 'Now it is not good to remain idle. Let us come upon these Musalmans all together, and let us neglect nothing to achieve our aim, and drive them from this city and kingdom.' So they all took up arms and sticks and stones and catapults, and set out. They surrounded the Khwāja and tried to harm him. The Khwāja was praying. His servants were disturbed, and brought the news to him. When he had finished his prayers, he rose up and he took up a handful of earth and recited the Throne-Verse over it, and then threw it towards his enemies. On whomsoever that earth fell, his body dried up and he lost his sense of feeling and power of movement; and they were all punished.

So when the infidels grew weak and saw that they had no power to resist such a perfect companion of God, they had to abandon the fight, and were filled with regret. They went into their idol temples which were their places of worship. In them there was a *dev*, in front of whom they cried out and asked for help. When the *dev* heard the truth of the matter, he stayed silent for a while, and then said, 'My friends, this darvīsh who has come is in his own faith very much a master of accomplishments. I shall not be able to overcome him except by magic and spells.'

He then taught them all magic and said: 'Recite as much as you can, so that the darvīsh will not have the strength to remain there.' The infidels did so, and then the *dev*, placing himself at the head of the band of the lost, set out. They came close to the

There he died. From lapse of time and general assent he became famous as a saint and his tomb became the circumambulation place of mankind.' *Akbarnāma*, vol. II, p. 540.

place where the Khwāja was, and these rebels taking shelter behind him, stood up and began to recite their spells. One of the Khwāja's disciples informed him of this and said: 'My pīr and protector, these filthy infidels have come back, led by their *dev*, and are reciting magic to put us in their power.'

'Their magic is all vain,' the Khwāja said, 'and will have no effect upon us. If God wills, their *dev* shall come into the true pathway.' He said these words and began to pray, until all those ill-fated ones came closer. When their glance fell upon the Khwāja their tongues lost the power of speech and their feet of movement, and they remained rooted where they stood, till the Khwāja had finished with his prayers. He then turned his blessed face towards them. The *dev* who was their leader, when he saw the perfect beauty of the Khwāja, trembled from head to foot like a willow tree. However much he tried to say 'Ram, Ram', it was 'Rahīm , Rahīm' that came from his tongue. When the kāfirs saw this, they were amazed and began to admonish him. At their behaviour the *dev* grew angry, and wherever he saw a stick or stone he took it up and beat their heads with it, so much that many of that band perished, and the remainder fled in disarray. The Khwāja, after much persuasion and search for him, praised God, and with his own hand gave a cup of water to a servant to take to that *dev*. The servant carried out his order and brought the water to him. Straightaway the *dev* took the cup from his hand and drank it with great keenness. He had no sooner drunk it than his heart was purified of the darkness of unbelief: he ran forward and fell at the Heaven-treading feet of 137 the Khwāja, and professed his belief, and said: 'Lord, from seeing your beauty I am exceedingly joyful.'

The Khwāja said: 'I also bestow on you the name of Shādī Dev [Joyful Dev].'

After the filthy infidels had been repelled, they went before the Mahārājā and related all of what had passed. The Mahārājā said, 'Try not to come before him impolitely, because it is not easy to drive away such darvīshes.'

At that time the camel-driver was present there, and he told the whole story of the camels.

'Have the camels not yet got up from there?' the Rājā asked.

'May you save me Mahārājā,' the camel-driver said, 'the camels have not got up from the moment when the words came forth from the tongue of that darvīsh, and have not even changed their position.'

'There is no cure for this,' the Mahārājā said, 'except you go to that darvīsh and put your head at his feet and implore him.'

The camel-driver went and did so; when the Khwāja had seen him imploring a great deal, he said: 'Go; your camels have got up.'

They straightaway brought the news to the Rājā who was amazed and concerned.

The Contest with Ajaipāl

It is related that in that country there was a Jogī called Ajaipāl, who had no equal in magic and sorcery in the whole of Hindustan.[17] He had a thousand and five hundred disciples, of whom seven hundred were reciters of spells, and the others fully accomplished in their own ways. The Mahārājā had great faith in him. He summoned him, sending an account of all that had happened. The Jogī when he heard this, gathered together all his disciples and came to the city to meet the Mahārājā. The Rājā pressed him hard to make him act in a way by which he would be revenged upon the darvīsh. The Jogī reassured him a great deal, and boasted more than can be described about his magic. The king believed what he was saying was true. Then the Rājā and Ajaipāl mustered all the men of the city and country, with many horses and attendants, and set out towards the Khwāja. Ajaipāl went flying along through the air on the skin of a deer.[18] Then they came close to the place where the Khwāja was and a
128 clamour broke out among the men. On the road itself, whenever Ajaipāl thought anything harmful about the Khwāja, he lost his sight and could not see. Every time he experienced this, he restored his sight by magic, until this had occurred seven times.

When the Khwāja heard of his coming, he completed his ablutions and rose up and drew a line around himself in a circle, and cheered his friends. Then these unlucky ones drew near, and much as they wanted, with the aid of their spells, to put their feet inside the circle, they could not do so. They saw Shādī Dev, who was standing with folded hands in the service of the Khwāja, and they lamented and said: 'O Dev, for year after year we have performed services for you, and spent sums of money with the object that you should aid our designs, and you have gone and become the slave of a Musalman.'

[17] The ruler of Ajmer almost immediately prior to Pithaurā was called Ajayapālā; this may be the source of the Jogī's name. D. Sharma, *Early Chauhan Dynasties*, p. 70.
[18] Deer-skins were commonly used by Muslim darvīshes. See F. W. Hasluck, *Christianity and Islam under the Sultans*, vol. 2, pp. 460–1.

Shādī Dev said nothing to them, and these unclean ones made even more noise and disturbance. The magicians were occupied with their own work till the Khwāja turned his face towards them and said: 'O you who have lost your way, what are you saying, and why are you discontented with me? Do you want everyone to be destroyed?'

'We wish to complain about our *dev*,' they said, 'whom we have worshipped for many years. He should belong to us, but has been turned away from us by your spells, so that now he does not listen to a word of what we say, nor give a glance at our condition.'

'If his heart inclines towards you,' the Khwāja said, 'when he is summoned and made glad he should come to you.'

Ajaipāl Jōgī and the infidels, however much they tried to lull the *dev* into contentment, and draw him back to them, by speaking soft words and rousing his hopes with promises, got no answer from him. Then the Khwāja said, 'Shādī Dev', and he replied immediately, 'Here I am, Sir.'

Then the Khwāja took up a cup, and gave it to him with his own blessed hand, and said, 'Shādī Dev, fill this cup from the lake of Ana Sagar, and bring it here, and as you fill it recite with your tongue the name of God "*Yā Badūh*".' Shādī Dev so reciting this blessed name of God, set out and came to the edge of the lake. As he was saying '*Yā Badūh*' and filling the cup, by a miracle of God, all the water of the lake came into the cup, and it seemed as if the lake had been dry for some time. Shādī Dev, holding that cup full of water, came back to the Khwāja and waited on him. When the infidels saw what had happened, they burned the more with rage, and tried even harder with their magic; for in their defective understandings they imagined that they would succeed by this means. From the hills they sent towards the Khwāja hundreds of thousands of snakes, and they tried to stone him. When those snakes arrived at the limit of the protecting circle, they put their heads down on the line and stayed there. The Khwāja commanded his companions to take up these snakes without fear, and throw them towards the hills, and in every place where the snakes fell, a plant sprouted from the ground and became a shady tree. Then the infidels rained fire in every direction, but not a cinder fell within the circle, and in the same way every spell which the magicians performed returned on their heads and injured them. Ajaipāl and the infidels grew weak, and he was shamed before the Rājā, so he came forward and said: 'I am Ajaipāl and now it befalls me to deal with you; so I have come upon you. Rise up, if you can, and take yourself

away from this place in safety. Otherwise you will see that at
this very moment I am going up into the sky to bring down such
a calamity upon your head that you will not be able to avert it.'

The Khwāja looked towards his companions and said, 'Do
you hear these words of a peasant bragging about himself and
threatening, like a dog which barks louder when it grows weak.'

Ajaipāl said some more words to frighten him, and the Khwāja
listened and smiled and said, 'O infidel, there is a proverb,

You have done your work on the earth well
That you should also be concerned with the sky.

Ajaipāl was put to shame by these words. He wound a
number of snakes around himself, and threw the deerskin into
the air, leapt up and sat upon it, and flew up into the sky, till he
had risen so far that the human eye could not see him. The
Khwāja looked towards his own shoes and said, 'O shoes of
130 mine, go and beat this luckless infidel so hard on the face that he
comes back to earth.' Then he made a sign to a companion to get
up and throw the shoes towards the infidel. He did as he was
ordered, and all saw that the shoes went up in the air till they hit
the head of Ajaipāl—whack, whack—sometimes on his head
and sometimes on his face, and brought him down to earth.[19]
When Ajaipāl landed and repented of his deeds, he came and
threw his head at the heaven-treading feet of the Khwāja, who
poured some water into a cup and gave it to him. Ajaipāl
immediately quaffed it, and all the false worship and darkness
which was in his heart was cleansed, and with a sincere heart he
recited the pure words of belief, and became a Musalman.

The Khwāja summoned him before him, and placed his hand
on his head and said, 'Ajaipāl, what is the wish of your heart?
Reveal it.'

Ajaipāl kissed the ground and spoke praises, 'O Khwāja,' he
said, 'seekers of God reach a state by their austerities and striving.
Bestow that state upon me from your miraculous power.'

'You will have knowledge of that state,' the Khwāja said,
'when you join the company of faqīrs and discipline yourself.'

'What you say, Sir,' Ajaipāl begged, 'is true, but I desire to
perceive now something of this.'

The Khwāja went into silent recollection, and after a while
opened his eyes and looked at Ajaipāl. Immediately the visible
world was lost to Ajaipāl's sight, and he found himself with the
Khwāja in the inner world. He saw that the Khwāja was flying

[19] Cf. Temple, *Legends of the Punjab*, vol. 3, p. 201; and *The Rehla of Ibn Battuta*, pp. 165–6.

up towards heaven, and he himself, Ajaipāl, was following him. They passed through the heavens, and each heaven which the Khwāja passed, Ajaipāl followed him through, and cried out: 'Sir, the angels of this stage do not let go the hem of my garment, for me to accompany you.' When the Khwāja turned round a voice came from the unseen: 'O Angels, let Ajaipāl also pass: he is the friend of Mu'īn al-dīn.'

They went on till they reached a place where Ajaipāl's awe increased, for it was a strange and pleasant place, pleasant beyond description. Then he saw a band of angels who came, company on company, and paid their respects to the Khwāja, 131 saying: 'Mu'īn al-dīn, the Friend of God, has come. Happy is he who meets him and does him service.'

'Ajaipāl,' the Khwāja then said, 'beyond this is a difficult place and the road is narrower. Although I am going there they will not let you pass, as you have not yet shown yourself worthy of it. So it is better for you to return from here.'

'Whatever you command,' he said.

'Close your eyes,' the Khwāja told him, and he closed them. Then he said, 'Open them.'

Ajaipāl opened his eyes and found himself in front of the Khwāja in the same place where they had been before. The Khwāja turned to him and said: 'Ajaipāl, have you seen what your heart desired?'

'O Khwāja, I have seen even more than that.'

'What else do you want?' the Khwāja asked.

'I wish to live forever,' he said.

The Khwāja considered this and went into silent communion. God's command came to him: 'O Mu'īn al-dīn, ask for him everything that he wants so that I may answer your prayer.'

The Khwāja opened his eyes and performed the prayers, and everything he asked for was granted. Then he summoned Ajaipāl before him and put his blessed hand over his head and face, and gave him the tidings of his life until the Day of Judgement, but that he should remain hidden from the eyes of men; and so it was, for people say that he still lives in those hills of Ajmer, and some men have met him, but his appearance is such that no man recognizes him. Once a woodcutter met him, and he fed the woodcutter on rice-milk. In short, from the blessings of the pure company of the Khwāja, he attained the ranks of the perfect, and received a cloak of succession. They say that to this day every Thursday night he comes to the radiant tomb of the Khwāja. And this would not be surprising.

After this, when the Rājā, and other Rājās, and all the band of

infidels beheld this state of affairs, they abandoned all hope from Shādī Dev and from Ajaipāl as well, and went away beaten and with yellow faces. Then Shādī Dev and Ajaipāl suggested to the Khwāja, that he should now set up a place in the city, where the populace might benefit from his holy arrival. The Khwāja accepted this suggestion, and ordered one of his special servants called Muhammad Yādgār, to go into the city and set in good order a place for faqīrs.[20] Muhammad Yādgār carried out his orders, and when he had gone into the city, he liked well the place where the radiant tomb of the Khwāja now is, and which originally belonged to Shādī Dev, and he suggested that the
132 Khwāja should favour it with his residence.

When he had settled there, he afterwards sent several persons to the Rājā, and said to them: 'Go to that lost infidel, and say: "O stony heart, those on whom you believed have by God's will become Musalmān. For your own good you should also testify to the oneness of God; otherwise you will be sorry." '

Then those who were appointed for this mission went before the Rājā and invited him to accept Islam, but their words had no effect at all upon him, and the lock of darkness was not opened from his heart:

The blanket of someone's luck is woven black:
It cannot be made white by the water of the stream of Paradise.

They therefore returned and related what had passed. When the Khwāja heard the truth of the matter, he went into silent communion, and after a while he opened his eyes and straightaway said: 'If this unlucky man has not believed in God, I give him into the hands of the army of Islam, to fall a prisoner alive.'[21]

And so in the end it befell: for after a little while Sultān Shihāb al-dīn awoke, he marvelled at this dream and related it to wise and accomplished men. They all praised God and foretold his victory, and reassured him, till with this encouragement of the Khwāja, he set out for Hindustan. After traversing the distance in between, he arrived at Ajmer. He gave battle to the Rājā of Ajmer several times, till finally the wind of victory blew on the flags of the Sultān's standards, and as the Khwāja had said, that infidel Rājā fell alive into the hands of the warriors of Islam. They made him prisoner and sacked his kingdom, and the Sultān, thanks to the encouragement and aid of the Khwāja,

[20] Cf. *Siyar al-'Ārifīn*, p. 11. Here Muhammad Yādgār remains at Hisar and does not accompany Mu'īn al-dīn to India.
[21] Cf. *Akhbār al-Akhyār*, p. 47.

returned fortunate and victorious to Delhi, where, after a great
slaughter, Rājā Pithaurā was also made prisoner. In the year AH
806/1403–4 he sat on the throne of Delhi, and after four or five
133 years he went back to Khurasan .... .

The reason for the name Ajmer is that there was a rājā named
Ajsā who ruled over territories stretching up to the boundaries
of Ghaznīn. In the Hindi language 'mīr' means mountain. When
this Rājā erected a building on a mountain he named it 'Ajmer'.
The first mountain-top building is at Ajmer.[22]

It is said by Qutb al-dīn Bakhtyār Ūshī, 'For a long time I was in
the service of Muʿīn al-dīn, my pīr. Muʿīn al-dīn never objected
to anyone. But one day Muʿīn al-dīn went into an alcove and
one of his disciples came taking with him a man named Shaykh
'Alī who owed him some *dirhams* as repayment of a loan. The
disciple grabbed hold of him and started to abuse him. When
Muʿīn al-dīn saw this happen he stepped forward to conciliate
them saying, "Give him a few more days." However, Muʿīn
al-dīn's suggestion made no difference. Muʿīn al-dīn became
very angry and put the shawl which he wore over his shoulders
on the ground. Through a miracle of Allāh that shawl was filled
with *dirhams*. Muʿīn al-dīn gestured the disciple towards it
saying, "Take from all this what you are owed." The man put
his hand out towards the *dirhams* intending to take more than
his rightful share of the money. His hand withered up. He
started protesting, "O Hazrat, I want to repent and I no longer
want my rightful share. I promise not to behave like this again."
Muʿīn al-dīn became kind and prayed with his hands upwards in
supplication saying, "O Allāh, when he has sincerely repented
by your mercy and beneficence heal his hand." Immediately the
disciple's hand was cured; he placed his head on Muʿīn al-dīn's
feet and for the rest of his life he served Muʿīn al-dīn entering the
group of *khuddām*.'

It is related that one day Muʿīn al-dīn was sitting down when a
man came and kissed the soil at his feet. He sat down and said,
'O Hazrat it has long been my ambition to meet you and serve
you. Praise be to Allāh that this great blessing has now been
bestowed on me.' When he said this Muʿīn al-dīn looked at him
and smiled. After a while he said, 'Come forward and do
whatever you have come to do.' As a result of this the man
started to tremble and he shook like someone in ecstasy. He put
his head to the ground and approached with humility saying, 'O
Hazrat, it is revealed to you that I have been sent to kill you and

[22] Cf. ibid., p. 52.

that I was ordered to do so but in my heart that was not my
intention.' Then he put his hand under his arm, removed his
134 weapon and placed it before the audience. Mu'īn al-dīn said,
'People's secrets should never be revealed. Never reveal anyone's
secret.' Then that man came forward and put his head on the feet
of Mu'īn al-dīn and said, 'O Hazrat, order them to punish me
and even to kill me.' Mu'īn al-dīn replied, 'O dear one, my way
is to benefit those who harm me. You did not even harm me.'
He said this and lifted the man's head. He prayed for him saying,
'Help this man to do good.' Simply through this prayer his heart
became gentle and he entered the service of Mu'īn al-dīn. By the
blessing of Mu'īn al-dīn's prayer he made 45 hajj and he is buried
by the blessing of Allāh near the Ka'ba in the graveyard of the
local people of holy Mecca.[23]

It is related that one day Mu'īn al-dīn was sitting performing
dhikr with Shaykh Ahad al-dīn Kirmānī, and Shaykh Shihāb
al-dīn Suhrawardī. Suddenly Sultān Shams al-dīn passed by
them with a bow and arrow in his hand. The glance of Mu'īn
al-dīn fell on him and he said at once, 'O my friends, this boy
will be the King of Delhi. I have seen it written that this
individual will not leave this world until he has become the
Sultān of Delhi.' It came to pass that after a short time this boy
did become the Sultān of Delhi.[24]

It is said that Mu'īn al-dīn went to Delhi twice during the
reign of Sultān Shams al-dīn. The first time he returned from
Delhi to Ajmer, he got married. The then Governor of Ajmer
was Mīr Saiyid Wajīh al-dīn Mashhadī. He had a daughter who
was pious and righteous. Her name was Bībī Asmat. When she
reached the age of puberty her father wanted her to get married,
but he could not find anyone suitable. He was anxious about
this when he saw in a dream the Amīr of believers, Imām Ja'far
Sadiq, who said to him, 'O Wajīh al-dīn, the Holy Prophet
orders you to marry your daughter to Mu'īn al-dīn Hasan
al-Husainī.' When he woke up, he went to Mu'īn al-dīn and told
him what had happened. Mu'īn al-dīn said, 'Although I am an
135 old man, I cannot refuse as it is an order of the Holy Prophet.'
So the marriage was performed and he took Bībī Asmat, whose
uncle was the late Mīr Saiyid Husain Khing Sawār, to his home.
After seven years Mu'īn al-dīn died. According to this calculation
his age was then 97.[25] However, some say that he lived for

---

[23] Cf. the story of the attempted murder of Farīd al-dīn Shakar Ganj,
      Fawā'id al-Fu'ād, p. 153.
[24] See also *Futūh al-Salātīn*, p. 119.
[25] Cf. *Siyar al-'Ārifīn*, p. 16.

17 years after his marriage; this would mean that he died at the age of 107. Mu'īn al-dīn had a second wife for the following reason: one night he saw the Holy Prophet in the flesh. The prophet said, 'You are not truly of my religion if you depart in any way from my sunnat.' It happened that the ruler of Patli fort, Malik Khitāb, attacked the unbelievers that night and captured the daughter of the Rājā of that land. He presented her to Mu'īn al-dīn who accepted her and named her Bībī Umiya.[26]

A daughter, whom he named Bībī Hāfiza Jamāl, was born to him by that crown of womanhood. Bībī Hāfiza Jamāl was extremely pious and righteous. She occupied herself in spiritual striving and asceticism before her father so she became one of his perfect khalīfas. The grave of this pious lady is at the feet of Mu'īn al-dīn. Her husband was Shaykh Razi al-dīn and by him she had two sons both of whom died during their childhood. Some people say that Bībī Hāfiza Jamāl was not the true daughter of Mu'īn al-dīn but that she was his adopted daughter. This idea is absolutely wrong. I have quoted the above from authentic sources; the claims of the common people have no reliability. They also claim that none of the sons of Mu'īn al-dīn were really his. However, it is a fact that three sons were born to Mu'īn al-dīn—Abū Sa'īd, Khwāja Fakhr al-dīn, and Hazrat Husām al-dīn. There is a controversy over which of the sons were born
136   by Bībī Asmat and which by Bībī Umiya. The eminent scholar, Saiyid Muhammad Gesūdarāz, attests that a group of darvīshes are agreed that all three sons are by Bībī Asmat. Others say that Abū Sa'īd is by Bībī Asmat, and the other two are by Bībī Umiya. Beyond this there is no other statement on the subject of Mu'īn al-dīn's descendants or forefathers.[27] Therefore, Shaykh Farīd, the grandson of Shaykh Hamīd al-dīn Nāgaurī, has quoted his pious grandfather as saying, 'When my Khwāja had fathered his sons, he said one day to me, "O Hamīd al-dīn, before I became a young man, Allāh granted to me everything for which I wished and asked. But now I have become an old man and my sons are born, my prayers are not answered and I do not get what I want immediately." He asked whether such things had happened before. "O Hazrat, before Jesus was born by Mary, without help and without labour she was given from the Unseen the fruit of summer in winter and found it in the *mihrāb*. When Jesus was born Mary expected to receive the fruit as usual but the order came to her to shake two branches of a date-palm. She

---

[26]   This is a new tradition for which there is no historical evidence.
[27]   Cf. *Akhbār al-Akhyār*, p. 250.

did so and immediately riches fell around her.[28] There is a great difference between times past and times present, but there is no difference in the regard and status of the Friends of Allāh before Him. The powers of their *wilāyat* is still alive." Hazrat liked this reply and he said, "This is true." ' [Details of Mu'īn al-dīn's descendants follow].

137   It is related that a man came into the presence of Shaykh Farīd al-dīn Shakar Ganj, kissed his feet and said, 'O Hazrat, in a dream once I saw Mu'īn al-dīn give me six *nan*, and from then until the present day, about sixty years, this has come to me without fail.' Farīd al-dīn said, 'This is not a dream but it is by the mercy and kindness of Allāh that Mu'īn al-dīn has been so generous to you that you will never suffer poverty.'

Quotations of Mu'īn al-dīn's teachings from the *Dalīl al-'Ārifīn* follow.

140   It is related that Mu'īn al-dīn had forty khalīfas: Qutb al-dīn Bakhtyār Ūshī, Fakhr al-dīn the son of Mu'īn al-dīn , Qāzī Shaykh Hamīd al-dīn Nāgaurī, Shaykh Wajīh al-dīn, Shaykh Hamīd al-dīn Sufī, Shaykh Burhan al-dīn (known as Badū), Shaykh Ahmad, Shaykh Muhsin, Shaykh Sulaiman Ghazī, Shaykh Shams al-dīn, Khwāja Hasan Khayāt, Salar Mas'ūd Ghazī, Ajaipāl Jōgī (known as 'Abdullāh) and Bībī Hāfiza Jamāl. ...

141   It is related that one night after the *'Ishā* prayer Mu'īn al-dīn went to his own cell and closed the door securely. The inhabitants of the dargāh were close by all night and listened to the noise of his feet. When they heard this noise they thought Mu'īn al-dīn was in *wajd*. From late at night until the dawn prayer he was silent. They knocked at the door and spoke, but this had no effect and there was no reply. At last they opened the door and saw that Mu'īn al-dīn had passed away.

It is related that during the night when Mu'īn al-dīn died the Holy Prophet came to various people in their dreams and said, 'The Friend of Allāh, Mu'īn al-dīn Hasan is coming. I have come to receive him.'

It is related that when Mu'īn al-dīn passed away the people saw that 'The Lover of Allāh has died in the Love of Allāh' had been inscribed by the Unseen on his pious forehead.[29]

Thus, on 6 Rajab in the year AH 633 Mu'īn al-dīn died.

[28] Cf. *Surūr al-Sudūr*, quoted Nizami, *Religion and Politics*, pp. 202–3. Also Quran, 19: 22–7.
[29] Cf. *Akhbār al-Akhyār*, p. 48.

All the raw materials from which the later hagiographers constructed their pictures of Mu'īn al-dīn have been assembled above. They borrow from each other and elaborate on each other, but their basic resources are to be found in the four texts, *Siyar al-Awliyā'*, *Siyar al-'Ārifīn*, the apocryphal *malfūzāt*, and the *Siyar al-Aqtāb*.

The development of the legend suggests that there was a demand for information about Mu'īn al-dīn, which requires explanation.

With the rise of the Chishtī shaykhs to a position of great influence and prestige at the time of Nizām al-dīn Awliyā', interest was stimulated in the lives of their predecessors. The spiritual authority of a shaykh was legitimized and explained by the hereditary nature of spiritual power; a saint owed his spiritual success to his pīr.[30] Thus, with the immense reputation of Nizām al-dīn, in his own time as well as later, the importance of Mu'īn al-dīn became paramount. The line of spiritual inheritance in the Chishtī *silsila* in India reverted to him, and through him to the family of Muhammad.[31]

But Mu'īn al-dīn's importance did not derive solely from being a precursor of Nizām al-dīn. He had a unique position of his own as a pioneer of Islam in India, and the founder of the Chishtī *silsila* in India. It is to emphasize this that the hagiographers focus on Mu'īn al-dīn's arrival in Ajmer and his settling there in spite of opposition.[32]

This theme already appears in the *Siyar al-Awliyā'* where Mu'īn al-dīn is instrumental in the conquest of India.[33] Sultān Mu'īzzi al-dīn conquers India to avenge Mu'īn al-dīn's suffering at the hands of the Hindu ruler. The *Akhbār al-Akhyār*[34] accepts this tradition which recurs, greatly elaborated, in the

---

[30] Hence the fabrication of the stories of the transmission of the *tabarrukāt* and the apocryphal traditions of Mu'īn al-dīn's initiation with his murshid, 'Usmān Hārwanī, and Mu'īn al-dīn initiating his murīd, Qutb al-dīn Bakhtyār Ūshī. See above, pp. 43–7, 51.

[31] Hence the name Mu'īn al-dīn Hasan al-Husainī (*Siyar al-Aqtāb*, p. 100) and the complete genealogies which appear in subsequent compilations. See also *Hasht Bahisht*, p. 8.

[32] *Siyar al-'Ārifīn* is an exception possibly because of Jamālī's *Suhrawardī* affiliations.

[33] *Siyar al-Awliyā'*, p. 44.

[34] *Akhbār al-Akhyār*, pp. 477–8.

Siyar al-Aqtāb.[35] Here, the story of Mu'īn al-dīn's coming to Ajmer and attempts by recalcitrant Hindus to displace him form the major part of the narrative.

Allāh Diyā Chishtī relates how astrologers had warned of Mu'īn al-dīn's imminent arrival in India and the Rājā had issued orders that he should be killed on sight; but 'the Khwāja and his forty companions travelled openly and no one had any power over him.'[36]

To settle in Ajmer, before dealing with the local secular ruler, Mu'īn al-dīn had to overcome the local deity, Shādī Dev, and Jōgī Ajaipāl, 'who had no equal in the whole of Hindustan.'[37] Mu'īn al-dīn's encounter with Shādī Dev is not without interest. Having settled his opposition and converted him to Islam, Mu'īn al-dīn, at Shādī Dev's suggestion, moves into his former temple. The take-over of 'pagan' sites is a recurrent feature of the history of the expansion of Islam. The most obvious precedent is to be found in the Muslim annexation of the Hajar al-aswad at Mecca. Jamālī tells how 'Usmān Hārwanī converts a group of fire-worshippers and moves into their temple for two and a half years after which he leaves them in the hands of the original priests who are now Sufi shaykhs.[38] Sir Thomas Arnold remarks that 'in many instances there is no doubt that the shrine of a Muslim saint marks the site of some local cult which was practised on the spot long before the introduction of Islam.'[39]

There is evidence, more reliable than the tradition recorded

---

[35] *Siyar al-Aqtāb*, pp. 123–33.
[36] Ibid., p. 124.   [37] Ibid., p. 127.
[38] *Siyar al-'Ārifīn*, pp. 8–9. See also Digby, 'Jogis in Indian Sufi Hagiography', pp. 13–14.
[39] Quoted Digby, 'Jogis in Indian Sufi Hagiography', p. 13. Elsewhere Arnold gives some more examples of this: 'The tomb of Salar Masud is said to occupy the site of a former temple of the sun, and the mosque of Shaykh Saddu at Amroha was also originally a temple. The *Panj Pir* are undoubtedly reminiscent of the *Pandavas*, the five hero brothers of the Mahabharatta, and it is significant that the shrine of Sakhi Sarwar (in the Dera Ghazi Khan District) contains, besides the tomb of the saint and his wife, a shrine dedicated to Babu Nanak, and a temple to Vishnu, and that Hindus believe that Shah Madar is an incarnation of Lakshman, the brother of the God Rama.' 'Saints and Martyrs (Muhammadan)', *Encyclopaedia of Religion and Ethics*, vol. 11, p. 72.

in the *Siyar al-Aqtāb*, to suggest that this was the case in Ajmer. Sculpted stones, apparently from a Hindu temple, are incorporated in the Buland Darwāza of Mu'īn al-dīn's shrine. Moreover, his tomb is built over a series of cellars which may have formed part of an earlier temple. Tradition says that inside the cellar is an image of Mahadeva in a temple on which *sandal* used to be placed every day by a Brahman.[40] The shrine still employs a Hindu family to prepare the *sandal* which is now presented on the grave of Mu'īn al-dīn. A tradition, first recorded in the *'Anis al-Arwāh*, suggests that the Sandal Khāna is built on the site of Shādī Dev's temple.[41]

These relics of Hindu buildings and practice imply that there is some substance behind the *Siyar al-Aqtāb*'s story of Mu'īn al-dīn moving into Shādī Dev's tomb. At the least it serves as a useful explanation to his followers of why Mu'īn al-dīn, elsewhere portrayed as a powerful evangelist, is buried on ground sacred to the Hindus.

Mu'īn al-dīn's arrival in India and his survival in Ajmer has become a source of strength to later generations of Indo-Muslims who found themselves a religious minority. Mu'īn al-dīn's achievement is magnified by hagiographers who exaggerate the opposition against him. It is emphasized how the series of battles, requiring the deployment of a wide range of supernatural weapons, against the king, the *dev* and the Jogī, all took place in the very heartland of the Hindu world. Thus, at Ajmer 'there was one temple to reverence which the Rājā and

---

[40] H. B. Sarda, *Ajmer, Historical and Descriptive*, p. 90. A variant of this tradition is found in Irvine, *Topography of Ajmer*, pp. 61–2: 'At one place (where the Seth burial-ground now is) there was an ancient shrine sacred to Mahadeva, the *lingam* of which was hidden by the leaves and rubbish. To this wood the Khwāja (Mu'īn al-dīn) had retired to contemplate during forty days; and every day he hung up his small *mussuq* of water on a branch of a tree overhanging the *lingam*. The water constantly dropped on this. At length Mahadeva became highly pleased, both at the sanctity and unexpected libation of the saint, and spoke out of the stone commending his virtue. From this tradition (related by one of the most learned *khadīms*) the Hindus equally venerate the Khwāja with the Mahomedans.' The present writer heard a further variation on the same theme; this time the *lingam* was located beneath the grave of Mu'īn al-dīn.

[41] *Ta'rīkh-i Khwāja-i Ajmer*, p. 56.

all the infidels used to come.'[42] Near Ajmer was the holy lake of
Pushkar, where the 'Hindus worship ... and gather together
and bathe for six days every year.'[43] Not only was Ajmer at the
centre of the sacred world of Hindus but it was also the secular
centre, the first city to be fortified and the city from which the
Chauhan dynasty ruled from Ajā Rājā, the eponymous founder
of the city, down to its last representative, Rāi Pithaurā, whom
Mu'īn al-dīn and the Sultān with his army vanquished.[44]

So the demand for information about Mu'īn al-dīn was established. It remains to explain how the rest of the legend developed,
but that requires an understanding of the hagiographer's aims.

Apart from the desire to communicate what is known of a
saint's life, a hagiographer wishes to edify his readers and to
increase the prestige of his subject. Fabrications can generally
be explained in terms of this dual motivation.[45]

In his attempt to satisfy the devout curiosity of his readers
the hagiographer can draw on two sources—the stories, true or
apocryphal, of other saints, and the stereotypes of a shared
religious milieu. However, the two sources will tend to merge
as idealized versions of the lives of saints replace historically
recognizable portraits. The hagiographer uses the saint as a
vessel into which he can pour the ideals of his religious understanding and from which, therefore, the vagaries of personality
are emptied. This process is facilitated and hastened if very
little is known of the saint's actual life (as for Mu'īn al-dīn). The
saint comes to embody (often to a superhuman degree) all the
virtues of an exemplary life. In the case of Mu'īn al-dīn, the
virtues which he came to epitomize under the guidance of the
hagiographer were those of an idealized Chishtī shaykh, and in
painting such a portrait the hagiographer achieves his twin aims
of edifying his reader and glorifying his hero. However, the
idealized shaykh of hagiography does not necessarily reflect
faithfully either the ideal shaykh as understood by himself or
portrayed by his teachings. The hagiographer projects his own

---

[42] *Siyar al-Aqtāb*, p. 125.   [43] *Akhbār al-Akhyār*, p. 52.
[44] Ibid., pp. 52–3; *Siyar al-Aqtāb*, p. 133.
[45] H. Delehaye of the Société des Bollandistes has arrived at similar
generalizations in the context of the hagiography of Christendom: See *The
Legends of the Saints*, pp. 54, 68, 69.

understanding of the ideal shaykh into his writing; the two visions of the *'Perfect man'* will not always coincide.

As an 'ideal shaykh' Muʿīn al-dīn is shown in the legend to practise many of the things which the Chishtīs are known to have regarded as important. The distinguishing characteristics of the Chishtī shaykhs were examined in Chapter 2. The way in which the Muʿīn al-dīn of legend both fits with this ideal and differs from it will be illustrated below by reference to the nine general principles outlined on page 65 above.

Obedience of the Murīd to the Murshid. 'After receiving the blessing of becoming the disciple of 'Usmān Hārwanī, I spent the next twenty years in his service. Never for a second or a minute did I spend time on my own comfort rather than in his service during all those twenty years.'[46] His loyalty to his murshid is further demonstrated in his conversation with 'Abd al-Qādir Jīlānī where he says he would never go into retreat except at the command of his pīr, that his pīr was without defect and 'more than that, I do not consider my pīr as being separate from Allāh.'[47]

Renunciation of the Concerns of the Material World. Jamālī tells how 'he was whole-heartedly disillusioned with his property and house.' 'He sold all his property and chattels.'[48] The *Siyar al-Aqtāb* relates how 'he withdrew from wordly affairs, and the world and its business lost its attraction for him ...'[49] His clothing consisted of one patched garment,[50] and 'wherever he gained a little fame or if anyone recognized him he used to leave that place so no-one would know him.'[51]

Independence of the State. There is no record of Muʿīn al-dīn himself having any dealings with a Muslim ruler or government.[52]

---

[46] *Siyar al-Awliyā'*, p. 43, cf. *Siyar al-Aqtāb*, p. 103, *Akhbār al-Akhyār*, p. 47, *Dalīl al-'Ārifīn*, pp. 4–5.
[47] *Siyar al-Aqtāb*, pp. 107–8.   [48] *Siyar al-'Ārifīn*, p. 5.
[49] *Siyar al-Aqtāb*, p. 102.   [50] Ibid., p. 101; *Siyar al-'Ārifīn*, p. 7.
[51] *Siyar al-'Ārifīn*, p. 8; cf. *Siyar al-Aqtāb*, p. 123.
[52] It is worth noting that one of the sons of Muʿīn al-dīn travelled to Delhi to secure a title to a *jāgīr* village which he claimed as his own. *Siyar al-Awliyā'*, pp. 49–50.

Approval of Samā'. The *Siyar al-Aqtāb* testifies that Mu'īn al-dīn 'always used to listen to *samā'* and that he 'had a great taste for *samā'* and when he listened to *samā'* he became ecstatic.'[53]

Strenuous Personal Routine of Prayers and Devotion. Mu'īn al-dīn 'busied himself in study, and spiritual exercises and striving.'[54] He 'was in such a strange state of austerity and spiritual striving that after seven days he broke his fast with a charred cake of bread weighing 5 *misqāl* and wetted with water.'[55] He was 'continually in a state of contemplation.'[56] He 'always used to fast during the day and pray during the night.'[57] He performed the *chillā* at Jīlān.[58] He learnt the whole Quran by heart and used to recite it fully twice every day.[59] 'For seventy years his Ablution was not broken without him washing before prayer.'[60] He seldom slept at night so busy was he in his devotions.[61]

Dependence on either the Cultivation of Wasteland or on Unsolicited Offerings. There is little information regarding Mu'īn al-dīn's livelihood. It is nowhere suggested that he contradicted the Chishtī axiom that the shaykh should never depend on anyone else except as the recipient of voluntary offerings. Jamālī tells of Mu'īn al-dīn preparing to eat a fowl which he himself has caught outside Balkh.[62] The avoidance of prohibited forms of sustenance is made easier when the hagiographers credit him with supernatural means of support.[63]

Disapproval of Displays of Miraculous Powers. This is the area in which the Mu'īn al-dīn of legend diverges most radically from the tenets of Chishtī practice as they are revealed in the historically reliable sources. This divergence was predictable in a world where spiritual elevation was inevitably accompanied by miraculous powers. The hagiographers constantly remind the reader of Mu'īn al-dīn's elevated position. His proximity to

[53] *Siyar al-Aqtāb*, pp. 101, 103.
[54] *Siyar al-'Ārifīn*, p. 5.
[55] Ibid., p. 7.
[56] *Siyar al-Aqtāb*, p. 101.
[57] Ibid.
[58] Ibid., p. 108.
[59] *Siyar al-'Ārifīn*, pp. 5, 8; and *Siyar al-Aqtāb*, p. 101.
[60] *Siyar al-Aqtāb*, p. 101.
[61] Ibid.
[62] *Siyar al-'Ārifīn*, p. 11.
[63] *Siyar al-Aqtāb*, p. 137.

Allāh is illustrated by the way in which Allāh communicates directly with him. The reader is left in no doubt of Allāh's love and regard for him. Thus, in the *Siyar al-Aqtāb*, after every recitation of the Quran, a voice comes from the Unseen world saying, 'O Muʿīn al-dīn, your recitation has been accepted.'[64] While at the Kaʿba a voice was heard, 'Muʿīn al-dīn is my friend. I have accepted him and exalted him.'[65] At Medina a voice came from the tomb of the Prophet, returning Muʿīn al-dīn's greeting.[66] At the Kaʿba on another occasion Allāh says, 'O Muʿīn al-dīn, I am pleased with you and have accepted you. Ask for whatever you desire and I shall give it to you.' Muʿīn al-dīn asks that all his murīds should be accepted into Paradise, a request which is immediately granted.[67] Later Muʿīn al-dīn is summoned by a voice emanating from the tomb of the Prophet at Medina and ordered to go to India and settle in Ajmer.[68]

During the night when Muʿīn al-dīn died the Holy Prophet came to various people in their dreams and said, 'The Friend of Allāh, Muʿīn al-dīn Hasan, is coming. I have come to receive him.'[69]

When Muʿīn al-dīn was dead the inscription—The Lover of Allāh died in the Love of Allāh—appeared on his forehead.[70]

This proximity to Allāh, which the hagiographers take such pains to demonstrate, inevitably (in the minds of the hagiographer and his readers) endows Muʿīn al-dīn with miraculous powers. The miracles which occur in the legend of Muʿīn al-dīn may be classified into three types: miraculous predictions; miraculous help to those in difficulty; and miraculous conversions.

Only his miraculous predictions will be considered here. The other classes of miracle can more usefully be discussed in connection with Muʿīn al-dīn's position *vis-à-vis* the remaining two principal characteristics of Chishtī practice below.

According to the *Siyar al-Aqtāb*, Muʿīn al-dīn was miraculously aware that a particular visitor had come to kill him. Muʿīn al-dīn's glance is enough to change the mind of the intruder, who repents, enters the service of Muʿīn al-dīn and

---

64 Ibid., p. 101.
65 Ibid., p. 103.
66 Ibid., also *Anīs al-Arwāh*, p. 5.
67 *Siyar al-Aqtāb*, pp. 103–4.
68 Ibid., p. 123.
69 Ibid., p. 141.
70 Ibid., p. 141; *Akhbār al-Akhyār*, p. 48.

later makes the pilgrimage to Mecca and Medina forty-five times.[71] On another occasion, Mu'īn al-dīn notices a youth passing by 'with a bow and arrow in his hand' and he prophesies that the same youth (Sultān Shams al-dīn) would become the Sultān of Delhi.[72] Predictions of this sort have an instrumental effect. The author of the *Siyar al-Aqtāb* clearly interprets Mu'īn al-dīn's prophecy of Sultān Mu'izz al-dīn's successful invasion of India in this light; Allāh Diyā Chishtī explicitly tells how Mu'īn al-dīn not only foretold the invasion but that he was the cause of it, appearing in a dream to the Sultān and summoning him with his army to India.[73] Similarly, Mu'īn al-dīn's prediction of the youth becoming the Sultān could be interpreted as his causing the youth to become the Sultān; for it is not unknown for Sufis to perform a king-making role.[74]

Miraculous predictions of this kind serve to remind the reader of Mu'īn al-dīn's proximity to Allāh and knowledge of His plans for this world.

Service to Others. Mu'īn al-dīn is represented in the hagiographies as a teacher. All the hagiographers reproduce a considerable corpus of his sayings which are plagiarized or quoted from the apocryphal *malfūzāt*.[75] His ability to serve other people in more practical ways is enhanced by his miraculous powers. Thus, his *langar khāna* can operate on a spectacular scale: 'In the kitchen of Mu'īn al-dīn so many meals were cooked every day that all the impoverished people of the whole city could eat their fill.' But Mu'īn al-dīn was able to fund this enterprise by miraculously producing treasure from beneath his prayer rug.[76]

---

[71] *Siyar al-Aqtāb*, pp. 133–4.

[72] Ibid., p. 134.   [73] Ibid., p. 132.

[74] See, among others, a portrait by Bichitr showing Mu'īn al-dīn Chishtī handing over the insignia of imperial office to Akbar (who remains out of the picture). For a discussion of this important picture, see below pp. 106–7. In the Windsor MS of the Shāh Jahān Nama (Folio 204 verso) there is a similar picture in which the orb and sceptre are being entrusted to Shāh Jahān. A. Ahmad, 'The Sufis and Sultans in pre-Mughal India', *Der Islam*, 38, 1968, 142–53 is also relevant in this context.

[75] The extent to which these diverge from Chishtī teachings as revealed in the reliable sources has been discussed in Chapter 2.

[76] *Siyar al-Aqtāb*, p. 104.

His miraculous powers meant that Mu'īn al-dīn could help all those who came to him in distress. Thus, he miraculously restored the boy who had been kidnapped by a *dev*, to his bereft father,[77] restored the innocent man, who had been beheaded, to life,[78] ensured that justice was done in the case of the debt of *dirhams*, and posthumously provided a daily supply of bread for a man who would otherwise have suffered poverty.[79]

Tolerance and Respect of Other Religions. The *Siyar al-'Ārifīn* relates a tradition wherein Mu'īn al-dīn is believed to have referred to a local Hindu as a saintly man of God.[80] This would have been in accord with the attitudes of many Chishtī shaykhs but such men are exceptional in Islam; the followers of Muhammad and readers of the Quran are exhorted to 'fight for Allāh's cause'.[81] So, predictably, this tradition about Mu'īn al-dīn was dropped by later hagiographers who represented him instead as an evangelist.

'Through his [Mu'īn al-dīn's] coming to Hindustan the Way of Islam was established there. He destroyed the darkness of unbelief.'[82] 'Because of his coming ... the darkness of unbelief in this land was illumined by the light of Islam.'[83] Amīr Khurd includes two verses which contrast the situation in India before and after Mu'īn al-dīn's arrival. Before,

All India was ignorant of the orders of religion and law.
All were ignorant of Allāh and His Prophet.
None had seen the Ka'ba.
None had heard of the greatness of Allāh.

After Mu'īn al-dīn arrived in India,

Because of his Sword instead of idols and temples there are Mosques, *Mimbar* and *Mihrāb* in the land of Unbelief.
In the land where the sayings of the idolaters were heard There is now the sound of 'Allāhu Akbar'.[84]

Again it is Mu'īn al-dīn's miraculous powers that enable him to be a spectacular success as a proselytizer. In the *Siyar al-*

[77] *Siyar al-Awliyā'*, p. 42.
[79] Ibid., pp. 133 and 137.
[81] Quran, 61: 4.
[83] *Siyar al-Awliyā'*, p. 44.
[78] *Siyar al-Aqtāb*, pp. 122–3.
[80] *Siyar al-'Ārifīn*, p. 14.
[82] *Siyar al-Aqtāb*, p. 101.
[84] Ibid.

Ārifīn, which depicts Muʿīn al-dīn as a respecter of Hindus, these powers are deployed to bring erring Muslims back to the true way. Thus, his glance is enough to convince the evil ruler, Muhammad Yādgār, of his sin and to persuade him to become a follower.[85] A bite of Muʿīn al-dīn's meal of roast fowl is sufficient to convince Hakīm Ziyāʾ al-dīn of the truth of the Sufi path.[86] While at Baghdad, 'All ardent unbelievers who saw the face of Muʿīn al-dīn became Muslims, so that at that time no unbelievers lived [there].'[87]

In the later hagiographies, where the picture of Muʿīn al-dīn's tolerance is replaced by a portrait of him as a warrior for Islam, his miraculous powers are used to enhance his success as an evangelist. He brings the seven fire-worshippers to Islam because they see that fire has no power to burn him,[88] and it is through his miraculous powers that Shādī Dev and Jōgī Ajaipāl are converted.

Muʿīn al-dīn's eminence is increased by the belief that he visited most of the cultural and religious centres of Islam. In the *Siyar al-Awliyāʾ*, geographical references are limited to his crossing of the Tigris, his arrival in Ajmer, his visits to Delhi and a reminder, in his name, that he comes from Sijistan.[89] This lack of experience of the Muslim world is soon remedied by the later hagiographers. In the *Siyar al-ʿĀrifīn* he is made to visit Samarqand, Bukhara, Sijz, Jīl, Baghdad, Hamadan, Tabriz, Ūsh, Isfahan, Khirqan, Astarabad, Herat, Sabzawar, Hisar, Balkh, Ghazni, Lahore, and Delhi, before arriving at Ajmer. The *Siyar al-Aqtāb*, which concentrates less on Muʿīn al-dīn's travels than on his arrival in Ajmer, also credits him with an exacting tour of the principal centres of learning and sanctity in the Muslim world. While this mentions fewer places, it does incorporate the tradition (which Jamālī does not use) from the apocryphal *malfūz* that Muʿīn al-dīn visited Mecca and Medina.[90]

---

[85] *Siyar al-ʿĀrifīn*, pp. 9–10.
[86] Ibid., pp. 11–12.   [87] *Siyar al-Aqtāb*, p. 104.
[88] Ibid. The consumption of a piece of food or a drink which has been in contact with the shaykh, as a way to enlightenment, is a common motif in Sufi hagiography—see also Muʿīn al-dīn's illumination at the hands of Ibrāhīm Qundūzī.
[89] *Siyar al-Awliyāʾ*, pp. 42–4, 49–51.
[90] *Siyar al-Aqtāb*, pp. 103–4, 123; *Anīs al-Arwāh*, p. 5.

The legend of Muʿīn al-dīn also connects him with many Muslims of religious significance whose lifetime approximately coincided with his own. The exalted position of these acquaintances is underlined by reference to their miraculous powers: Ibrāhīm Qundūzī converts him to the mystic path by giving him a morsel of bread to eat.[91] At ʿUsmān Hārwanī's order Muʿīn al-dīn picks up a brick which immediately turns to gold.[92] Jamālī tells how ʿUsmān converts a group of fire-worshippers near Isfahan.[93] Between ʿUsmān's two fingers Muʿīn al-dīn was able to see 'eighteen thousand spheres'.[94] At Damascus ʿUsmān miraculously produces gold coins from beneath his prayer rug and Awhad al-dīn Kirmānī touches a stick which turns to gold.[95]

A difference emerges between the *Siyar al-ʿĀrifīn* and the *Siyar al-Aqtāb* in their approaches to these encounters. In the earlier work they are seen as part of Muʿīn al-dīn's training and discipleship, whereas in the *Siyar al-Aqtāb* he has become so exalted, even early on in his career, that shaykhs such as Shihāb al-dīn ʿUmar Suhrawardī come to 'kiss his feet' and 'just to receive spiritual benefit'.[96] When he meets ʿAbd al-Qādir Jīlānī the impact of his replies silences the shaykh.[97]

In the legend Muʿīn al-dīn also comes to represent virtues which are valued in a wider Muslim context and associated less specifically with the lives of Sufis. He was a Saiyid by descent.[98] He did not depart in any way from the sunna.[99] The ʿulamāʾ could not fault him,[100] and he performed the hajj.[101]

Muʿīn al-dīn's is not merely an exemplary human life; it is more than that. He shows forth the virtues of Muslim life, as understood by the Chishtī shaykhs, in a way which is only possible because of his close relationship with Allāh and his consequent miraculous powers. As the hagiography develops, Muʿīn al-dīn is elevated to this position of supranormal proximity

---

91 *Siyar al-Aqtāb*, pp. 101–2; *Siyar al-ʿĀrifīn*, p. 5.
92 *Siyar al-Aqtāb*, p. 103; *Anīs al-Arwāh*, p. 5.
93 *Siyar al-ʿĀrifīn*, pp. 8–9.
94 *Anīs al-Arwāh*, quoted M. Habib, 'Mystic Records', p. 18.
95 *Dalīl al-ʿĀrifīn*, p. 45.   96 *Siyar al-Aqtāb*, p. 103.
97 Ibid., p. 108.   98 Ibid., p. 101.
99 Ibid., p. 135.   100 Ibid., p. 101.
101 *Anīs al-Arwāh*, p. 5; *Siyar al-Aqtāb*, pp. 103–4, 123.

to Allāh and he becomes an intermediary between men and Allāh.[102]

The list of the principal *tazkirāt* which refer to Mu'īn al-dīn (see pp. 25–6) continues to grow. The substance of the legend changes very little as can be seen from the text of the *Hasht Bahisht* (c. 1900). The narrative tends to expand with time as more miracles are ascribed to Mu'īn al-dīn, and as authors attempt to reconcile conflicting sources. Two twentieth-century English-language hagiographies illustrate this point. Begg talks of Mu'īn al-dīn's '4,600 miracles', while Sharib credits him with five separate journeys to India in an attempt to reconcile the differing itineraries of Mu'īn al-dīn which the author has encountered in earlier compilations.[103]

However, it is not necessary to examine closely these later *tazkirāt*. The development of the legend of Mu'īn al-dīn has been discussed in detail up to the point when Mu'īn al-dīn has been exalted to a position where he can effectively act as an intermediary between Man and Allāh. In the mind of his devotees, Mu'īn al-dīn, the Muslim darvīsh, has become the 'Prophet of India' (*nabī al-Hind*).[104]

---

[102] For the place of intermediaries in Islam, see above, pp. 15–19.
[103] Begg, *Hazrat Khwāja Mu'īn al-dīn Chishtī of Ajmer*, p. 97. Sharib, *Khwaja Gharıb Nawaz*, pp. 24–5.
[104] *Siyar al-Aqtāb*, p. 101.

4

A History of the Shrine of Mu'īn al-dīn Chishtī

Chroniclers of the shrine have (predictably), limited themselves to recording the patronage and pilgrimages of ruling families and other outstanding individuals. Historical information is therefore sketchy but it can be supplemented by a survey of the practices and motives of contemporary visitors to the shrine.

The first recorded visitor to the shrine of Mu'īn al-dīn was Muhammad bin Tughluq.[1] The exact date of the Sultān's pilgrimage is difficult to ascertain, but it was probably in 1332.[2] In the first year of the reign of Firūz Shāh Tughluq (1351–2) the important Chishtī, Zain al-dīn, the khalīfa of Burhan al-dīn Chishtī, who was himself the khalīfa of Nizām al-dīn Awliyā', made a pilgrimage to Ajmer.[3]

A further reference to regular pilgrimage to Ajmer in the latter half of the fourteenth century occurs in the conversations of Saiyid Muhammad Gesūdarāz recorded in 1399–1400 AD. Gesūdarāz was talking about his refusal to impart further instructions to one Husām al-dīn, who had previously received Sufi teaching from other shaykhs. An unnamed darvīsh approached Gesūdarāz and gave him a résumé of what he might have imparted to him. This included an injunction to perform the *ziyārat* of the *Panj Pīrs* (five pīrs) who, as explained in the anecdote, are the five great Chishtī shaykhs who preceded Gesūdarāz, viz. Nasīr al-dīn, Nizām al-dīn, Farīd al-dīn, Qutb al-dīn, and Mu'īn al-dīn.[4]

[1] Isamī, *Futūh al-Salātīn*, p. 460.
[2] Digby, *Early Pilgrimages*, p. 2.
[3] 'Abd al-Majid, *Rawzat al-Awliyā'*, pp. 101–2, quoted Digby, *Early Pilgrimages*, p. 3.
[4] *Jawāmi al-kilm*, p. 183, quoted Digby, *Early Pilgrimages*, p. 3. For the *Panch Pirs* of Indian Islam see Crooke, *Encyclopaedia of Religion of Ethics*, vol. 9, p. 600. Also Crooke, *Popular Religion and Folk-Lore*, pp. 202–3; Husain, *L'Inde Mystique*, pp. 30–2.

Between the death of Firūz Shāh Tughluq (1388) and the invasion of Timur (1398), Zafar Khān, progenitor of the Sultāns of Gujarat, made the pilgrimage to Ajmer from Nandalgarh. He dismounted at a distance of three *kos* from Ajmer and went on foot to the shrine where he performed the appropriate ceremonies.[5]

The Khiljis of Malwa and Mandu had close connections with the shrine in the last half of the fifteenth century. Sultān Mahmūd Khiljī visited Ajmer in 1455. The Muslim population of Ajmer resented their Hindu governor, so Mahmūd marched on Ajmer. On the fifth day he captured the fort and appointed his own Muslim governor. 'He then payed his respects to the shrine and distributed offerings among its attendants in thanksgiving for his successful campaign.'[6]

Firishta records that Mahmūd also built a mosque near the shrine.[7] However, there is no evidence, epigraphical or otherwise, to support this statement beyond a popular tradition which ascribes the construction of the mosque, known as the *Sandal Khāna*, to Sultān Mahmūd Khiljī.[8]

At that time there was still no proper mausoleum to house the tomb of Muʿīn al-dīn. According to ʿAbd al-Haqq Dihlawī, it was Shaykh Husain Nāgaurī, a descendant of Hamīd al-dīn Savālī Nāgaurī and pīr of Sultān Ghiyās al-dīn Khiljī, who first remedied this situation.[9]

Ghiyās al-dīn (1469–1500) himself was a devotee of Muʿīn al-dīn and it was almost certainly he who funded the construction of the Buland Darwāza, one of the ceremonial gates of the dargāh, and so-called because of its great height.[10] The Buland Darwāza is sometimes attributed to ʿAlā al-dīn Khiljī—some refer today to it as the ʿAlāʾī Darwāza—but this is unlikely, and is no doubt the result of a confusion between the Khiljīs of Malwa and Mandu, and ʿAlā al-dīn Khiljī of Delhi

[5] *Mirʾāt-i Sikandarī*, p. 18, quoted Digby, *Early Pilgrimages*, p. 3.
[6] Firishta, vol. 2, p. 490.   [7] Ibid., vol. 4, p. 222.
[8] Cf. A. A. Tirmizi, 'Persian Inscriptions at Ajmer', *Epigraphia Indica, Arabic and Persian Supplement*, 1957, p. 44 (I). Tirmizi published a second article on the Persian Inscriptions at Ajmer in the Arabic and Persian Supplement of the *Epigraphia Indica* in 1959 (II).
[9] *Akhbār al-Akhyār*, p. 48. See Fig. 4.1, pp. 104–5.
[10] Sarda, *Ajmer*, p. 88.

(1298–1316).[11] The Buland Darwāza, can, therefore, more acceptably be attributed to Ghiyās al-dīn Khiljī.

At the beginning of the sixteenth century Maulānā Jamālī, author of *Siyar al-ʿĀrifīn*, undertook the pilgrimage to Ajmer. He refers to the existence of families of attendants long-established at the shrine, and the significant quantity of gifts brought to it by Hindus as well as Muslims.[12]

The *Taʾrīkh-i Daudī* mentions that in 1554 Sher Shāh himself went to Ajmer to have the *ziyārat* of Hazrat Khwāja Muʿīn al-dīn Chishtī, gave large alms to the faqīrs of that *khānqāh* and performed the necessary ceremonies of going around it.[13] However, there is no other evidence for this visit, and bearing in mind that the *Taʾrīkh-i Daudī* is based largely on oral tradition, it remains questionable whether Sher Shāh ever visited Ajmer.

In AH 939/1532–3 the cupola of Muʿīn al-dīn's mausoleum was embellished as is indicated by an inscription in golden letters on the northern wall of the tomb.[14] There is nothing to suggest who was responsible for this decoration; however, a certain 'Muaʿzzam' was the chronogrammatist. Tirmizi believes that this might have been Khwāja Muaʿzzam, the uncle of the Emperor Akbar.[15]

Akbar was the first Mughal Emperor to take an interest in Muʿīn al-dīn, and with his imperial patronage the fortunes of the shrine dramatically improved. He visited the grave of Muʿīn al-dīn fourteen times.[16] The *Akbarnāma* records how his interest in the saint was kindled:

[11] 'The style of the building, with its elegant, lofty and narrow, slightly ogee central arch, the row of irregularly shaped merlons on the inner side, and the twin *chatris*, which crown it on the outer side, is unacceptable as a product of the reign of ʿAlā al-dīn Khiljī, but it can be closely paralleled in the later fifteenth century buildings of Mandu.' Digby, *Crosscurrents*, I, p. 19.

[12] *Siyar al-ʿArifīn*, p. 13.

[13] Quoted K. R. Qanungo, *Sher Shah*, p. 332.

[14] Tirmizi, 'Persian Inscriptions', I, pp. 49–50.

[15] Ibid. If this is correct, it establishes the earliest Mughal connection with Ajmer, for neither Humāyūn nor Bābur ever visited Ajmer, although Bābur did visit the shrine of Qutb al-dīn at Mehrauli, Delhi. See *Bāburnāma*, tr. Beveridge, p. 475.

[16] *Akbarnāma*, vol. 2, pp. 243, 477, 496, 511, 516, 530, 539; vol. 3, pp. 63, 111, 233, 259, 303, 363, 405. *Muntakhab al-Tawārīkh*, vol. 2, pp. 45, 108, 174, 188, 258, 262, 280.

One night His Majesty went off to Fathpur to hunt and passed near by Mandhakar which is a village on the way from Agra to Fathpur. A number of Indian minstrels were singing enchanting ditties about the glories and virtues of the great Khwāja, Khwāja Muʿīn al-dīn—May his grave be hallowed—who sleeps in Ajmer. Often had his perfections and miracles been the theme of discourse in the holy assemblies. His Majesty, who was a seeker after Truth, and who, in his zealous quest sought for union with travellers on the road of holiness, and showed a desire for enlightenment, conceived a strong inclination to visit the Khwāja's shrine. The attraction of a pilgrimage thither seized his collar.[17]

The Emperor's subsequent devotion to the shrine was remarkable. He made it a rule for himself 'that he should go every year in the beginning of *Rajab* (the time of the ʿurs) to the holy shrine'.[18] But his visits were not confined to attending this annual festival:

As the expeditions of just rulers are a source of soothment to mortals, and are market-days of justice, His Majesty was disposed to travelling and hunting especially when in this way he could make a pilgrimage to the shrine of some great ascetic.[19]

Akbar also visited the shrine regularly to give thanks after important military victories. Thus, he went there after the conquest of Chittor in 1568 and of Bihar and Bengal in 1574.[20] His gratitude to Muʿīn al-dīn for his military successes is illustrated in the following anecdote from the *Muntakhab al-Tawārīkh*:

During the first days of the month of Rabiʿ al-Ākhir (AH 984/1576). ... I [Badāyūnī] prostrated myself in the Audience-Chamber at Fathpur and delivered the despatches of the *amīrs*, together with the elephant [a spoil of war after the victory of Kokandah]. The Emperor asked, 'What is its name?' I replied, '*Ram-Prasad* [Gift of Rama].' His Majesty replied, 'Since all this [success] has been brought through the pīr [Muʿīn al-dīn], its name should henceforth be *Pīr-Prasad*.'[21]

[17] *Akbarnāma*, vol. 2, p. 237.
[18] Ibid., vol. 3, p. 361. For explanation and description of ʿUrs, see below pp. 117–29.
[19] Ibid., p. 298. It is worth noting that Nizām al-dīn Awliyāʾ, who became the murīd of Farīd al-dīn Shakar Ganj, first heard of his future murshid from a wandering singer (*qawwāl*), who came to his home-town (Badaʾon) when he was aged twelve. See *Fawāʾid al-Fuʾād*, pp. 252–3.
[20] *Akbarnāma*, vol. 2, p. 496; vol. 3, p. 110.
[21] *Muntakhab al-Tawārīkh*, vol. 2, p. 243.

Akbar believed the birth of his son, Prince Salīm, in 1570 to have been the result of the successful intercession with God by Salīm Chishtī, a darvīsh whose marble mausoleum may still be seen at Fathpur Sikri. This reinforced the Emperor's faith in the Chishtī order and was the occasion of his most striking display of devotion to Mu'īn al-dīn.

He, at the time when he was seeking for a son, had made a vow to his God that if this blessing should be attained, he would perform an act of thanksgiving which would be personal to himself, viz., that he would walk from Agra to the shrine of Khwāja Mu'īn al-dīn Chishtī and there pay his devotions to God.[22]

He repeated the visit on the birth of his second son later in the same year, though this time he only walked the last stage of the journey.[23]

Each of Akbar's visits to Ajmer was celebrated by his making substantial offerings at the shrine, conferring endowments on it and beautifying it.[24]

His Majesty also arranged for the management of the shrine, and for the treatment of pilgrims, and for the extension of mosques and *khānqāhs* in the territory.[25]

Badāyūnī records how in the year 1573–4

a lofty college and high spacious palaces were built on the road to Ajmer. And the cause of this was as follows: His Majesty's extreme devotion induced him every year to go on a pilgrimage to that city, and so he ordered a palace to be built at every stage between Agra and that place, and a pillar to be erected and a well sunk at every *kos*. Ever so many hundreds of thousands of stags' horns, which the Emperor had killed during the course of his life were placed on these pillars as a memorial to the world. ... Would that instead of these he had ordered gardens and caravanserais to be made![26]

In 1571 Akbar initiated the building of the mosque which is named after him at the shrine, and in 1579 he had the mausoleum of Mu'īn al-dīn further embellished. This is mentioned in an

---

[22] *Akbarnāma*, vol. 2, p. 510.   [23] Ibid., p. 516.
[24] Ibid., pp. 233, 516; vol. 3, p. 111. The details of his benefactions are given below in Appendix IV.
[25] Ibid., p. 511.
[26] *Muntakhab al-Tawārīkh*, vol. 2, p. 176.

inscription painted in golden *nasta'līq* lettering inside the dome
of the mausoleum.[27] Badāyūnī states incorrectly that this was
Akbar's first visit to Ajmer in fourteen years. However, he
does make the point that 'while he [Akbar] had rejected the
foundation of everything'—in other words he had rejected
Islam in favour of his new religion, the Dīn-i Ilāhī—he had
retained his faith in Mu'īn al-dīn.[28]

For early topographical descriptions of Ajmer and its shrine,
reliance must be placed on the foreign travellers who went
there. Contemporary local authors give no such descriptions.
W. Finch, who was in India between 1608 and 1611, left the
following account of the shrine:

Ajmer is only famous for the sepulchre of Hoghee Mundee (Khwāja
Mu'īn al-dīn), a saint much respected by the Mughals. ... Before you
come to this tombe you passe three faire courts, of which the first
contayneth neere an acre of ground, paved all with black and white
marble,... . On the left is a faire tanke enclosed with stone. The
second court is paved like the former, but richer, twice as bigge as the
Exchange in London, in the midst whereof hangs a curious candlesticke
with many lights. Into the third you passe by a brazen gate curiously
wrought; it is the fairest of the three, especially neere the doore of the
sepulchre, where the pavement is curiously interlayed; the doore is
large and inlayed with mother of pearle, and the pavement about the
tombe of interlaid marble; the sepulchre very curiously wrought in
work of mother of pearle and gold with an epitaph in the Persian
tongue. A little distant stands his seate in a darke obscure place,
where he sat to fore-tell of matters, and is much reverenced. On the
East-side stand three other courts, in each a fine tanke; on the North
and West stand divers faire houses, wherein keep their sides (*Saiyids*)
or churchmen.[29]

So it was not only Akbar and the Khiljī Sultans who adorned
Mu'īn al-dīn's tomb. By the early seventeenth century the
dargāh was clearly an impressive establishment with a considerable staff financed by the endowments and offerings of

[27] Tirmizi, 'Persian Inscriptions', 1957, pp. 49–50. The text of these
inscriptions is given in Appendix I.

[28] *Muntakhab al-Tawārīkh*, vol. 2, p. 280. Akbar's lasting devotion to
Mu'īn al-dīn was also celebrated by the Court miniaturists; see the *Akbarnāma*
in the Victoria and Albert Museum, 77/117, Akbar travelling on foot to
Ajmer; and 23/117, Akbar at the Ajmer dargāh.

[29] *Early Travels in India*, ed. W. Foster, p. 171.

devotees. There was already accommodation for the staff, facilities for the pilgrims' ritual ablutions, a monumental gateway (the Buland Darwāza), at the entrance of the shrine, and a lavishly decorated mausoleum for the saint. Finch mentions that there were many tombs within the precincts of the dargāh. There is no doubt that the cult of the saint was sufficiently developed for many men of distinction to be buried in his vicinity. Most remarkable of them, at the time Finch was writing, was the grave of Nizām, the water carrier who saved the Emperor Humāyūn's life. In his gratitude, the emperor promised that he would seat the water carrier on his throne. Humāyūn did not fail to keep his word and the humble *bhishtī* was able to dispense imperial authority for a period which varies in the sources from two hours to two days. By the time Aurangzēb visited Ajmer (1659) the water carrier's grave was so elaborately decorated that the Emperor mistook it for that of the saint. He ordered that it should be stripped of its embellishments.[30]

The next addition to the shrine of any significance was the gateway to the north of the mausoleum, adjacent to the present Mahfil Khāna (Figure 4.1). The inscription above the gate records that it was built by Mīr Shamanī in AH 1021/1612–13. The identity of Mīr Shamanī is not known.[31]

The Emperor Jahāngīr lived at Ajmer 'for five days less than three years'.[32] The prospect of going there pleased him:

In this undertaking two things were agreeable to me, one a pilgrimage to the splendid mausoleum of Khwāja Mu'īn al-dīn Chishtī, from the blessings of whose soul great advantages had been derived by this dignified family and whose venerable shrine I had not visited after my accession to the throne.[33]

Accordingly, on Monday, 5 Shawwāl (18 November 1613)

the hour for entering Ajmer was fixed. On the morning of the said day I went towards it. When the fort and the buildings of the shrine of the revered Khwāja appeared in sight, I traversed on foot the

[30] Muhammad Akbar Jahān, *Ta'rīkh-i Khwāja-i Ajmer*, pp. 56–9.
[31] Tirmizi, 'Persian Inscriptions', 1957, p. 52.
[32] *Tuzuk-i Jahāngīr*, vol. 1, p. 340.
[33] Ibid., p. 249.

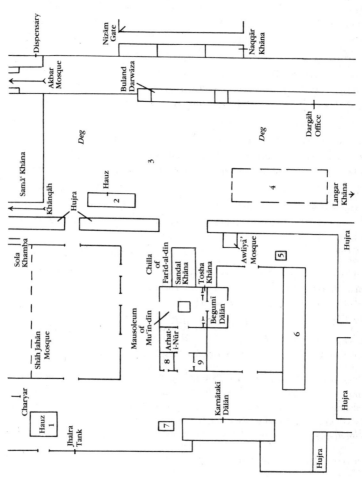

Figure 4.1 *Plan of the Mausoleum of Muʿīn al-dīn Chishtī*

Key

Mausoleum of Muʿīn al-dīn: Originally built under Husain Nagaurī and often embellished and redecorated subsequently.

Buland Darwāza: So-called because of its great height. Probably built by Sultān Ghiyās al-dīn Khiljī.

Akbarī Mosque: Built by the Emperor Akbar and completed in 1571. It now houses a Madrasa.

Shāh Jahāni Mosque: Built by Shāh Jahān and completed in 1637–8.

Naqqār Khāna: Sometimes called Shāh Jahāni Darwāza. It houses two immense drums, believed to be the spoils of war, and is staffed by six hereditary musicians.

Begumī Dālān: Built at the wish to Jahān Āra, daughter of Shāh Jahān, and a devotee. of Muʿīn al-dīn.

Karnātakī Dālān: Built by the Nawab of Karnātak as a shelter for pilgrims in 1793.

Samāʿ Khāna: Built by Sir Asman Jah in 1888 for the performance of *samāʿ*.

Nizām Gate: The main gate to the shrine. Built by the Nizam of Hyderabad in 1915.

Sandal Khāna: A small mosque which is believed to have been built on the site of the converted *dev*'s temple.

Awliyā' Mosque: Another small mosque believed to have been built on the site where Muʿīn al-dīn immobilized the Rājā's camels.

Arhat-i Nūr: An enclosure which is believed to contain the tombs of Muʿīn al-dīn's daughter, Hāfiza Jamāl, and his granddaughter. It is used by female pilgrims for reading the Quran.

Charyar: An enclosure containing many tombs some of which are supposed to house the remains of the fictitious forty companions of Muʿīn al-dīn.

Langar Khāna: The kitchens from which *langar*, a porridge made of barley, is distributed free of charge to the poor.

Shiffā Khāna: A charitable dispensary run by the dargāh. It offers traditional medicine to all, and employs a *hakīm*, nurse and compounder.

Sola Khamba: The mausoleum of Shaykh ʿAllā al-dīn, a Sajjāda-Nishīn from the reign of Shāh Jahān. So-called after its sixteen pillars. Adjacent to it stands the *Mausoleum of Shaykh Husain*. Husain was the Sajjāda-Nishīn who was banished by Akbar. The mausoleum is now full of tombs of later Sajjāda-Nishīns.

Hujra: These are small shelters in the walls surrounding the various courtyards of the shrine. They are owned by *khuddām* and are often leased out to pilgrims as accommodation during the ʿurs.

1. *Hauz* used for the ablutions necessary before prayers in the Shāh Jahāni mosque. This site marks a ghat built by Shāh Jahān to give access to Jhalra Tank. In 1901 it was converted to its present use.
2. *Hauz* repaired and roofed at the expense of Queen Mary after her visit to the shrine in 1911.
3. A domed pavilion used as a shelter by pilgrims.
4. A shelter for poor pilgrims conveniently situated adjacent to the *Langar Khāna*. Built 1974–5.
5. Tomb of Nizām the *bhishtī*.
6. Shelter reserved exclusively for female pilgrims.
7. Mausoleum of Shāh Qulī Khān.
8/9. Enclosures believed to contain the graves of Muʿīn al-dīn's sons and grandsons.

remainder of the road, about one *kos*. I placed trustworthy men on both sides of the road, who went along giving money to faqīrs and the necessitous. When four *gharīs* of the day had passed, I entered the city and its inhabited portion, and in the fifth *gharī* had the honour of visiting the venerable mausoleum.[34]

In fact, this was not Jahāngīr's first independent visit to Ajmer. In AH 990/1582–3, Badāyūnī records that

the Prince Salīm went to Ajmer to meet Gulbadan Begum and Salīma Sultān Begum, who had returned from pilgrimage. On this occasion they paid a gratuitous visit to the shrine of the saint Mu'īn al-dīn and left their gifts there.[35]

A year after his first visit to Ajmer as Emperor, Jahāngīr decided outwardly to symbolize his devotion and gratitude to the saint:

During my illness it had occurred to me that when I completely recovered inasmuch as I was inwardly an ear-bored slave of the Khwāja [Mu'īn al-dīn] and was indebted to him for my very existence, I should openly make holes in my ears and be enrolled among his ear-marked slaves. On Thursday, 12th Shariwar, corresponding to the month of Rajab, I made holes in my ears and drew into each a shining pearl. When the servants of the palace and my loyal friends saw this, both those who were in the presence and some who were in the distant borders, diligently made holes in their ears and adorned the beauty of sincerity with pearls and rubies, until by degrees the infection caught the *ahādīs* and others.[36]

That Jahāngīr believed that he owed not only his 'very existence' to Mu'īn al-dīn but also his throne is suggested by a miniature by Bichitr which shows Mu'īn al-dīn proferring the orb and crown of imperial office to Jahāngīr (who is out of the picture). On the orb is inscribed 'The key of victory over the two Worlds is entrusted to thy hand.'[37]

[34] Ibid., vol. 1, p. 253. There are two outstanding miniatures of Jahāngīr at Ajmer in 1613. See 'Tuzuk-i Jahāngīr' MS at Rampur; the relevant miniature is published in P. Brown, *Indian Painting under the Mughals*, Plate 20, and the MS at Prince of Wales Museum, Bombay; the relevant miniature is published in *Indian Art*, Prince of Wales Museum, Bombay, 1964, Plate 33.

[35] *Muntakhab al-Tawārīkh*, vol. 2, p. 320.

[36] *Tuzuk-i Jahāngīr*, vol. 1, p. 267.

[37] T. W. Arnold, *A Catalogue of the Indian Miniatures, The Library of A. Chester Beatty*, vol. 1, p. 30, Miniature Number 14 of the Royal Albums.

A notice in the *Tuzuk-i Jahāngīr* mentions that later in the same year he presented '732 pearls of the value of 36,000 rupees to the servants, who, by way of loyalty, had bored their ears.'[38] In the three years he was at Ajmer, Jahāngīr visited the shrine nine times.[39] He gave the dargāh one of its cauldrons (*degs*) and on the inaugural occasion he lit the fire beneath it himself and the contents of the pot fed five thousand poor, as well as himself and his wife, Nūr Mahal.[40] In 1616, Jahāngīr

had made a vow that they should place a gold railing with lattice-work at the enlightened tomb of the revered Khwāja. On the 27th of this month (Rabīʿ II) it was completed and I ordered them to take and affix it. It had been made at a cost of 110,000 rupees.[41]

The Emperor Shāh Jahān visited Ajmer five times during his reign (1627–58). The Shāh Jahānī mosque at the shrine is the chief monument of his devotion to Muʿīn al-dīn. He ordered the mosque to be constructed in fulfilment of a vow made during his Mewar campaign. The result is a building of striking quality, its beauty enhanced by the enclosure, paved in polished marble and bounded by a marble balustrade, which stretches before the mosque itself. According to the *Siyar al-Aqtāb*, Shāh Jahān built 'such a splendid mosque that no former ruler has ever built a mosque to rival it anywhere on the face of the earth. May Allāh preserve this building for ever.'[42]

In the *Catalogue* the figure in this painting by Bichitr is identified as Shah Daulat. This is incorrect as a glance at a named portrait of Shah Daulat painted by Dilwarat, also in the Chester Beatty Collection, will demonstrate (see vol. i, p. 34). The figures represented are in no way similar. However, the individual in the Bichitr miniature is recognizably the same as several named pictures of Muʿīn al-dīn. See, among other things, Clive Album at the Victoria and Albert Museum, Folio 86a of I.S. 133–1964. For this information I am grateful for the assistance of Mr Robert Skelton of the Indian Department of the museum. (Note that the king-making function of Sufi shaykhs was alluded to above, p. 92, and frontispiece).

[38] *Tuzuk-i Jahāngīr*, vol. 1, p. 279.
[39] Ibid., p. 341.
[40] *Observations of Thomas Coryat, Haklyutus Posthumus, or Purchas His Pilgrimes*, vol. IV, pp. 491–2; and pp. 123–6 below.
[41] *Tuzuk-i Jahāngīr*, vol. 1, p. 329.
[42] *Siyar al-Aqtāb*, p. 141.

Tirmizi has noted the details of the mosque's construction thus:

It measures 148 feet in length and 25 feet in width, having in front an enclosure measuring 150 feet by 53 feet. This enclosure, paved with polished marble, is surrounded on the south, north and east of an elegant balustrade having five entrances, one in the south, one in the north and the remaining three in the east, each reached by a flight of stairs.

The mosque proper is on a plinth, which is again reached by a flight of stairs. Under the roof of the mosque there is an exterior row of eleven arched entrances running parallel to an interior row of the same number, all the twenty-two being identical to one another. The back-wall has five niches in which the fundamental creeds of Islam are inscribed in letters of gold. Over the frieze of the facade there is an inscription in Persian verse.[43]

The chronogram yields the date AH 1047/1637–8.[44]

Shāh Jahān is also believed to have constructed a ghat to give access to the Jhalra tank, which is adjacent to the south side of the dargāh.[45]

A second monumental gateway was built outside the Buland Darwāza during Shāh Jahān's reign. The inscription on the gateway indicates that it was built to commemorate a victory of Shāh Jahān over some non-Muslim power. One of the verses reads:

During the reign of Shāh Jahān, the religious-cherishing king, the son of Faith has wiped away the darkness of infidelity completely. Year 29 (1654).[46]

This gateway is variously known as the Shāh Jahāni Darwāza and the Naqqār Khāna, the latter because it was used to house two immense drums, which came from Bengal. An earlier reference suggests, however, that there was some kind of naqqār khāna before the reign of Shāh Jahān.

Early in *Ramazan* [1574] the atmosphere of Ajmer became fragrant from the storm raised by the musk-like hoof of royal horses. [The king]

---

[43] Tirmizi, 'Persian Inscriptions', 1957, p. 62. See Appendix I for the text of this inscription.

[44] *Ta'rīkh-i Khwāja-i Ajmer*, pp. 50–5.

[45] Sarda, *Ajmer*, p. 95. No other reference to this could be traced. Sarda's source was perhaps local oral tradition.

[46] Tirmizi, 'Persian Inscriptions', 1957, p. 69.

went straight to the shrine of Khwāja Mu'īn al-dīn and duly observed the necessary religious ceremonies there, and from the spoils of Bengal, two big drums, which from the first day had been kept apart to be presented to the Khwāja, were brought and presented to the Naqqār Khāna.[47]

The unknown benefactor responsible for the above inscription may have merely embellished the original structure, or razed it and constructed an entirely new one.

Shāh Jahān's daughter, Jahān Ārā Begum, was a loyal follower of Mu'īn al-dīn and, as an expression of her devotion, she had a porch of white marble built over the main entrance to the saint's mausoleum.[48] This is known as the Begumī Dālān and has been recently decorated. In 1888 the walls and pillars were painted a rich red, gold and blue at the expense of the Nawab Mushtak 'Alī Khān of Rampur. A wealthy Muslim merchant from Bombay funded the embellishment of the roof, and there have been further additions of electric lights and fans, and modern clocks.[49]

Another account of Ajmer and its shrine by a European traveller dates from Shāh Jahān's reign. Peter Mundy describes 'a great resort of people continuously from all parts thronging in and out'. Evidently the saint's reputation as a miracle worker was widespread. Mundy heard 'a world of false miracles' attributed to him. Mu'īn al-dīn was well-known in Agra as being effective against poisonous snakes: Mundy met

by the way four or five who carried faggots of rodds like switches. I asked what they meant. I was told that by the Holynesses of Qfauz Mondeene [Khwāja Mu'īn al-dīn] whoever had a rodd of those in his hand should not be bit by any venemous thing, a snake, scorpion etts; and they carried them to Agra where they sold them for five or six pice each, bringing them from Adzmeere where they grow and where also is the Tombe of their said Sainte.[50]

---

[47] *Tabaqat-i Akbarī*, quoted Sarda, *Ajmer*, p. 87. See also *Muntakhab al-Tawārīkh*, vol. 2, p. 188, which gives a similar account of the provenance of the drums.

[48] For her devotion to Mu'īn al-dīn, see her *Mu'nis al-Arwāh*.

[49] *Ta'rīkh-i Khwāja-i Ajmer*, pp. 43–6.

[50] *The Travels of Peter Mundy*, vol. 2, pp. 238–9.

Mundy also records how, when he visited the shrine, 'one presented me with a rodd, another with seedes, another with sandal, another with water etts. all belonging to their Saint.'[51]

The Emperor Aurangzēb was not wholly in favour of pilgrimages to the shrines of saints: 'He forbade the roofing over of buildings containing tombs, the lime-washing of sepulchres, and the pilgrimage of women to the grave-yards of saints, as opposed to Quranic law.'[52] Even so Aurangzēb himself did not fail to visit the shrine of Mu'īn al-dīn when he was at Ajmer in 1659 after his victory over Dārā Shikōh; he presented Rs 5,000 to the attendants as a thanks-offering for the victory.[53] However, there are no lasting monuments in the shrine of Aurangzēb's reverence of Mu'īn al-dīn. But in spite of the lack of any obvious imperial patronage at this time, there seems to have been no drastic decline in the popularity of the shrine. Thevenot noted in 1666 that 'the famous Hogea Munday (Khwāja Mu'īn al-dīn) is reverenced at Azmer; and from all parts, they come in pilgrimage to his tomb.'[54]

The era of the Great Mughals was a time of unusual stability in the history of Ajmer. The cult of Mu'īn al-dīn and his shrine had developed unhindered by political and territorial disputes. This relative tranquillity ended with the death of Aurangzēb, when Ajmer entered a period of uncertainty and political turbulence. The city became the focus for Rajput expansionist ambitions.

In 1709 Ajīt Singh of Jodhpur conquered Ajmer. He left shortly afterwards with a fine of Rs 45,000 which he had collected from the governor.[55] Aurangzēb had actively oppressed the Hindus. In April 1669 he had ordered the provincial governors 'to destroy the temples and schools of the Brahmans ... and to utterly put down the teachings and religious practices of the infidels.'[56] Ajīt Singh determined to reverse the situation after Aurangzēb's death. Ajīt Singh

[51] Ibid., p. 244.
[52] Sarkar, *History of Aurangzeb*, vol. 3, p. 101.
[53] Ibid., vol. 2, p. 188.
[54] *Indian Travels of Thevenot and Coreri*, ed. S. R. Sen, p. 69.
[55] Sarda, *Ajmer*, p. 175.
[56] Sarkar, *Anecdotes of Aurangzeb and Historical Essays*, p. 12.

again showed his disobedience and rebellion by oppressing Musalmans, forbidding the killing of cows, preventing the summons to prayer, razing the mosques which had been built after the destruction of the idol-temples.[57]

In 1719 Ajīt Singh re-took Ajmer, but this time did what he could to mollify Muslim opinion.

On entering Ajmer he rebuilt mosques which had been destroyed by his orders, allowed the butchers to kill cattle for food, and withdrew his prohibition of the Muslim call to prayer. He then wrote to court a humble petition promising that, if he were allowed to retain Ajmer, he would be loyal and submissive in future, and this was granted.[58]

This situation did not last. Muhammad Shāh, the new Mughal Emperor, recaptured Ajmer in 1722. But by 1730 Ajmer was again in Rajput hands.[59] It has been suggested that the visit to Ajmer planned by Nādir Shāh was no more than a cover for political designs: 'At Delhi Nādir Shāh talked of making a pilgrimage to the tomb of Shaykh Mu'īn al-dīn Chishtī at Ajmer. This journey was really intended for the spoliation of the Rajput states because Ajmer is in the heart of Rajputana.'[60]

Ajmer was the centre of endless disputes in the mid-eighteenth century, but stability returned when it was annexed by Scindia of Gwalior in 1791. It remained in his hands until it was ceded to the British government in 1818.[61] The turbulent history of Ajmer is a factor in the growth of its shrine. Nādir Shāh was not alone in realizing that journeys to shrines could be used for military or political ends. The strategic importance of Ajmer may help to explain the interest temporal rulers (including non-Muslims) took in the shrine. Geographically Ajmer is the gateway to much of Rajasthan. Its position, combined with the precipitous nature of the hill on which its fort is built, made the city of supreme strategic interest. As Sarda somewhat ornately puts it:

History tells us that from the twelfth to the nineteenth century Ajmer was not only the cynosure of all eyes, but adorned the brow of the

[57] Elliot and Dowson, *History of India*, vol. 3, p. 404.
[58] *Cambridge History of India*, vol. 4, p. 347.
[59] Sarda, *Ajmer*, p. 186.
[60] Irvine, *Later Mughals*, vol. 2, p. 374.
[61] *Cambridge History of India*, vol. 5, p. 381.

victor in the race for political supremacy in India. The possession of Ajmer by a Power is the index to its political predominance in Upper India....[62]

Pilgrimage to Ajmer could provide an apparently innocent reason for visits to a military outpost. Observations of historians of the period substantiate this. According to Rizvi, Akbar's interest in Ajmer was certainly not confined to the spiritual; he used the town as a military base from which he could direct campaigns against disaffected Rajput chiefs.[63] Digby thinks it probable that Zafar Khān's pilgrimage to Ajmer was also 'an attempt to extend his military power northwards into Rajasthan' with an eye on Delhi itself.[64] Patronage of the shrine was a useful instrument in gaining the loyalty of subjects in a politically sensitive area.[65]

Thus, even during the political upheavals in Ajmer in the nineteenth century the dargāh was not entirely neglected. A succession of Mahārājās endowed it with a series of villages (see Chapter 9). The Rathor of Jodhpur removed the balustrade which Jahāngīr had installed to surround Mu'īn al-dīn's grave, but it was replaced by Mahārāja Jai Singh of Jaipur in *c.* 1730. This contains approximately 42,961 *tolas* of silver.[66]

The advent of Scindia rule in Ajmer in 1791 was marked by the Nawāb of Arcot wishing to repair the dargāh buildings which had become dilapidated. Rao Scindia co-operated in this and was presented with a telescope in return. From the correspondence between the two, it is clear that there was much rivalry to gain the privilege of funding this repair work. The Nawāb was considerably alarmed by the potential competition, but the Mahārāja was able to assure him that all was well and no-one would interfere with the Nawāb's requests.[67]

[62] Sarda, *Ajmer*, p. 137.
[63] S. A. A. Rizvi, *Religious and Intellectual History of the Muslims in Akbar's Reign*, p. 68.
[64] S. Digby, 'Early Pilgrimages to the Graves of Mu'īn al-dīn Sijzī and Other Indian Chishtī Shaykhs', p. 3.
[65] While this theme is not explored in any detail here, it is, no doubt, relevant to many visits to Ajmer and the dargāh made by leading political figures.
[66] Sarda, *Ajmer*, p. 92.
[67] *A Calendar of Persian Correspondence*, vol. 9, Nos. 1556/7.

In spite of being Hindu, the Scindia family was devoted to the shrine. Bishop Heber, who visited Ajmer shortly after the beginning of British rule noted that 'the Scindia family, while masters of Ajmer, were magnificent benefactors of its shrine.' They spent Rs 2,000 annually on the distribution of food to the poor at the two Id festivals.[68]

In 1793 the Nawāb of Karnātak, Muhammad 'Alī Khān Wala Jah, built the Karnātakī Dālān as a shelter for pilgrims to the shrine.[69] In 1800 the Mahārājā of Baroda presented a *chatgiri* with which to cover the ceiling of the mausoleum of Mu'īn al-dīn. This was replaced in 1959 by Ghulām Dastgir of Hyderabad.[70]

The next architectural tribute to the importance of the shrine came in 1888 when Sir Asman Jah initiated the construction of the Mahfil Khāna where *samā'* is held every night during the 'urs.[71] The Nizām of Hyderabad's patronage of the dargāh began when he gave a *jāgīr* to the shrine in 1851.[72] A crown-like pinnacle for the apex of the mausoleum was presented in 1896 by Nawāb Haidar 'Alī Khān.[73] In 1901 the Akbarī mosque was repaired at the expense of Nawāb Gafur 'Alī of Danapur.[74] The eastern and southern doors of the mausoleum were then plated with nickel thanks to the generosity of Sadutullah Khān of Jaora, and Shāh Jahān's ghat was converted into a square *hauz* for the ritual ablutions before prayers in the Shah Jahānī mosque.[75]

On 23 December 1911, Queen Mary of Britain visited Ajmer and its shrine. She gave Rs 1,500 to pay for the repair and roofing of the tank in front of the Mahfil Khāna.[76]

[68]   Heber, *Narrative of a Journey*, vol. 2, p. 49.
[69]   *Ta'rīkh-i Khwāja-i Ajmer*, pp. 46–7; Tirmizi, 'Persian Inscriptions', pp. 51, 195. For its inscription see Appendix I.
[70]   Begg, *Biography of Hazrat Khwaja Mu'īn al-dīn Chistī*, p. 121.
[71]   *Ta'rīkh-i Khwāja-i Ajmer*, pp. 83–4.
[72]   *Ajmer Documents*, ed. Ma'nī, pp. 338–9. This is a collection of documents relating to the Ajmer shrine. It was published in a very small edition in 1952. The documents, having been collected together for the purpose of producing this volume were mislaid and cannot now be found. So for early documentary evidence of the shrine this volume is heavily relied upon.
[73]   Begg, *Biography of Hazrat Khwaja Mu'īn al-dīn Chistī*, p. 122.
[74]   Sarda, *Ajmer*, p. 88.
[75]   Ibid., pp. 95, 91, n. 1.
[76]   *London Times*, 27 Dec. 1911; and *The Statesman*, 28 Dec. 1911.

The present main gate of the dargāh was built by the Nizām of Hyderabad in 1915. It stands outside the Naqqār Khāna. The raised steps beneath this new gateway were, actually, built during Akbar's reign in order to prevent flooding.[77] Distinguished individuals continue to visit the shrine. Thus, in 1951 Dr Rajendra Prasad, then President of India, paid a visit to the dargāh, as did the wife of President Fakhr al-dīn 'Alī Ahmad in 1975, and Indira Gandhi in 1977.

The dargāh has been enlarged still further more recently. In 1975 a modern, western-style guest house was completed to house the more important and wealthy visitors to the shrine. A second guest house of similar design is at present under construction. Another shelter for the poorer pilgrims was completed in 1976.

Mention was made above of Nizām the Bhishtī's tomb. Numerous individuals since then have elected to be buried within the precincts of Mu'īn al-dīn's shrine. Not only is this exceptionally holy ground, but the saint is believed to be able to intercede on behalf of those buried near him and ensure for them the mercy of Allāh. Two of these graves are outstanding architecturally: the first is that of Husain, the Diwan whom Akbar banished but Jahāngīr pardoned. This mausoleum is almost identical to that of Mu'īn al-dīn himself. The chronogram of the inscription yields the date AH 1047/1637.[78] The building is now in a poor state of repair and is congested with smaller graves of various later Diwans and their families.[79] The second of the two graves is the edifice known as the Sola Khamba on account of its sixteen pillars. It houses the remains of Shaykh 'Allāh al-dīn, Diwan during Shāh Jahān's reign.[80]

There are many other, less impressive, graves within the dargāh, but only some of the occupants can be identified. The earliest belong to Mu'īn al-dīn's immediate family. His daughter, Hāfiza Jamāl, and her daughter are buried in the Arhat-i Nūr, adjacent to the southern side of Mu'īn al-dīn's mausoleum.

---

[77] Sarda, *Ajmer*, p. 87.

[78] Tirmizi, 'Persian Inscriptions', 1957, pp. 61–2.

[79] *Ta'rīkh-i Khwāja-i Ajmer*, pp. 66–7.

[80] Ibid., p. 67, and for a detailed architectural description see Sarda, *Ajmer*, p. 97. For inscription, see Appendix I.

In two enclosures next to this are various graves which are supposed to be those of some of Muʿīn al-dīn's grandsons. This, however, is unlikely as his grandsons are not known to have resided in Ajmer.[81]

Another of the graves belongs to Shāhbāz Khān, one of Akbar's leading generals. There is a curious story behind his burial at the shrine:

Shāhbāz had expressed a dying wish to be buried in Ajmer within the hallowed enclosure of Muʿīn al-dīn Chishtī. But the custodians of the sacred shrine refused to comply [no reason for this is given] and Shāhbāz was buried outside. At night, however, the saint appeared in the dream of the custodians, and told them that Shāhbāz was his favourite, whereupon the hero was buried inside, north of the tomb.[82]

Near the Karnātakī Dālān is the mausoleum built by Muhammad Tāhir Bakhsh, entitled Shāh Qulī Khān, who had been Subadar of Ajmer. Anxious to be buried near Muʿīn al-dīn, he had this small mausoleum built, but he died in Agra in 1605 and nobody thought to return his body to Ajmer.[83]

The enclosure behind the Shāh Jahānī mosque is called the Charyar after the forty companions of Muʿīn al-dīn who are supposed to have arrived in Ajmer with him, and whose remains are believed to be buried there. There is no reliable evidence which supports this. The area is now used as the graveyard for various families associated with the shrine. The oldest datable tomb there is dated AH 1022/1613–14.[84]

Ghiyās al-dīn entitled Naqīb Khān, who was made a commander of 1500 at the beginning of Jahāngīr's reign, and died in 1614, is also buried in the Ajmer dargāh with his wife beside him. Badāyūnī thought highly of him and described him as being 'endowed with angelic qualities and adorned with the graces and perfection of learning, has no equal either in Arabia or Persia in his knowledge of works on travel, of history, and of chronicles.'[85]

[81] See below, pp. 150–1.
[82] Abu 'l-Fazl, *Aʾīn-i Akbarī*, vol. 1, p. 401.
[83] Sarda, *Ajmer*, p. 94; *Taʾrīkh-i Khwāja-i Ajmer*, pp. 47–8.
[84] Sarda, *Ajmer*, p. 95; *Taʾrīkh-i Khwāja-i Ajmer*, pp. 55–6.
[85] *Muntakhab al-Tawārīkh*, vol. 3, p. 150.

In 1616 Ḥūr al-Nisā', daughter of Shāh Jahān, is believed to have died of smallpox and to have been buried just to the west of Muʿīn al-dīn's tomb.[86]

Outside the Begumī Dālān are several tombs, one of which houses the remains of Shaykh Mīr, commander of Dārā Shikōh's forces and Aurangzēb's father-in-law. Another contains the body of Shāh Nawāz Khān, Aurangzēb's general. They were both killed in the battle of Ajmer fought between Dārā Shikōh and Aurangzēb in 1658–9.[87]

In the same courtyard is the tomb of Mīrzā ʿĀdil, governor of Ajmer under the Scindias. The chronogram on the tomb gives the date AH 1182/1768–9. Close to the grave of Mīrzā ʿĀdil is that of his son, Nawāb Mīrzā Chaman Beg, who was Subadar of Mālwa under the Scindias.[88]

It was only a small minority who had the means to record their respect for the saint in the form of architectural monuments, or who were in a position to select the dargāh of Muʿīn al-dīn as their last resting place. While these monuments are crucial to the task of tracing the development of the cult, they represent only a very limited range of the saint's followers. Since its inception, the cult of Muʿīn al-dīn has always been a popular movement. The nature of this popular support is traced in Chapter 5.

[86] Sarda, *Ajmer*, p. 93.   [87] Ibid., p. 94.
[88] Tirmizi, 'Persian Inscriptions', 1957, pp. 49–50.

5

The Pilgrimage to Ajmer

Isolated references in the historical sources indicate that it was not just highly-placed individuals who travelled to Ajmer for the *ziyārat* of Mu'īn al-dīn. Jamālī mentions the large numbers of Muslims and Hindus who visited Ajmer to make offerings at his tomb.[1] The Emperor Akbar made arrangements for the 'treatment of pilgrims' at Ajmer.[2] Pelsaert, in Jahāngīr's reign, noted the existence of the cult of Mu'īn al-dīn 'who is buried in a very costly tomb at Ajmer, whither pilgrims journey annually from distant places.'[3] From the reign of Shāh Jahān there is Peter Mundy's evidence that at Mu'īn al-dīn's shrine there was 'a great resort of people continuously from all parts thronging in and out'.[4] Thevenot, who visited Ajmer in Aurangzēb's reign, records how 'from all parts they come in pilgrimage to his [Mu'īn al-dīn's] tomb.'[5]

While devotees visit Ajmer throughout the year, the chief occasion for the pilgrimage is the anniversary of Mu'īn al-dīn's death, a festival known as the 'urs.[6]

The figures of the attendance at the 'urs between 1879 and 1976 show that Mu'īn al-dīn has lost none of his popular appeal:

[1] *Siyar al-'Ārifīn*, p. 13.
[2] *Akbarnāma*, vol. 2, p. 511.
[3] *The Remonstratie of Francisco Pelsaert*, p. 70.
[4] *The Travels of Peter Mundy*, vol. 2, p. 244.
[5] *Indian Travels of Thevenot and Coreri*, p. 69.
[6] 'Urs was originally the term used for marriage festivities, as opposed to *nikāh*, the marriage ceremony. However, it has come to be used to designate 'the ceremonies observed at the anniversary of the death of any celebrated saint'. Used in this way the word 'urs has 'a subtle reference to the unitive stage attained by him (the saint) in his lifetime and consummated at the time of his death'. Subhan, *Sufism: Its Saints and Shrines*, p. 114; also Hughes, *Dictionary of Islam*, p. 655.

from 20,000 pilgrims in 1879, the figures have risen steadily, to about 100,000 every year.[7]

The pilgrims come from all over the Indo-Muslim world. This does not limit the catchment area to the subcontinent of India. Indo-Muslims who have emigrated still return to Muʿīn al-dīn's shrine. Pilgrims from South Africa, Canada, Yemen

[7] These figures, except for those of the last three years which come from newspaper reports, are taken from the Annual Administration Reports of the Ajmer-Merwara District. The figures can only be taken as an approximate guide. Where the decennial Census Reports refer to attendance at the ʿurs

Attendance at ʿUrs			
1879	20,000	1925	40,000
1891	40,000	1926	50,000
1892	30,000	1927	21,000
1893	50,000	1928	50,000
1894	50,000	1929	70,000
1896	60,000	1930	100,000
1898	10,000	1931	60,000
1899	5/6,000	1932	100,000
1904	80,000	1933	50,000
1905	200,000	1934	60,000
1906	200,000	1935	70,000
1907	100,000	1936	60,000
1908	50,000	1937	70,000
1909	60,000	1938	64,500
1916	60,000	1939	43,000
1917	2,000		
1918	40,000		
1919	100,000	1960	150,000
1920	150,000	1961	50,000
1921	50,000		
1922	40,000		
1923	125,000	1975	300,000
1924	100,000	1976	100,000

there is a wide discrepancy between the different sets of figures. For instance, the Census Report of 1931 records 15,000 pilgrims at the ʿurs, while the Administration Report for that year records 60,000. No details for attendance at the ʿurs could be found for the period prior to 1879. Early newspaper reports do not give attendance figures so they could not be used to fill in the gaps left by the Administration Reports. 1879 was the year in which the railway connection to Ajmer was opened. This, no doubt, led to an increase in the numbers of pilgrims. The sudden fall in attendance can often be explained in terms of extraneous conditions. Thus, in 1898, 1899 and 1917 there were serious outbreaks of plague. In 1909 there was an unusually heavy

and the United Kingdom were interviewed (as well as many from India and Pakistan) during the 'urs of 1975 and 1976.[8] Hindus also visit the shrine, but their catchment area seemed to be limited to the immediate locality of Ajmer. None of the Hindu devotees encountered at the shrine had travelled far. The goal of the pilgrimage is the mausoleum of Mu'īn al-dīn. Once they have achieved the inner sanctum of the shrine, the devotees bow low and kiss the tomb. Prayers are offered in thanksgiving for favours received, and petitions made for favours required. The prayers are a form of spiritual bargaining; offerings to the shrine will be made if the devotee's prayers are answered. As an earnest of their offerings, devotees tie strings to the pierced-marble screens that surround parts of the mausoleum. These strings are removed when the prayers have been answered and the offerings submitted. The devotees scatter red rose-petals over the tomb, and the privileged are given petals which have been lying there to keep as *tabarruk*

---

monsoon and in 1915 and 1939 the monsoon failed. In 1927 the 'urs occurred during a particularly severe winter and in 1921 there was a shortage of coal which prevented the railways from operating on schedule. All these explanations are furnished by the Administration Reports. In 1976 the low attendance was due to a fear of a repeat of the heavy monsoon which badly damaged parts of Ajmer and killed several people during the 'urs of 1975. There was also a general fear among Muslims in India that they were subject to victimization in the sterilization campaign during the political emergency. The fact that the date of the 'urs is organized by the Muslim lunar calendar means that it is continually changing in relation to the seasons and agricultural cycle. This must also have an effect on the numbers attending the 'urs. The peak attendance occurred in 1975. The overall trend is an increase in attendance. But how this increase compares with the increase of the population cannot be established without more exhaustive statistical research. Others have noted that there is a general increase in numbers of people on pilgrimage. See Bhardwaj, *Hindu Places of Pilgrimage in India*, p. 5; Jameson, 'Gangaguru. The Public and Private Life of a Brahmin Community of North India', p. 3; V. Turner, 'The Centre Out There: Pilgrims' Goal', *History of Religions*, vol. 12, p. 196.

[8] Those émigrés who cannot manage to travel to Ajmer for the 'urs organize their own festival in their local community. This usually centres around someone who claims descent from the saint and can act as his regional representative. Thus, the Indo-Muslims of Wembley, London, have had their own 'urs in 1976 and 1977. See *The People's Weekly*, July 13 1976; and *Wembley Observer*, July 15 1977.

or to eat.[9] Pilgrims also spend time circumambulating the mausoleum, and sitting in its vicinity in passive and receptive silence to absorb the spiritual presence of the saint and to meditate on his life and teachings.[10] There is a special enclosure, immediately adjacent to the mausoleum—the Arhat-i Nūr— where women may sit in silence and read the Quran. The men may read the Quran inside the mausoleum itself.

The pilgrims then visit various other places associated with Mu'īn al-dīn and his family and entourage. The anecdotes of Mu'īn al-dīn's coming to Ajmer are all located and comme- morated by monuments. Thus, the pilgrim may go to his *chillā* where he is believed to have lived before being accepted into the city. Next to this shelter cut out of the rock is the cell where Qutb al-dīn, his khalīfa, is believed to have performed his ascetic exercises. The converted *dev*'s temple is now the site of a mosque, as is the place where Mu'īn al-dīn immobilized the Rājā's camels. The pilgrim visits the place where Mu'īn al-dīn died, now marked by a building known as the *khānqāh*. Farīd al-dīn Shakar Ganj, the khalīfa of Qutb al-dīn, is believed to have sat and prayed in a place which is also an object of veneration.[11]

Two other major shrines visited by pilgrims are the dargāh of Mu'īn al-dīn which is situated at the foot of Taragarh hill, and, halfway up the hill, an imposing white edifice known as the

---

[9] There is a tradition according to which Muhammad declared the red rose to be the manifestation of the glory of Allāh. *Tabarruk* is something particularly laden with *baraka*, usually through close physical association with the saint or his shrine.

[10] The original meaning of the root hajj was 'to describe a circle'. So the pilgrimage to Mecca received its name from the rite of the circumambulation, which reflects its importance as part of the pilgrimage ritual. The prescribed number of circuits is seven at Mecca, and the same custom is observed at Ajmer. The tradition is ancient; it is attested in pre-Islamic Arabian poetry, and found in Jewish ritual 'in which at one time during the Feast of the Tabernacles the altar was circled once on each of the first six days, and seven times on the seventh'. Von Grunebaum, *Muhammadan Festivals*, pp. 29–30.

[11] There is no evidence to support this tradition of Farīd al-dīn's visit to Ajmer. This brief summary of the sacred geography of Ajmer is based on observations made *in situ*. Both Sarda, *Ajmer*, pp. 86–98, and *Ta'rīkh-i Khwāja-i Ajmer*, pp. 38–67, describe most of these sites.

chillā of 'Abd al-Qādir Jīlānī. 'Abd al-Qādir never visited India but tradition relates that a faqīr from Ajmer visited his shrine near Baghdad and returned with two bricks from the mausoleum. When the faqīr died these bricks were buried with him and in c. 1800 a shrine was built over these relics. Pilgrims then continue up the hill until they achieve the fortifications which crown the summit and house the dargāh of Mīrān Husain Khing Sawār, Governor of the fortress, who is believed to have died in an attack by the Rajputs in 1202.[12] Abu 'l-Fazl records that 'From lapse of time and general assent he became famous as a saint and his tomb became the circumambulation place of mankind.'[13] His dargāh was not built until the reign of Akbar.[14] The rise of the cult of Mīrān Sahib is clearly associated with the growth of interest in Ajmer as a sacred centre under the imperial patronage of Akbar himself, and perhaps helped by a confusion over the identity of Mīrān Sahib. There is a lively cult of Mīrān Sahib in other parts of northern India, with shrines dedicated to him not only at Ajmer, but also at Amroha, in the Muradabad district, at Banaras and at Bundi. Popular belief regards these shrines as being dedicated to the same Mīrān Sahib, whose identity is further confused with 'Abd al-Qādir Jīlānī.

According to folk lore

[Mīrān Sahib] is said to have been a magician, and to have subdued to his service a *jinn* named Zain Khān, whom he treated with great cruelty. One day the *jinn* surprised his master in a state of uncleanness and slew him, but even then he was unable to escape from the influence of this arch-magician, who rules him in the world of spirits. Mīrān Sahib is said to be buried at Ajmer.[15]

It, therefore, seems reasonable to speculate that this association of Mīrān Sahib, the government servant, with the Mīrān Sahib of the folklore of northern India and even more remotely with 'Abd al-Qādir Jīlānī, enabled the cult to establish itself and provide a useful additional source of income to the inhabitants of Taragarh Hill.

[12] Sarda, *Ajmer*, p. 55. Sarda notes that the Rajput attack of 1202 is nowhere mentioned by contemporary historians.
[13] *Akbarnāma*, vol. 2, p. 540.
[14] Sarda, *Ajmer*, p. 57.
[15] Crooke, *Popular Religion*, pp. 216–17.

Returning from the dargāh of Mīrān Sahib, pilgrims pass the Adhar Silla. This is a large boulder which is said to have been magically thrown at Mīrān Sahib by his Hindu enemies. Mīrān Sahib saw it coming and spoke to it saying, 'If thou art from God, fall on my head; if magic sent thee, stay there.'[16] But evidently he enjoyed the favour of Allāh, for the missile fell at his feet and the old lady who attends the Adhar Silla shows pilgrims where his fingers and horse came into contact with it.

At all these objects of veneration pilgrims make offerings in cash or kind, and the path between these sacred places is lined by beggars to whom they give alms. Cowries are still negotiable currency here. At the bottom of Taragarh Hill pilgrims buy a weight of shells and distribute them as they wind their way upwards.

Most parties of pilgrims present a *chādar* at Mu'īn al-dīn's mausoleum. This cloth to cover the tomb varies from the coarsest and cheapest material to richly-worked embroidered silks and velvets costing several thousand rupees. The pilgrims, led by musicians, proceed through the bazars to the shrine, holding the *chādar* above their heads. Others clamour to touch the cloth which will have such close contact with the sacred tomb and impart their personal blessing to it.[17]

It is not only the pilgrims who give to beggars. The dargāh administration distributes food to the destitute twice daily from the langar khāna, at an annual cost of approximately Rs 55,000. Chishtī foundations have always believed in distributing food to the needy whenever possible. The medieval Chishtī *khānqāhs* kept open kitchens and this tradition is continued by the Ajmer dargāh.[18] The British administration was clearly impressed by this aspect of the dargāh's activities. The Rajputana District Gazetteer of 1904 reports that

[16] Sarda, *Ajmer*, p. 58.

[17] According to *The Times of India* (Thursday, 8 July 1976) during the 'urs of 1976 'about 3,000 *chādars* costing over Rs 5 lakhs (500,000) were offered at the tomb [of Mu'īn al-dīn].'

[18] Some *khānqāhs* also keep up the tradition. During the monsoon floods which destroyed many houses around the Ajmer dargāh during the 'urs of 1976, the head of a *khānqāh* situated near the dargāh fed and housed all those who found themselves without shelter after the devastation.

ordinary private charity in times of famine cannot much be counted upon to supplement government aid ... an exception is, perhaps, the institution attached to the Dargāh Khwāja Sahib [Mu'īn al-dīn] at Ajmer, known as the langar khāna, the only permanent poor-house in the district. Two maunds and six seers of grain with six seers of salt are cooked and distributed to all comers before daybreak in the morning, and the same quantity before five o'clock in the evening.... Besides the 1,570 maunds of grain which are thus yearly consumed, 644 maunds are annually distributed to infirm women, widows, and other deserving persons at their own houses.[19]

Food is also cooked in large quantities in the two *degs* which were presented to the dargāh for the purpose of providing for the poorer pilgrims. This practice has changed over the years and now the contents of these cauldrons are sold to those who can afford it. By comparing the following two nineteenth-century accounts of the practices associated with the *degs*, with a description of the same performance today, it can be seen how the details have changed. Broughton gives the following account:

On either side of this archway [the Buland Darwāza], within the court, is an enormous copper boiler fitted into solid masonry, the larger of which is capable of holding seventy maunds or five thousand, four hundred pounds of rice, and the smaller twenty-eight maunds. When princes or other great men visit Ajmer, it is usual for them to order these vessels to be filled, which is accordingly done, with rice, sugar, butter, sweetmeats, etc. It requires the whole night to boil this mess, which is distributed in the morning among the hungry pīr-zādas. The mode in which the distribution is conducted affords the chief amusement to the pious donor, who is generally seated halfway up the gateway to witness the extraordinary spectacle. Some of the oldest of the pīrzādas are entitled to certain portions of the com-position, and when this quantity is taken out and distributed, large shovelfuls are thrown among the rest of these holy persons who scramble for them with such avidity that they soon begin fighting, while some, who have taken the precaution to wrap old clothes around their bodies and limbs, plunge bodily into the boilers, where a battle royal takes place for every handful; but should an unfortunate stranger presume to intrude upon their prescriptive rights, and try his luck for a share of the *tabarruk* (for it is all consecrated), they join

[19] *Rajputana District Gazetteer*, vol. 1-A, pp. 76–7.

instantly to drive away the intruder and make him pay dearly for his temerity.[20]

The *Rajputana Gazetteer* of 1879 records the practice somewhat differently

Pilgrims to the shrine according to their ability and generosity propose to offer a *deg*. The smallest amount which can be given for the large *deg* is 80 maunds of rice, 28 maunds of ghee, 35 of sugar, and 15 of almonds and raisins, besides saffron and other spices; and the minimum cost is one thousand rupees. The larger the proportion of spices, sugar and fruit, the greater the glory of the donor ... The donor of the large *deg*, besides the actual cost of its content, has to pay about 200 rupees as presents to the officials of the shrine and as offerings at the tomb.[21] The small *deg* costs exactly half the large one.

When this gigantic rice-pudding is cooked, it is looted in a state of boiling heat. Eight earthen pots of the mixture are first set aside for the foreign pilgrims and it is the hereditary right of the people of Inderkot, and of the menials of the dargāh to despoil the chaldron of the remainder of its contents.[22] After the recitation of *fātiha*, one Inderkoti seizes a large iron ladle, and, mounting the platform of the *deg*, ladles away vigorously. All the men who take part in this hereditary privilege are swaddled up to the eyes in cloth to avoid the effect of the scalding fluid. Each takes a ladleful of the stuff in the skirt of his coat, and not uncommonly finds the heat so overpowering that he is obliged to drop it. When the chaldron is nearly empty, all the Inderkotis tumble in together and scrape it clean. ... There is no doubt that the custom of looting the *deg* is very ancient, though no account of its origin can be given. It is generally counted among the miracles of the saint that no lives have ever been lost on these occasions, though burns are frequent.[23]

[20] Broughton, *Letters from a Mahratta Camp*, p. 256, quoted Sarda, *Ajmer*, p. 89.

[21] When Jahān Shāh, son of Bahadur Shāh, wished to have the large *deg* cooked as a thanksgiving on the occasion of the birth of his son, he sent Rs 2,000 to cover the costs. One quarter of this money was claimed by officials of the shrine as their right by tradition. See *Ajmer Documents*, p. 271.

[22] Inderkot is a particular quarter of the city of Ajmer. According to the *Census Report of the Province of Ajmer-Merwara* for 1881, the Inderkotis 'describe themselves as the descendants of the soldiers who came here in the time of Shihāb al-dīn and are a particularly dark race; they own no land but get their livelihood by farming the gardens around Ajmer' (p. 95).

[23] *Rajputana Gazetteer*, vol. 1-A, p. 63.

The Inderkotis still loot the *degs*, sell the contents and keep the proceeds. The cooked food goes to those who can afford it, rather than to the hungry and destitute. This practice is now against the law which states that 'no portion of the food so cooked shall be sold.'[24] However, the dargāh authorities lack the executive power to enforce the law and a tradition is recounted to discourage anyone from attempting to do so:

There is a story that Imdad Khan, a *risaldar* of Jodhpur, wished on one occasion to make a fair and equable division to all, and partially accomplished his object; but, on his return from the festival, he was stricken by a bullet directed by an unseen, if not supernatural, hand and died.[25]

The various families from Inderkot work as teams to secure as much of the food as they can for themselves. When the *degs* are cooked and *fātiha* has been recited, the cloth cover, laden with ghee, is torn from over the contents, and the *deg*-men, wrapped in rags against the heat, begin frenziedly to empty the cauldron by the bucket-load. When the level of food inside the *deg* is such that the emptiers can no longer reach it with facility, they leap into the gruel, eager to salvage as much as they can for themselves. Steam envelops the fighting Inderkotis. A sweet sickening smell of sugared rice pervades the entire courtyard which is packed with spectators. The whole scene resembles some Goyaesque fantasy on the smouldering furnaces of hell. The heat inside the *deg* is intense; some of the Inderkotis collapse and are dragged senseless from the cauldron to be revived when the hectic looting is over. The looters are well rewarded for their struggle. They auction oil-drums full of the looted food for as much as Rs 400 (1976 prices) to entrepreneurs who then sell the rice in small bowls or on leaves to pilgrims.[26] The food is regarded as *tabarruk* ; in other words it is thought to be laden with *baraka* so that

[24] Dargāh Khwāja Sahib By-Laws, 1958, Section 27c., *Gazette of India*, II, 198.

[25] *Rajputana Gazetteer*, vol. 1-A, p. 63.

[26] Three lists of the ingredients cooked in the *deg* reproduced in *Ajmer Documents* (pp. 275–6) show that the food was not always sweet rice. Meat was also used, but out of deference to Hindu devotees of Muʿīn al-dīn and their vegetarian principles the practice of cooking meat was ended.

none may be wasted. Those who cannot afford to buy a portion may be seen licking the protective clothing of the Inderkotis. The surrounds of the *degs* are washed and the slops carefully conserved and drunk.

During the 'urs the most important official function is the *samā'* which is held every evening after the *'Ishā* prayer in the Samā' Khāna. Whatever Sufi theoreticians have written in the past about the dangers of *samā'* to the spiritually immature, there are no restrictions on attendance at the *samā'* at Ajmer for men. Women are, however, forbidden to attend.

Before the singers (qawwāls) begin, a *Fātiha Khwān* ceremony is performed. Hereditary *fātakhwān* officiate; there are seven incumbents of this post at present. They all hold other jobs as well; most are government clerks or railway employees. They start by reciting the *Sūra Fātiha* once and then the *Sūra Ikhlās* three times.[27] The *Sūra Falaq* and *Sūra Amān* then follow. After this a special sweet, called *dallī*, is distributed among the audience.

The living representative of the former saint (the Diwan or Sajjāda-Nishīn) sits at one end of the Samā' Khāna under a silken canopy (*shamiana*) supported on ornate silver posts. Facing the Diwan's *gadī*, at the other end of the hall, sit the musicians. Between the Diwan and the musicians are ranged the most privileged members of the audience, sitting tightly packed into neat rows, cross-legged on the floor. Two hereditary officials, called *chobdārs*, clad in *angarkhas* (white robes tied across the chest and widening out below the waist into billowing pleated skirts), control the audience and usher respected guests to the best seats. They carry long silver staffs of office. The rest of the audience is kept at bay outside the central area of the Samā' Khāna. The music is relayed by a loudspeaker system to all parts of the dargāh, so that women who are forbidden to enter the Samā' Khāna, and those men who were too late to find space in the audience hall, may still have the benefit of hearing the *samā'*.

[27] Muhammad is believed to have said, 'One who recites *Fātiha* and *Ikhlās* three times before going to bed will be raised on the Day of Resurrection among my people. He will enter into paradise after the prophets. His place will be near Isa.'

The group of musicians consists of a drummer, a harmonium player, and at least two other singers. The same musicians do not perform all night. Substitute groups of qawwāls are brought on as energy and repertoire begin to fail. When particularly moved or impressed by the musicians' performance, individuals from the audience present money to the musicians through the Diwan. They take their rupees to him, bowing low as they approach. The Diwan puts the money to his forehead and then hands it to an attendant (a son of the *chobdār* who is there to learn his father's business), who takes the offering over to the musicians. Often a member of the audience will not take his money direct to the Diwan, but will use an intermediary in order to show his humility and give another the privilege of approaching the Diwan.

Responses to the music differ. Many appear to be bored by the whole proceeding and there is a constant background of shuffling and whispering. Some evidently find the music and the poetry 'uplifting' and an aid to the contemplation of the essentials of their religion as the qawwāls sing of the Prophet, his descendants and entourage, and of the exploits of Mu'īn al-dīn and his murshid and murīds. Others react ecstatically to the performance.

al-Hujwīrī remarked that ecstasy tended to be of two different kinds: it either agitated because of ardent longing, or calmed by contemplation.[28] This observation was supported by the present-day evidence of the Ajmer *samā'*. In the first case, the ecstatic would suddenly fall forward prostrate on the floor, an expression of agonizing bliss across his face and a finger pointing upwards to Allāh. Then he begins to roll over and over across the floor keeping time to the music, further and further with each beat of the drummer. Soon he collapses, awareness of the present seeps back, then helping hands guide the weakened devotee back to his seat. Or else, another leaps to his feet and dances round and round with small shuffling steps, the pace quickening until the ecstatic is whirling like a spinning-top, till he collapses and returns to a more normal state of consciousness. Where ecstasy calms rather than agitates, the devotee remains

[28] al-Jujwīrī, *Kashf al-Mahjūb*, p. 414. A miniature, *c.* 1660–70, from the Warren Hastings Collection, Victoria and Albert Museum, London, contains an imaginary depiction of Mu'in al-dīn himself presiding over the *samā'*.

seated, rocking to and fro with the rhythm of the music until he
gradually attains the state of *wajd*.

When *wajd* is achieved the Diwan, and the whole audience
with him, rise to their feet to honour the ecstasy of the devotee.[29]
The qawwāl repeats the couplet that has so inspired the ecstatic
until the latter's spiritual thirst is quenched and he returns to
this world.[30]

The *samāʿ* is interrupted at 3 a.m. when tea, flavoured with
saffron and cardamom, is brought into the Samāʿ Khāna by
servants of the shrine dressed in long velvet dresses. The tea is
served only to the Diwan and his party, and VIP visitors who
sit in the front rows of the audience. The qawwāls continue for
another hour, after which the proceedings are brought to an
end with the *fātiha* being read again. Bowls containing rose
water which has been used to wash Muʿīn al-dīn's tomb, are
then passed around. A fortunate few are able to sip from them
before the rest is sprinkled over the crowd. The Diwan rises,
and with him the whole congregation, which then loses all self
control, pushing forward in an attempt to gain a position from
which the Diwan may be touched on his way out. Officials
eventually manage to clear a path for him.[31] The Diwan and his
entourage walk down the aisle thus created. The *samāʿ* is over.

The only official *samāʿ* is that held every night during the
ʿurs, one in the morning on the final day of the ʿurs which may

[29] Nizām al-dīn Awliyāʾ said, 'When a darvīsh claps his hands in ecstasy all
the sins of his hands are removed, and when he shouts all evil desires are
destroyed.' With such a high regard for ecstatic states in the *samāʿ* it is
possible that many of the shouts of 'Allāhu Akbar' and other standard
Muslim imprecations at the Ajmer *samāʿ* are less involuntary than they
should be. Sufi theoreticians often warned against feigned ecstasy. See,
among other things, al-Hujwīrī, *Kashf al-Mahjūb*, p. 419.

[30] The conditions in the Samāʿ Khāna are conducive to trance. The following factors have been found to help produce trance states and are present in
the Samāʿ Khāna—rhythmic stimulation (the drums), strict limitation of
movement (the audience is obliged to sit crosslegged on the floor throughout
the five hour performance), overcrowding, theatricality, group excitement,
and strong models for trance states. See: V. Crapanzano, *The Hamadsha, A
Study in Moroccan Ethnopsychiatry*, pp. 234–5; M. M. Gill and M. Brennan,
Hypnosis and Related States, pp. 123–9; A. Alland, 'Possession in a Revivalistic
Negro Church', *Journal for the Scientific Study of Religion*, vol. 1, 212.

[31] The local boy-scouts volunteer for crowd control during the ʿurs. They
are supported by considerable numbers of police.

be attended only by invitation from the Diwan himself, and a weekly *samā'* on Thursday evening. However, the dargāh is continuously filled with the sounds of qawwāls singing for the devotees who gather around them in various courtyards of the shrine. Private *samā'* parties are organized by groups of pilgrims in the houses where they are staying, and by the few *khānqāhs* that still exist in Ajmer outside the dargāh.

On the last day of the 'urs, all the pilgrims gather together in and around the dargāh to pray before returning home. Every flat space in the mosques and courtyards of the shrine, on the rooftops and in the streets of the surrounding bazars is occupied by pilgrims. They arrive several hours before the prayers, so they can secure a position close to the centre of the dargāh from which the call to prayer is broadcast by a public address system over the whole shrine and adjacent parts of the town.[32]

At the end of this *namāz* a gun is fired, the Jannatī Darwāza of the mausoleum, only opened for the duration of the 'urs, is closed, and the festival is officially ended. The pilgrims begin to leave the city, but many stay on until the ninth day of the 'urs (9 Rajab) when the entire shrine is ceremonially washed and cleaned. Only the *khuddām* (servants of the shrine) may wash the saint's grave and the inside of the mausoleum. This they do with rose water which is then sold as *tabarruk*. The pilgrims buy special brooms made from long reeds with which they sweep the rest of the dargāh.[33]

This ritual washing (*ghusl*) is the final ceremony associated with the 'urs. The life of the shrine returns to normal and the population of pilgrims diminishes.[34]

[32] If the period covered by the 'urs includes a Friday, this so-called *barī namāz* is performed twice—once on 6 Rajab and once on the Friday.

[33] This practice appears to be borrowed from the rituals performed at the Ka'ba where the sharif sprinkles the inside of the building with rose-water, and washes the walls with a broom made of palm leaves. The pilgrims then buy similar brooms from the *mutawwifs* and sweep the surrounding area. The water used for the washing of the Ka'ba is considered particularly charged with *baraka* as is the water used for the cleaning of the tomb of Mu'īn al-dīn.

[34] A survey was not conducted on the numbers of pilgrims visiting the shrine outside the time of the 'urs, so no exact figures can be given. However, the *khuddām* gave the impression that there was a steady flow of pilgrims throughout the year. The daily routine of the dargāh will be described in the next chapter.

Motive for the Pilgrimage

In order to understand why people in such large numbers visit the tomb of Mu'īn al-dīn, it is necessary to understand that death does not prevent the shaykh from playing his two roles of healer and spiritual guide. He is believed to live on in the place where he is buried and to continue to help his followers in the way he did during his earthly life. It is this belief which inspires his followers through the ages to continue to make the pilgrimage to his grave.[35]

The specific motives which take devotees to Ajmer fall into two categories which correspond closely to the roles of the shaykh as healer, and as guide: the practical or material, and the spiritual or ritual.

Practical or Material Motives

The commonest motive for making the pilgrimage to a saint's shrine is to ask him to fulfil a need or to thank him for help already received. This was certainly the case historically. We have noted in Chapter 4 how it was through the intervention of a saint that Prince Salīm was believed to have been born, and it was to give thanks that the Emperor Akbar made his pilgrimage on foot to Ajmer.[36] He also travelled to Mu'īn al-dīn's tomb to give thanks for his military victories.[37]

Scholars who have dealt with the veneration of saints in Islam agree that this is the most important motive. Thus, Goldziher says that people who are troubled by illness, poverty, etc. turn to the saint in their distress.[38] Mrs Meer Hasan Ali, referring to the shrine at Lucknow, stated that 'all who assemble at this *melā* ['urs] have some prayer to offer, or acknowledgement to make, for they depend on the abundant power and influence of the saint's spirit to supply their several wants and desires.'[39] She continues: 'Recovery from sickness, preservation

---

[35] This is certainly true of the generality of pilgrims. Some may have a more sophisticated rationale for their devotion to the saint's tomb. This will be examined below.

[36] *Akbarnāma*, vol. 2, p. 510; *Tuzuk-i Jahāngīr*, vol. 1, p. 267.

[37] *Akbarnāma*, vol. 2, p. 496; vol. 3, p. 110.

[38] Goldziher, *Muslim Studies*, vol. 2, p. 283.

[39] Mrs Meer Hasan Ali, *Observations on the Mussulmans of India*, p. 373.

from any grievous calamity, danger or other event which excites grateful feelings, are the usual inducement to visiting the dargāh.[40] Likewise, among the Hamadsha in Morocco Crapanzano noted similar motives: the desire for a child, a spouse, success in business, etc.[41]

Examples to substantiate these generalizations in the context of the Ajmer pilgrimage could be multiplied almost indefinitely. However, a few cases are enough to make the point.

A cow-herd from a Rajasthani village, who was unable to have children, visited the shrine of Mu'īn al-dīn in Ajmer with his wife. After ten years of a childless marriage they now have three sons. The cow-herd said 'All my milk is from the Khwāja [Mu'īn al-dīn].' A welder from Rampur found his lost brother through Mu'īn al-dīn's help and had come to the shrine to thank the saint. A government servant from Aurangabad had come with his wife to the shrine to pray for a child. During the same visit to Ajmer they visited a gynaecologist (with whom I was staying). The doctor pronounced that the woman was unable to have a child. However, the doctor later received a letter from the couple saying the wife was pregnant and that they would be returning to Ajmer to thank the saint for his help. A refugee from Bangladesh, who had lost everything, had come to the shrine to pray for a gift of Rs 5,000. A textile merchant from Southall, London, had had no children until he and his wife visited the shrine. A year later twins were born to them, and they had returned to give thanks.

However, in the sample interviewed in Ajmer it was only a minority who came to request specific things or give thanks for specific favours received. The prayers—either of supplication or of thanksgiving—of the majority were on a more general level: thanks for their well-being and prayers for their continued prosperity.[42]

Ajmer is not only a sacred centre, it is also a market place. Many of the visitors come to exploit its commercial possibilities.

---

[40] Ibid., p. 35.   [41] Crapanzano, *The Hamadsha*, p. 170.
[42] Similar motives have been found to inspire pilgrims in the Hindu context. See: Vidyarthi, *The Sacred Complex in Hindu Gaya*, p. 9; Bhardwaj, *Hindu Places of Pilgrimage*, p. 151; Jameson, 'Gangaguru', pp. 28, 365.

During the 'urs prices of commodities and services soar. Businessmen come for the duration of the festival to sell their wares. Shops in the bazars around the shrine are leased for this short period at a rent which would normally only be paid for a whole year lease. These short-term traders specialize in regional products and objects associated with the cult of Mu'īn al-dīn—pious compilations of anecdotes about him, hats to be worn in the shrine, rose water to be scattered over the mausoleum, petals to be placed on his grave, and embroidered cloth covers to adorn it.[43]

These traders are not necessarily devotees of Mu'īn al-dīn, but there is a class of trader who attends the 'urs to combine business with piety. Amongst those interviewed, a sherbet-seller, bangle-maker, cobbler, perfume-seller, several prostitutes and tea-stall holders, fell into this category. So too does the large population of itinerant beggars who do the rounds of religious festivals and only come to Ajmer for the 'urs.

Both sides benefit from these transactions, regardless of the motivation. The saint is believed to perform a service for the devotee in return for which offerings are made. Likewise, the beggars, in return for the alms which they receive, enable pilgrims to observe one of the demands of their faith and earn religious merit.[44] With pilgrim traders the transaction is more strictly of a commercial kind. The religious transactions are of a similar order to the secular ones and appear to be modelled on them.

Ritual Motives

It is frequently mentioned in the literature on the subject of sacred centres that pilgrimages are made at particular times in

[43] Other items include popular, brightly-coloured prints of the saint and the mausoleum.

[44] See Quran II: 261–4; XIII: 20–3; LVII: 7; LXX: 24–5, etc. Life in this world (*al-dunyā*) according to the Quran, is controlled in terms of eternal 'Reward' and 'Punishment'. In the next world men will either go to the Garden (*al-Jannah*) or to the Hell-Fire (*al-Jahannam*). 'The presence of *Jannah* and *Jahannam* must make itself felt in the form of the moral conscience whenever a man does something, whenever a man acts in this world. It is the very source of the moral values' (Izutsu, *God and Man in the Koran*, pp. 88–9). By observing the tenets of his faith a Muslim will earn a place in the Garden. Hence the use of the word 'merit' here.

the life cycle.[45] Writing towards the beginning of this century, Rose noted that Muslim birth observances demanded a pilgrimage to Ajmer:

A blue cotton thread, called *beri*, is tied to the left foot of a child in the name of Mu'īn al-dīn Chishtī of Ajmer, and when it is three or four years old it is taken to the shrine of that saint, and the parents there make an offering of 5¼ seers of *maleda* (a thick bread pounded and mixed with ghee), two pice and a trouser-string.[46]

No trace of this particular life-cycle ritual could be found. Amongst those interviewed, one couple had come to present their son's hair at the grave of the saint, but until further research is undertaken it is not possible to gauge accurately the importance of the performance of life-cycle rituals today as a reason for pilgrimage to Ajmer. However, as only one couple out of a sample of 200 said they were at the shrine for purposes linked with life-cycle rituals, it may be assumed that this motive is of declining importance at Ajmer.

Spiritual Motives

The shrine of Mu'īn al-dīn is a source of power and pilgrims travel there to establish a relationship with this power. The *baraka* of the saint is contagious and may be absorbed by close contact with his grave and with anything associated with it.[47] This power of the saint is not simply valued for the material and physical help that it can bring, it is also a spiritual power[48] which works by a kind of spiritual osmosis. The saint's *baraka* imbues the places and things which are close to him; thus, the pilgrim kisses his tomb, eats the rose petals which have touched it, touches the *chādar* which will adorn it, buys the rose water which has washed it and eats the food which has been cooked near it.

[45] Cf. Bhardwaj, *Hindu Places of Pilgrimage*, p. 150; Vidyarthi, *Sacred Complex*, p. 9; Jameson, 'Gangaguru', pp. 365–6; Mrs Meer Hasan Ali, *Mussulmans of India*, p. 383.

[46] Rose, *Glossary*, vol. 1, p. 269.

[47] The idea of the contagious nature of sanctity antedates Islam and accounts for some of the practices associated with the Ka'ba. See A. Guillaume, *Islam*, p. 9.

[48] In India, where Islam has often borrowed from Hinduism, the word *darshan* is often used in this context. This implies that *baraka* is transferred by sight rather than contact, but the effect is the same.

The models for such behaviour are to be found in the hagiography where unbelievers are converted by eating food which Muʿīn al-dīn has chewed and by the power of his glance. His power is still believed to be communicated by sight and touch, and benefits all those who come within reach of it.[49]

The possibility of spiritual benefit at the shrine is not limited to a passive absorption through physical proximity to the interred saint. The shrine can be used as an aid to contemplation.

The pilgrim in this case fixes his heart or soul wholly on that of the saint, the result being that it experiences an ecstatic communion with this in the Spirit World, whereby it is greatly strengthened and rejoiced on its return to the earthly plane. It is not, we are expressly told, because the soul of the saint is supposed to linger about his tomb that the mystic goes thither for his *murāqaba*; but because it is easier for the mystic to banish all outside thoughts and fix his heart wholly and exclusively on that of the saint in the place which is hallowed by associations with the latter.[50]

Here we are presented with a more sophisticated rationale of pilgrimage. But this, too, is of declining importance and only relevant to the small band of darvīshes and Sufis who still pursue the *tarīqa*. There is, however, a mid-way position: 'The better educated among the strictly orthodox visit such shrines out of respect for the holy man and in order to salute the place where his remains repose.'[51] Associated with this is often a belief that prayers offered on such holy ground have a peculiar efficacy. But there is no belief that the saint in some way lives on at his shrine, or that the saint can be used as an intermediary to God.

Thus, there are different kinds of motives depending on the intellectual and religious status of the pilgrim. Only the very orthodox find no justification for pilgrimage to anywhere except Mecca. The diverse motives for the pilgrimage means that the pilgrims are not drawn from any one class, rank or even religion.

The belief that pilgrimage is an act of penitence provides a further motive for the pilgrimage to Ajmer. The Prophet is traditionally claimed to have held the view that 'Pilgrimage is a sort of punishment',[52] and that 'Pilgrimage effaces the

[49] Hasan Ali, *Mussulmans of India*, p. 373.
[50] Gibb, *A History of Ottoman Poetry*, vol. 1, p. 180, n. 2; cf. Spencer-Trimingham, *Sufi Orders*, p. 212. [51] Ibid.
[52] Quoted A. J. Wensinck, 'Pilgrimage', *Encyclopaedia of Islam*, vol. 2, p. 197.

sins committed after the previous pilgrimage'.[53] al-Hujwīrī
and Junaid both regarded pilgrimage as an act of mortifica-
tion.[54]

Linked with this is the belief that physical misfortune can
have a spiritual cause. In this way, the spiritual and physical
motives for pilgrimage can become intermingled. Misfortune
can be caused by sin; pilgrimage, as a penitential act, can erase
the sin and counteract the misfortune.

There is another, subconscious, category of motives for the
pilgrimage; the observer who stands outside the belief system
involved may search further for these.

An 'urs offers a holiday. The attraction of the pilgrimage
journey, the picnics, the companionship and the music must
exercise a considerable pull on the individual bound up in the
routine of everyday life.[55]

Victor Turner, an anthropologist who has recently turned
his attention to the phenomenon of pilgrimage in general,
similarly contrasts the stability of the pilgrim's social life at
home with the 'total process of pilgrimage'.[56] The structured
nature of society is particularly marked in India, where, in spite
of the Muslim belief in equality 'the influence of caste has
certainly made itself felt ... Muslims were and are divided into a
large number of groups of graded status.'[57]

Pilgrimage offers a means of escape from the hierarchy and
obligations of the social structure. The pilgrim leaves behind
his social role and 'the role-playing games which embroil his
personality in manifold guiles, guilts and anxieties.'[58] Instead,

[53] al-Bukharī, *Les Traditions Islamiques*, Chapter 1, XXVI.

[54] al-Hujwīrī, *Kashf al Mahjūb*, p. 328.

[55] W. Crooke, 'Pilgrimage', *Encyclopaedia of Religion and Ethics*, vol. 10,
p. 27; cf. *Fawā'id al-Fu'ād*, p. 334; Mujib, *The Indian Muslims*, p. 384;
Bhardwaj, *Hindu Places of Pilgrimage*, p. 3. The consequences of this
'movement of people on pilgrimage', though not directly relevant here, are
no less important. See B. S. Cohn and McKim Marriott, 'Networks and
Centres in the Integration of Indian Civilisation', *Journal of Social Research*,
vol. 1, 1–9; and M. E. Oppler, 'The Extensions of an Indian Village', *Journal
of Asian Studies*, vol. 16.

[56] V. Turner, 'The Centre Out There: Pilgrim's Goal', *History of Religions*,
vol. 12, 1973, pp. 191–230; and *Dramas, Fields and Metaphors*, 1975, pp. 167–8.

[57] Dumont, *Homo Hierarchicus*, p. 206; cf. Ansari, *Muslim Caste in
India*, p. 110.   [58] Turner, *Dramas, Fields and Metaphors*, p. 203.

he associates only with those who share similar values, and who are reaffirming those values by the act of pilgrimage, and through the rituals performed and witnessed at the shrine. The fact that these values are shared is emphasized in the rituals; the differences between the participants are minimized and their equality and relatedness are stressed.

At Ajmer, in spite of differences of caste, class and religion, all the pilgrims get on their knees to sweep and wash the precincts of the shrine—a communal activity particularly remarkable in India where normally only members of an untouchable caste would perform such a menial task. The pilgrims all pray together in public. They eat the same food from the *degs*. At the *samā'* they drink from the same bowl of rose water. They have come, whatever their individual motivations, to venerate the one saint.[59] The contrast between life at home and at the pilgrimage centre is further shown during the *samā'* when normal patterns of behaviour may be abandoned and individuals are encouraged to lose conscious control of their bodies and enter a state of trance. According to Mary Douglas, trance is an expression of 'social solidarity without differentiation'.[60]

Where trance is not regarded as at all dangerous ... I would expect to find a very loosely structured community, group boundaries unimportant, social categories undefined.[61]

This closely describes the community of pilgrims at the shrine and is almost the inverse of the situation that obtains in their everyday life. At the shrine the pilgrims behave in a way which would be impossible and unacceptable in their homes. They are freed from the obligatory everyday constraints of status and role. Instead of the hierarchy of social structure the pilgrim lives temporarily in a community governed by the principles of equality and brotherhood.[62] In short, he experiences what Turner has called *communitas*.[63]

---

[59] This unifying effect of pilgrimage has been emphasized by others: Bhardwaj, *Hindu Places of Pilgrimage*, pp. 151, 173; A. Bharati, *Pilgrimage in the Indian Tradition*, p. 141; and Vidyarthi, *Sacred Complex*, p. 112.

[60] Mary Douglas, *Natural Symbols*, p. 111.   [61] Ibid., p. 109.

[62] Cf. Turner, 'The Centre Out There', p. 221.

[63] Turner, *The Ritual Process*, p. 96.

Pilgrimage is, therefore, a journey from *structure* to *communitas* and back to *structure* again.[64]

What we see is a social system, founded in a system of religious beliefs, polarised between fixity and travel, secular and sacred, social structure and normative communitas. ... Daily, relatively sedentary life in the village, town, city and fields is lived at one pole; the rare bout of nomadism that is the pilgrimage journey over many roads and hills constitutes the other pole.[65]

While the pilgrims travel to that pole occasionally, the mystic attempts to live there permanently. His life style contrasts with that of structured social life. The communities which were centred on a shaykh in Indian Islam were characterized by a lack of structure and hierarchy. Ideally they had no property, no privileges, no material pleasures and little or no clothing. They were cut off from the world of commerce and lived on the very fringes of society.

Pilgrims temporarily, and shaykhs permanently, inhabit a place peripheral to the social structure. But it is at this periphery that *communitas* is experienced. From here the mystic seeks communion with God and the pilgrim endeavours to experience more directly the sacred.[66] Thus, shaykh and shrine occupy a similar structural position mediating between this world and the next, the visible and the invisible, laymen and God. The community surrounding a shaykh in his *khānqāh* and the community of pilgrims at a shrine are strikingly similar. Both are set apart from the constraints of social life. In both, the ideals of religion can more easily be lived out,[67] for the community at a *khānqāh* or at a shrine is based on the Muslim ideal

---

[64] There is a parallel here with *Rites de Passage*. See Turner, 'The Centre Out There', pp. 204 and 213.

[65] Ibid., p. 195. The same contrasts may be made between the social structure and the liminal period in *Rites de Passage*. Cf. Turner, *The Ritual Process*, p. 96.

[66] Cf. Turner, 'The Centre Out There', p. 214.

[67] This 'ideal' version of Islam may differ between disciples at the *khānqāh* and pilgrims at the shrine. The pilgrim's understanding of his religion may diverge from that of the shaykh. But, in the present context, these differences are subordinate to the major contrast between *Communitas* and *Structure*: shaykh and shrine on the one hand, and social life as generally lived by the layman on the other.

of equality and exemplifies the principles of Islam. The shaykh and his disciples attempt to live exemplary Muslim lives and pilgrims are scrupulous in their performance of the obligatory prayers and spend time also in supererogatory prayer. The shrine is also a place for alms giving and reading the Quran, and for living as brothers, not as 'superiors' and 'inferiors'.

This parallel between the pilgrim and the mystic in Islam was pointed out by the Sufi theorists themselves. The layman's pilgrimage to the Ka'ba or some other sacred centre was understood by al-Hujwīrī as being parallel to the journey of the mystic within himself:

Pilgrimages, then are of two kinds: 1) in the absence of God and 2) in the presence of God. Anyone who is absent from God at Mecca is in the same position as if he were absent from God in his own house, and anyone who is present with God in his own house is in the same position as if he were present with God at Mecca. ... The true object of pilgrimage is not to visit the Ka'ba but to obtain contemplation of God.[68]

Thus, every step the mystic takes is a symbol of the journey to Mecca.[69] If the Sufi theorists say that the journeys of a pilgrim and mystic have something in common, it is legitimate to deduce that their destinations and life styles there are not dissimilar.

Life as lived by a shaykh and by a pilgrim at his destination is similar and contrasts with life as lived by laymen in their homes. The former occurs at the *communitas* pole of Society and the latter at the *structure* pole. The two are linked by a journey—a pilgrimage for the layman, and a spiritual journey for the mystic. Turner sees this movement between the two poles of society as essential for the healthy functioning of society:

[68] al-Hujwīrī, *Kashf al-Mahjūb*, p. 329. See also von Grunebaum, *Muhammadan Festivals*, p. 40.

[69] al-Hujwīrī has worked this out in detail: *Kashf al Mahjūb*, pp. 326–7. For this metaphorical understanding of pilgrimage see also Bhardwaj, *Hindu Places of Pilgrimage*, p. 2, and for a further example of the equivalence of spiritual journeys and physical journeys, see N. Allen, 'The Ritual Journey, A Pattern Underlying Certain Nepalese Rituals', in *Contributions to the Anthropology of Nepal*, 17, 19.

Social life is a type of dialectical process that involves successive experience of high and low, *communitas* and *structure*, homogeneity and differentiation, equality and inequality.[70] There would seem to be—if one can use such a controversial term—a human 'need' to participate in both modalities.[71]

Here the story of Lao-Tse's chariot-wheel may be apposite. The spokes of the wheel and the nave (i.e., the central block of the wheel holding the axle and spokes) to which they are attached would be useless, he said, but for the hole, the gap, the emptiness at the centre. *Communitas*, with its unstructured character ... might well be represented by the 'emptiness at the centre', which is nevertheless indispensable to the functioning of the structure of the wheel.[72]

If Turner is right about this 'need' to move between the two poles of *communitas* and *structure*, then we are furnished with an explanation of pilgrimage more fundamental than any discussed above. Moreover, this opposition between *communitas* and *structure* and their concomitant characteristics sheds further light on the 'need' for intermediaries in Islam.

Just as this world (*al-dunyā*) is dominated for the layman by the hierarchical structure of society, so too is his vision of the unseen (*al-ghā'ib*). In this world society is stratified into ashrāf, non-ashrāf, high- and low-caste converts, and infidels, and social relations are organized hierarchically. Similarly, in the unseen world there are the various ranks of the Awliyā', the prophets, Muhammad and Allāh. To petition Allāh, it is necessary first to approach an intermediary, just as to petition the local Deputy Commissioner his inferiors had first to approach the door-keepers.[73] The layman's ideas about relations between man and the supernatural are patterned on his understanding of relations between men.[74] Furthermore, these relations are maintained in the same way. It was noted above how the transactions between the pilgrim and the dead saint did not differ substantially from those between the pilgrim and the beggars or the merchants at the shrine.

The issue is complicated by the fact that this hierarchical

[70] Turner, *The Ritual Process*, p. 97.
[71] Ibid., p. 203. [72] Ibid., p. 127.
[73] See above, p. 17.
[74] Cf. Eickelman, *Moroccan Islam* pp. 160–1.

vision of this world and the next is opposed to the teachings of the Quran. According to the Quran all men are equal before Allāh and no-one approximates to Him in any way. However, such equality does not exist within society, except at its edge—in the shaykh's *khānqāh* for the disciples, and at the shrine for the pilgrims. The shaykh is an exemplar of the ideal Muslim, and the community that surrounds him during his life in his *khānqāh* exemplifies ideal Muslim society.[75] The life of the shaykh is closer to Quranic Islam than that of the layman, so it is inevitable that he will be regarded as somehow superior to the layman and, therefore, as a suitable intermediary between the layman and Allāh.

As the hagiography of Mu'īn al-dīn developed, he was transformed in popular belief from a darvīsh, about whom little was known, into an idealized shaykh—the 'Prophet of India'. Likewise, as the cult of Mu'īn al-dīn developed Ajmer came to be regarded as a threshold to the next world—a second Mecca.[76]

[75] In practice shaykhs may well not exemplify Muslim values, but in Sufi hagiography they invariably do, and it is to the idealized shaykh of hagiography that reference is being made here.

[76] For the way in which ritual at Ajmer is similar to ritual at Mecca, see above, pp. 120, 129.

6

The *Khuddām*

The *khuddām* are the servants of the shrine who have two distinct tasks, looking after the ceremonial life of the mausoleum, and looking after the pilgrims. These two roles will be examined in turn.

The rituals of the mausoleum are in the hands of a group of *khuddām* known as the *haft bārīdār*, or *haft chawkīdār*. During one of his visits to Ajmer, Shāh Jahān organized a rota system to ensure that the duties of locking and unlocking the mausoleum and performing the various ceremonies there were carried out efficiently and that the burden was spread equitably. A *sanad* was issued dividing the *khuddām* into seven groups, each group being responsible for the shrine for one day each week.[1] The system is still in force.

On their duty day, the *haft bārīdār* take charge of the keys of the mausoleum and dargāh treasury (Tosha Khāna), and assume responsibility for all that happens within. Their day begins before dawn when the main entrance of the mausoleum is opened. Devotees are allowed inside as far as the second door, but at this time only the *khuddām* may enter the inner sanctum itself to perform the ceremony of *khidmat*. The flowers from the previous day are removed from the tomb and fresh flowers are presented. The *chādars* which cover the tomb and were presented the previous day are removed. The surround of the tomb is swept with a brush of peacock feathers. When this is completed devotees are allowed right inside the mausoleum. *Khidmat* is performed for a second time every day at 3 p.m. On this occasion male devotees as well as the *khuddām* are allowed into the inner sanctum while the ceremony is being performed. The *Fātiha* is read and *sandal* presented.

---

[1] See *sanad* No. 11 of the reign of Shāh Jahān, *Ajmer Documents*, pp. 211–14. The date of the *sanad* is not legible.

The next daily ceremony is held fifteen minutes before the *maghrib* prayer. *Khuddām* take unlighted candles from near the Buland Darwāza to the mausoleum. Meanwhile the dargāh drummers in the Naqqār Khāna begin to play, and a crowd gathers around the tomb. The candles are placed in the four lamps at each corner of the tomb and lit. Holding the lamps above their heads, the *khuddām* recite some Persian verses in praise and honour of the saint.

When one fifth of the night has passed, a bell is rung five times. The duty *bārīdār* clear the mausoleum of devotees and again sweep around the tomb. They then pass out of the mausoleum and the bell is rung six times. The dargāh's *chawkī* of qawwāls then sing a special song (*kadkha*) which relates the history of Mu'īn al-dīn and tells of his life and works. At the end of the qawwālī the mausoleum is locked up for the night.

This daily routine is somewhat altered during the 'urs. The main entrance to the mausoleum is not closed at all at night. The Jannatī Darwāza, the west door of the mausoleum, is opened at 3 p.m. on the first day of Rajab (the beginning of the 'urs) and remains open day and night until the end of the final *namāz* of the 'urs. *Khidmat* is performed at 8 p.m. instead of 3 p.m., and the ritual of cleaning the mausoleum at 1 a.m. The latter is always a scene of fervent devotion to the saint during the 'urs. All the pilgrims are eager to participate and push desperately so they can reach and wash the outside walls of the mausoleum with their rose water, and scrub them with their clothing. Again, only the *khuddām* are allowed to wash the inside of the mausoleum.

Most *khuddām* depend on the pilgrims for their livelihood. They provide accommodation, escort them to the various ceremonies held at the shrine, and show them around the sacred sites of the city.[2]

A lasting relationship may build up between a *khādim* and a

---

[2] Another parallel with activities at the Ka'ba here presents itself: The *mutawwif* at Mecca perform a similar role to the *khuddām* at Ajmer. 'The *mutawwif* provides accommodation for the pilgrims ... He sees to it that the complicated rites are correctly performed' (von Grunebaum, *Muhammadan Festivals*, p. 40).

devotee, with the *khādim* becoming the devotee's *wakīl*. The *wakīl* performs all the functions of a *khādim* for that devotee and his family whenever they visit the shrine, and undertakes to pray for them at the shrine in their absence. In return, the devotee makes offerings to the shrine which the *wakīl* is entitled and expected to keep. The relationship is based on reciprocity—offerings in return for prayers and services.[3]

All regular visitors to the shrine, as well as outstandingly important ones, have their own *wakīl*. The relationship between pilgrim and *wakīl* is formalized in a document known as a *wikālatnāma*. A *wikālatnāma* was issued to Queen Mary when she visited Ajmer in 1911.[4]

The earliest *wikālatnāma* that could be traced was dated the second day of the year AH 1081 (22 May 1670).[5]

Those who go to the dargāh for the first time are soon taken in hand by the *khuddām*. An Enquiry Report of 1949 records that *khuddām* who needed more client pilgrims would wait at the railway station, and when devotees arrived they would be auctioned to the *khādim* prepared to make the highest bid.[6] Today the *khuddām* still wait at bus and railway stations and at the shrine itself, ready to pick up any unattended pilgrims.

The *khuddām* also solicit devotees through the post. Cards are sent out advertising their services and to remind devotees to make their offerings. During the 'urs the Ajmer post office is inundated with money-orders addressed to *khuddām* as offerings to the shrine. In 1949 one *khādim* was reported to spend

[3] Note the similarity of this relationship with the Hindu *Pānda-Jajmān* relationship at Hindu pilgrimage sites. See Bhardwaj, *Hindu Places of Pilgrimage*, p. 209; Jameson, 'Gangaguru', pp. 324, 335, 347 and Vidyarthi, *Sacred Complex*, p. 61.

[4] Quoted Maulvi Ghazi Khan, *The Khadims of the Khwaja Sahib of Ajmer and the Baneful Effects of the Dargah Khwaja Sahib Bill on their Rights*, pp. 11–12.

[5] *Ajmer Documents*, p. 245. A *wikālatnāma* of the Emperor Bahadur Shah shows how *wakīls* were expected regularly to pray for their clients at the shrine as well as look after them, their friends and their family when they visited the shrine. Bahadur Shah, in fact, never managed to get to Ajmer, but the existence of the *wikālatnāma* shows he was, nevertheless, a devotee of Mu'īn al-dīn (*Ajmer Documents*, p. 336.)

[6] *Report of the Dargāh Khwāja Sahib Committee of Enquiry*, p. 42, 1949.

somewhere between Rs 5,000 and 10,000 per annum on postage alone.[7] The *khādim* run offices from which their business is conducted, and often employ secretaries to do their clerical work for them—widening their clientele, encouraging client-devotees to make the journey to the shrine, and reminding them to make their offerings.

Documentary evidence confirms that the custom of making offerings to the shrine through individual *khuddām* is not a recent innovation. This was, and still is, the major source of the income of the *khādim* community. These offerings were usually in cash or in kind, but sometimes endowments of land were made in their favour. The substance of documents on this subject that could be traced is given in Appendix III. In addition to the individuals mentioned there, the Mahārājās of Udaipur were also clearly involved in the dargāh as is witnessed in a letter of AD 1868–9 which summons the Mahārājā's *wakīls* to see him in his palace in Udaipur as soon as possible. Details of his offerings to the shrine and his *wakīls* could not however be found.[8]

The *khuddām* were not only supported by individual devotees. They were regular recipients of endowments made by the Mughal court. These were in the form of *madad-i ma'āsh* grants. 'The grant of *madad-i ma'āsh* was theoretically an act of charity. ... All those who were engaged in service or in any trade and thus had other means of livelihood, could not properly hold grants.'[9] According to Abu'l-Fazl,

His Majesty, from his desire to promote rank distinctions, confers lands and subsistence allowances on the following four classes of men: first, enquirers after wisdom, who have withdrawn from all worldly occupation, and make no difference between night and daytime in searching for true knowledge; secondly, on such as toil and practise self-denial, and while engaged in the struggle with the selfish passions of human nature, have renounced the society of men; thirdly, on such as are weak and poor, and have no strength for enquiry; fourthly, on honourable men of gentle birth who, from want of knowledge, are unable to provide for themselves by taking up a trade.[10]

[7] Ibid.   [8] *Ajmer Documents*, p. 333.
[9] Irfan Habib, *The Agrarian System of the Mughal Empire*, p. 307.
[10] *Ā'īn-i Akbarī*, vol. 1, p. 268.

In the event, criteria for receiving these grants were rather wider than Abu'l-Fazl suggests.

Descendants of saints or religious divines and persons who had retired from the world, but most frequently, those simply belonging to families reputed for learning or orthodoxy, or just held to be respectable, were regarded, without particular reference to their individual merits, as eligible for receiving grants.[11]

The *khuddām* were thus eligible for such grants from the state. The grants came in the form of land.

The grantees were to enjoy the revenues (*hāsilāt*) from the land, and they were exempted from all obligations to pay the land-revenue (*mal-o jihāt*) as well as *ikhrājāt*, the petty burdens imposed by officials, who are then specified in detail [in the *madad-i ma'āsh* documents], and so, from all 'fixed obligations and royal demands' ... In other words, what was granted was the right to collect the land-revenue and to keep it.[12]

However, the grantee had no right to sell or transfer his *madad-i ma'āsh* land.

A digest of the Mughal *madad-i ma'āsh* documents that have been traced, which give an idea of the scale of support the dargāh at Ajmer received from the Mughal Court, is given in Appendix IV.

All these endowed lands, as well as all the land grants for which the records are not traceable, were annexed by the Indian Government in 1950 and the beneficiaries received compensation calculated as four times the average revenue of the holdings.[13] With this source of revenue cut off, the *khuddām* are left only the offerings they receive from their client devotees and the offerings made anonymously at Mu'īn al-dīn's tomb and in other parts of the dargāh.[14]

The Origins of the Khādim Community

The *khādim* community numbered, in 1976–7, approximately 1400, including women and children. Their exact provenance is

---

[11] Irfan Habib, *Agrarian System*, p. 309.   [12] Ibid., p. 304.
[13] *Ajmer Tenancy and Land Records*, Act XLII of 1950, p. 36.
[14] See below, pp. 176–80.

the subject of dispute. Some *khuddām* claim that they are descended from Mu'īn al-dīn himself, but this appears to be a deliberate misrepresentation to increase their prestige, and command greater respect and more generous offerings. Others make less demanding claims, that they are descended from the immediate entourage of the saint. The improbability of this applying to the entire *khādim* population is emphasized by the claim that some are descended from Muhammad Yādgār, who, according to the *Siyar al-'Ārifīn* lived in Transoxiana, and there is no record of any of his descendants migrating to Ajmer either during Mu'īn al-dīn's life-time or later.[15] It was only the later hagiographers who suggested that Muhammad Yādgār had accompanied Mu'īn al-dīn to India.[16]

There is an alternative tradition, that the *khuddām* are descended from converts originally belonging to the Bhīl tribe. It is said that there were five brothers called Laikhā, Taikhā, Shaikhā, Jhodā and Bhirdā. Jhodā and Bhirdā never accepted Islam and settled in Pushkar. The other three brothers became converts through Mu'īn al-dīn himself. They dedicated their lives to his service and, after his death, looked after his grave as have their descendants ever since. The only evidence to support this tradition is a document from the 15th year of Jahāngīr's reign (1619) which establishes what share of the offerings made at the shrine should be apportioned to the descendants of Taikhā.[17]

If this tradition is reliable it is certainly one which the *khuddām* would prefer to deny. A criminal court case of defamation was brought before the court of Ajmer in 1928.[18] Pamphlets had been circulated in Ajmer questioning the status of the *khuddām* and alleging that they were not of noble Muslim lineage, but were descended from converted Bhīl tribesmen. Mīr Sarfarāz 'Alī, representing the *khādim* community, sued the author of the pamphlets for defamation, and maintained that the said pamphlets were 'defamatory of *khuddām*

[15] *Siyar al-'Ārifīn*, p. 11; and Maulvi Ghazi Khan, *The Khadims and the Baneful Effects of the Dargāh Khwaja Sahib Bill on their Rights*, pp. 2–3.
[16] *Siyar al-Aqtāb*, p. 131.   [17] *Ajmer Documents*, p. 68.
[18] Judgement of Criminal Case No. 70, 1928, in the Court of the Treasury Office and Magistrate First Class, Ajmer.

and full of pain-giving matter, the result of which is that
khuddām are ridiculed wherever they go in the city, and the
pilgrims criticise our lineage and pecuniary loss thereby has
occurred.'[19] The Magistrate finally acquitted the accused on
the grounds that

All the fuss and fury spent in this case by the *khuddām* and com-
plainants is wholly mistaken and out of place ... It is admitted on all
hands that, there being no rigid caste system in Islam, a convert to
Islam, no matter to what caste or class he may belong, becomes a
social equal to all Mussulmans; so that a *Bhīl* or a descendant of a *Bhīl*
is not an object of contempt in Islam or Islamic society. ... To say that
so and so is *Bhīl* by descent does not itself lower that man intellectually
or morally or socially or in any other way in Islamic society.[20]

But, having declared that the *khuddām*'s complaints were
irrelevant to the tenets of their faith, the Magistrate added that
the weight of evidence suggested that the *khuddām* were not in
fact 'what they claim to be.'[21]

With this variety of traditions as to the ancestry of the
khuddām, it is unlikely that they are descended from any one
stock. But it is generally agreed that their ancestors have worked
as servants of the shrine since Mu'īn al-dīn's lifetime. While
some outsiders may have infiltrated their ranks there is no
reliable evidence of this. The commercial motive would have
complemented the possibility of social advancement. The attraction of the position is demonstrated by the fact that almost no
khuddām left Ajmer for Pakistan at the time of Partition.

[19] Ibid.
[20] Ibid.
[21] Ibid.

7

The Sajjāda-Nishīn

The spiritual authority (*wilāyat*) of a shaykh was inherited by a chosen disciple (khalīfa). The transmission of this authority was symbolized in the transference from the shaykh to his successor of various personal insignia of office. These insignia (*amānat*) consisted in the Chishtī *silsila* of the prayer rug (*sajjāda* or *musallā*), the staff (*'asā*), the cloak (*khirqa*) and less importantly, sandals and a begging-bowl.[1]

In the case of Mu'īn al-dīn these *tabarrukāt* were inherited by Qutb al-dīn Bakhtyār Ūshī. Qutb al-dīn did not live in Ajmer but established himself in Delhi.[2]

While the spiritual traditions, symbolized by the *tabarrukāt*, were continued by the chosen khalīfa and through further generations by a succession of murshid and khulafā, the original charisma of a shaykh was also transmitted to the physical site of his burial and through the ties of lineal descent.[3] Descendants of the saint usually tended his grave and fostered a lasting cult of the saint. The community which lived at the shrine would be led by the man who was most closely and most directly descended from the saint. This man was the Sajjāda-Nishīn and he was believed to represent the saint on earth and to symbolize the saint's continued activity and interest in the lives of his devotees.[4]

[1] *Siyar al-'Ārifīn*, p. 30; *Anīs al-Arwāh*, p. 35; *Dalīl al-'Arifīn*, p. 56; *Akhbār al-Akhyār*, p. 57; cf. Digby, *Crosscurrents*, II, 1.

[2] *Siyar al-'Ārifīn*, p. 23.

[3] Cf. R. M. Eaton, 'The Court and the Dargāh in Seventeenth Century Deccan', *Indian Economic and Social History Review*, Vol. 10, 51; and Digby, *Crosscurrents*, II, 15.

[4] So the Sajjāda-Nishīn at a shrine is not necessarily the inheritor of the original saint's prayer-carpet despite the suggestion of the title (*sajjāda* = prayer-rug). The division of the saint's charisma between two groups—the disciples and the descendants—can lead to controversy with one group

In keeping with this practice, the shrine of Mu'īn al-dīn has a Sajjāda-Nishīn as its spiritual leader. The holder of this office claims descent from the saint. His function is to be a figurehead: he has no administrative duties, and his ritual duties are far from exacting. He presides over the *samā'* held every night during the 'urs, and every week on Thursdays. But as the living representative of the most widely-revered Muslim saint in India, he is rewarded not only with reverence and deference, but by a substantial income and a rent-free official residence.[5]

The issue of the rightful claimant to be Sajjāda-Nishīn at the Ajmer dargāh is accompanied by intense rivalry and continual litigation.

The tradition that Qutb al-dīn inherited the *amānat* of the Chishtī *silsila* from Mu'īn al-dīn is not questioned by Mu'īn al-dīn's followers or descendants. The name Sajjāda-Nishīn for the titular leader of the community attached to the Ajmer shrine is therefore an anachronism. The suggestion that the Sajjāda-Nishīn of Ajmer inherited the Chishtī *amānat* is irrelevant, and recognized as such by all sides in the controversies. Thus the titular leader of the shrine is often called the Diwan, a title which carries no overtones of a legacy of *amānat* and *wilāyat*.

The Diwan and the devotees of Mu'īn al-dīn claim that this post has been occupied by an unbroken line of incumbents who have had ultimate responsibility for the shrine of Mu'īn al-dīn since his death, and who have all descended from him. These claims appear, however, often to rest on very tenuous evidence, which needs to be examined.

---

claiming both legacies. In the Chishtī *silsila* there was conflict between family and disciples on the occasion of the death of Qutb al-dīn Bakhtyār, and in the following three generations on the deaths of Farīd al-dīn, Nizām al-dīn and Nasīr al-dīn. The family of the dying shaykh in each case attempted to prevent leading disciples from gaining access to the death-bed, but they were never successful. The successors to the *wilāyat* never gained control of the tomb, neither did the family manage to inherit the *wilāyat*. Cf. Digby, 'Crosscurrents', II, 14.

[5] See below, pp. 180–2.

From Mu'īn al-dīn's Death to the Arrival of the British

Although a list of individuals holding the office of Sajjāda-Nishīn has been handed down through the centuries, there is very little evidence to substantiate the historical accuracy of these claims. Indeed, such evidence as there is suggests that the direct descendants of Mu'īn al-dīn had little connection with Ajmer.

The tradition claims that the first Sajjāda-Nishīn was Mu'īn al-dīn's son, Fakhr al-dīn. However, nothing is known for certain about Mu'īn al-dīn's sons. No details are given of their lives until the seventeenth century.[6] But even then no mention is made of them being the Sajjāda-Nishīn. In fact, Husām al-dīn is said to have disappeared into the company of the *abdāl*, and Fakhr al-dīn is said to have been 'a great man' and to have 'lived for 20 years after the death of Mu'īn al-dīn. He died in the town of Sarwar.'[7] There is still no information on the life of the third son, Abū Sa'īd. It is only in the later *tazkirāt* that the tradition of one of Mu'īn al-dīn's sons becoming Sajjāda-Nishīn makes its appearance: 'After the death of Mu'īn al-dīn, his son, Hazrat Saiyid Fakhr al-dīn, became his *Jā-nishīn* and for twenty years men of God received spiritual benefit from him.'[8] However, this author goes on to relate the tradition that Fakhr al-dīn died and was buried in Sarwar. It would be unlikely that the Sajjāda-Nishīn was buried anywhere other than within the precincts of the dargāh itself.

After Fakhr al-dīn's death, his brother, 'Abū Sa'īd, is believed to have assumed the sajjāda.[9] Again there is no evidence to support this. No details of the life of Abū Sa'īd are given in the early hagiographies.

Husām al-dīn Sokhta is listed in the pedigrees as the third Sajjāda-Nishīn. The *Siyar al-Aqtāb* gives a brief outline of his life:

[6] *Siyar al-Aqtāb*, p. 136.   [7] Ibid.
[8] *Hasht Bahisht*, p. 22. See the appended genealogy which was accepted as authentic by the Diwan in 1976 and is supported by hagiographer, W. D. Begg, *Biography of Hazrat Khwaja Mu'īn al-dīn Chistī*, pp. 76–7. See back endpapers.
[9] *Hasht Bahisht*, p. 22.

Khwāja Husām al-dīn, son of Khwāja Fakhr al-dīn, and the grandson of Mu'īn al-dīn, was named Sokhta. He was a pīr, a man of miracles and a great saint of his age. Spiritually he was a true descendant of his grandfather; he was extremely devoted to contemplation and asceticism. He was a companion of Sultān al-Mashā'ikh, Shaykh Nizām al-dīn Awliyā', and his grave is in the western part of Sanbhar.[10]

Again it will be noted that there is no reference here (nor in any of the other principal sources) of Husām al-dīn being Sajjāda-Nishīn, or even living in Ajmer.

Again there is no early reference to the fourth putative Sajjāda-Nishīn, Mu'īn al-dīn the Younger, having any link with Ajmer. The notice on him in the *Akhbār al-Akhyār* runs as follows:

Khwāja Mu'īn al-dīn the Younger is the older son of Shaykh Husām al-dīn Sokhta. He is called the Younger to distinguish him from the elder Khwāja. He was a perfect saint and, before he became a disciple, had, by his devotion and austerities, reached the stage where he could hold direct communion with Hazrat Khwāja [Mu'īn al-dīn Ajmerī]. At last, ordered by the Khwāja, he became a disciple of Shaykh Nāsir al-dīn Mahmūd and obtained from him the robe of khilāfat.[11]

Thus, there is no evidence to link either the sons or the grandsons of Mu'īn al-dīn with the Ajmer shrine. In the following generation, the evidence suggests that his immediate descendants were living either in Mandu or in Gujarat,[12] probably because of the contemporary political situation. Ajmer was annexed by the Hindus after the fall of the Tughlaq Empire in the early fifteenth century, and it is with the re-conquest of Ajmer by Sultān Mahmūd Khiljī in 1455 that the next phase of the history of the putative descendants of Mu'īn al-dīn is connected, for no mention can be found of either of the Sajjāda-Nishīns allegedly following the younger Mu'īn al-dīn.

After the conquest of Ajmer, Mahmūd Khiljī appointed a certain Tāj al-dīn Bāyazīd to the Ajmer dargāh. Tāj al-dīn Bāyazīd

[10] *Siyar al-Aqtāb*, pp. 136–7.   [11] *Akhbār al-Akhyār*, p. 251.
[12] Qutb al-dīn Chisht Khān, a descendant of Mu'īn al-dīn, attained the rank of 12,000 horse. His residence still stands on the edge of the plain in Mandu. See G. Yazdani, *Mandu*, pp. 108–9; also Amīn al-dīn Khān, *Kitab al-Tahqiq*, p. 3.

claimed descent from Mu'īn al-dīn through Qayām al-dīn Bābā Yaal, the son of Husām al-dīn Sokhta who settled in Gujarat. According to the *Siyar al-Aqtāb*, Tāj al-dīn

disappeared in his youth but after a long interval he reappeared during the reign of Sultān Mahmūd Khiljī. The Sultān gave him the state of Ajmer [*sic*]. After a time the people became intensely ill-disposed towards his sons. It reached the point when they went to the Sultān of that time. The Sultān collected 'ulamā', *fuzalā'* and mashā'ikh from the town and countryside and asked for their opinions on this matter. In the end, Shaykh Husain Nāgaurī and Maulānā Rustam, who were high-ranking among the 'ulamā', as well as many other well-known people, testified that Shaykh Bāyazid was descended from Shaykh Qayām al-dīn, the son of Khwāja Husām al-dīn Sokhta, son of Khwāja Fakhr al-dīn, son of Sultān al-'Ārifīn, Hazrat Khwāja Mu'īn al-dīn Hasan al-Husainī.[13]

The author does not say explicitly that Tāj al-dīn was appointed Sajjāda-Nishīn of the dargāh, but if his claims to descent were acceptable they would have qualified him to become the titular head of the community attached to the shrine. That the *khuddām* did not find him acceptable is predictable. With considerable vested interests at stake, it is to be expected that they would do all they could to keep the prestige and income deriving from the shrine exclusively to themselves and not share it by admitting a lineal descendant of the saint into their midst.

Shaykh Husain Nāgaurī was clearly convinced of the validity of Tāj al-dīn's descent for, having ensured that Tāj al-dīn would be allowed to remain at Ajmer, he married his own daughter to one of Tāj al-dīn's sons.[14]

It is fair to assume that, on Tāj al-dīn's death, the office was handed down by lineal descent; but nothing is known of the next three Sajjāda-Nishīns. It was not long, however, before the question of descent again arose, and this time it aroused the interest of the Emperor Akbar himself. When Akbar began to take an interest in the affairs of the shrine, he ordered another enquiry to be made into the ancestry of those who claimed descent from the saint.

The *Akbarnāma* records the following incident, occurring when Akbar visited the dargāh in gratitude for the birth of his first son:

[13] *Siyar al-Aqtāb*, p. 137. [14] Ibid.

As on the occasion of the division of the gifts, which came to a large
amount, those who claimed to be descendants of the Khwāja, and
who had the superintendence of the shrine—their chief was Shaykh
Husain—took possession of the whole of the money, and there were
disputes and quarrels between him [Shaykh Husain] and the attendants
on the shrine [*khuddām*], and there was the allegation that the
shaykhs who had charge of the shrine had told falsehoods with regard
to their descent, and as this dispute had gone on for a long time, His
Majesty appointed trustworthy persons to inquire into the matter
and report thereon. After much investigation it was found that the
claim of sonship [descent] was *not* genuine.[15]

Badāyūnī is more sympathetic to the cause of Shaykh Husain
than Abu'l Fazl and, because of its different approach, his
version is worth quoting in extenso:

It is commonly reported that he was a descendant of that pole-star of
holy men, and king of true lovers of God, Khwāja Mu'īn al-dīn Sijzī-i
Chishtī (may God hallow his soul!). Since the Emperor, in the days
when he first began especially to venerate his holiness the Khwāja of
Ajmer, happened to slight the claims of the Shaykh (to descent from
him) some perverse fellows, prompted thereto by certain shaykhs of
Fathpur, men who have endeavoured to the utmost to depose and
discredit those of their own class (may God reward them therefor!),
gave evidence against his claim to descent from the Khwāja, saying that
his holiness left no descendants, and the *sadrs* and *qāzīs* also issued
decrees to that effect, being guided by their time-serving dispositions ...
   Thus the hereditary trusteeship of the shrine which had come
down to him through so many years was transferred to others. The
Shaykh, who was a man of great estate, lived in that province like a
king, and the emperor's regal jealousy ... could not endure the
Shaykh's position, so he ordered him to leave India and to journey to
Mecca, and the Shaykh accordingly took formal leave of His Majesty
during the march to Banswala [1577], and, after successfully performing the pilgrimage to Mecca, returned. Having accomplished his
journey to the *Hijaz*, he paid his respects at Court, on his return ...;
but he would not conform to the ceremonies which have in these days
been established by those who have accepted a new faith and have been
recently converted to Islam, new followers of a new order of things.
   The Emperor, after studying the page of the Shaykh's life and the
lines of his forehead read there the signs of disaffection to himself,
and commanded that the Shaykh should be imprisoned in the fortress
of Bakkar. There he spent some years, and at last, in the year 1002 AH
[1593–4] owing to the efforts made on his behalf by certain courtiers

who had His Majesty's confidence, he was summoned from Bakkar to the Imperial presence .... He arrived at Court, and there they all paid their respects to his Majesty, and all, with the exception of the Shaykh, prostrated themselves. He, an old man of seventy years of age, utterly unaccustomed to the ceremonial of kingly courts and the correct fashion of waiting upon royal personages, made a slight inclination and a mere bow, after the old custom. The Emperor's displeasure with him was renewed, and the Mirzā was ordered to have a grant of three hundred *bīga* of land in Bakkar made out to him, as *madad-i ma'āsh*, and to dispatch the Shaykh thither once more.[16]

Badāyūnī was clearly contemptuous of the reasons for Shaykh Husain's dismissal and had a high regard for him:

I was not personally acquainted with him till recently, but now that he has returned from his pilgrimage to the Hijaz, and has suffered bonds, he appears to me to be a quantity of [heavenly] light, and an angel in bodily form. Never have I known him to speak of wordly matters, either in public or in private. He is ever employed in austerities, in worship, and in striving in the way of holiness, fasting continually and always watching at night.[17]

After the dismissal of Shaykh Husain, and his banishment to a remote corner of Sind, Muhammad Bukharī, 'distinguished among the Saiyids of Hindustan for knowledge and fidelity', was given charge of the dargāh.[18] There is no mention of his being descended from the saint; this was a secular government appointment to oversee the organization and administration of the shrine.

Prince Salīm, disturbed by his father's treatment of Shaykh Husain, interceded on the Shaykh's behalf and eventually procured his release. Shaykh Husain returned to Ajmer where he is buried within the dargāh. The faction that believes in a continuous line of descendants acting as Sajjāda-Nishīn at Ajmer argues that Shaykh Husain's family, having regained favour, once more succeeded to office in the person of Walī Muhammad, son of 'Abd al-Khair, the brother of Shaykh Husain.[19]

It will be clear by now that there is no evidence to suggest that there was a Sajjāda-Nishīn, in the usual sense of the word,

[16] *Muntakhab al-Tawārīkh*, vol. 3, p. 136.
[17] Ibid., p. 139.
[18] *Akbarnāma*, vol. 2, p. 511.
[19] Begg, *Hazrat Khwaja Mu'īn al-dīn Chistī*, p. 77.

at Ajmer during this period. None of the early sources refer to a Sajjāda-Nishīn at the shrine. Neither Akbar nor Jahāngīr mention meeting a Sajjāda-Nishīn when they visited the shrine. Furthermore, none of the *farmāns* or *sanads* dating from these reigns refer to the Sajjāda-Nishīn. The word used to describe the position of Shaykh Husain at the dargāh in both the *Akbarnāma* and the *Muntakhab al-Tawārīkh* is *Tuliyāt* (trusteeship). In a *farmān* issued by Jahāngīr in 1621 to sanction Shaykh Husain's return to Ajmer, he is described as 'descendant and *Sahib Maqam* of the saint Mu'īn al-dīn', and 'the *khuddām, muezzin* and all other officials and servants of the shrine' are ordered to carry out 'their duties in accordance with the advice and discretion of Shaykh Husain'.[20]

After the controversy over the antecedents of Shaykh Husain the government appointed a *mutawallī* (secular trustee) to take charge of administration of the shrine. With no more secular duties to perform, the titular head of the shrine assumed the title Sajjāda-Nishīn, which emphasized that his significance was solely derived from descent from Mu'īn al-dīn and his consequent spiritual eminence.

Under later Mughal rule Ajmer enjoyed greater political stability than at any time since the death of Mu'īn al-dīn. There were no more migrations of putative descendants who lived in Ajmer and those with the closest ties of descent successively assumed office.

In 1770 the Emperor Shāh 'Ālam endowed the office of Sajjāda-Nishīn with the revenue from three villages—Hokran, Kishenpura and Dilwara. The Sajjāda-Nishīn automatically became *jāgīrdār* of these villages. The control of succession to office passed from the dargāh itself to the government. There is, however, no record of any disputes in this period subsequent to that of Shaykh Husain's claim to descent.

Evidence about the office of Sajjāda-Nishīn from Mu'īn al-dīn's death until the beginning of the nineteenth century is very sparse, but certain tentative assumptions can be made about this early period. The immediate male descendants of Mu'īn al-dīn appear to have had nothing to do with Ajmer at all.

[20] 'Abd al-Qādir Beg, *Collection of Persian, Urdu and English Documents*, Persian Document No. 4.

Until the appearance of Tāj al-dīn Bāyazīd, there is no evidence to suggest that there had always been a titular head of the shrine with pretensions to direct descent from the saint. During this period, the shrine would have been attended by the *khuddām* with no Sajjāda-Nishīn to preside over them. From Tāj al-dīn to Shaykh Husain, there was a series of titular heads with both sacred and secular authority. These individuals, claiming direct descent from Mu'īn al-dīn, were believed to have inherited the saint's charisma, a legacy which substantiated their authority and earned them respect as the living representatives of the deceased saint. This situation would appear to have continued uninterrupted until the advent of British rule in Ajmer in 1820. But after the British annexation of Ajmer, there are extensive records of further disputes.

From the Advent of British Rule to the Present Day

The first such dispute in which the British Government had to take a hand, occurred on the death of Diwan Mehdi 'Alī in 1838. Imām 'Alī, the brother of Mehdi 'Alī, claimed prior right to succession over the former Diwan's (Sajjāda-Nishīn's) son, Hadi 'Alī, on the grounds that the son's mother was of dubious reputation and lowly birth, and that he was not, therefore, qualified to occupy the honoured position of Sajjāda-Nishīn.

The Superintendent of Ajmer decided the case against Imām 'Alī, who then appealed to the Commissioner, Colonel J. Sutherland. The Commissioner reversed the decision of his subordinate and decided that Sirāj al-dīn, the son of Imām 'Alī (Imām 'Alī had died while the case was being heard) should be recognized as Diwan. Sutherland decreed that the Diwan should be of respectable birth on both sides of his family; only shaykh-zāda, saiyid-zāda, or pīr-zāda families could qualify. The incumbent should also be of suitable moral stature.[21]

This emphasis on the social qualifications of the Diwan constitutes a significant shift away from traditional Muslim precepts whereby the social position of the mother is irrelevant

[21] The case is conveniently summarized in a letter from the Chief Commissioner, Col. Watson, presented to the Court of the Civil Judge, Ajmer in 1945.

in determining the status of the child. However, Sutherland's criteria have been generally accepted ever since.[22]

Diwan Sirāj al-dīn died in November 1865, having nominated his son Ghiyās al-dīn as his successor in a letter written on his death-bed. This nomination was confirmed and approved by the then Deputy Commissioner of Ajmer, Major Davidson. Ghiyās al-dīn died in 1909. Imām al-dīn, the son of Ghiyās al-dīn's father's brother, Munīr al-dīn, succeeded to office. This was disputed by a certain Rashīd al-dīn, but the objection was dismissed by the executive authorities. Imām al-dīn died in 1912. After an enquiry the Chief Commissioner appointed Sharf al-dīn 'Alī Khān. Although Sharf al-dīn was closely connected with Imām al-dīn by marriage through the female line, his relationship in the male line was remote and could only be traced by returning through seven generations to the common ancestor, 'Abd al-Fath, through his second son, Shams al-dīn.

The death of Sharf al-dīn left nineteen rival candidates for office. It was the duty of Colonel Watson, Commissioner of Ajmer, to consider the merits of each candidate and arrive at a decision as to whose claim was the strongest. In his summing up of the case in court, Watson said:

It is common ground between the parties that the nearest male heir to the deceased Diwan through the male line has the prior right to succeed provided he has the other qualifications required in a diwan by family custom. Each claim is based on this propinquity to Diwan Sharf al-dīn 'Alī Khān and on the assertion that the other claimants who may be nearer by blood are debarred by some disability or disqualification.[23]

Only one claimant, Saiyid Munawar 'Alī, was descended in the same male line as the former Diwan, but he was disqualified because he was an illegitimate son and had been sentenced in 1912 for smuggling cocaine. Six candidates claimed descent from various sons of Saiyid 'Abd al-Fath; five from his eldest son, the former Diwan Sirāj al-dīn, and one from his fourth son, Saiyid 'Atāullāh. Of the five, Mehreban 'Alī's case was dismissed because his grandfather's mother had been a concubine; Rashīd al-dīn's case was dismissed because his father was discovered to be the illegitimate son of Diwan Saiyid Sirāj al-dīn

[22] Ibid.   [22] Ibid.

'Alī Khān II; the case of the brothers Imdād and Akbar Husain was dismissed because they eventually admitted that their mother had been a prostitute before she was married.

Watson decided:

Whatever may have been the case in ancient times, the recent custom has been to demand a worthy lineage on both sides from candidates for diwanship. The sons of a prostitute cannot have, in the eyes of the Muslim world, the pure noble descent which is required, and on this ground their claim should be rejected.[24]

Shihāb al-dīn was the fifth candidate descended from Diwan Sirāj al-dīn I. Watson observed that Shihāb al-dīn was

undoubtedly the popular favourite in Ajmer; he has managed to enlist the support of the *khuddām* who are the hereditary opponents of the Diwan in all matters of perquisites and privileges. The late Diwan, who was over eighty when he died and not a man of strong character, was greatly under his influence, and during his term of office said and did all that he could to strengthen Shihāb al-dīn's claim to succeed on his death. He has the strong support of the ladies of the family—the widow of the Diwan Imām al-dīn and the sister of Diwan Sharf al-dīn—who fear that their position and maintenance will be imperilled if an outsider [Saiyid 'Alī Rasul] whose family has been away from Ajmer for two hundred years be appointed to succeed.[25]

In spite of such popular approval of Shihāb al-dīn, Watson disqualified him because his mother was a Hindu. Furthermore,

so far as I can judge, the candidate has no special qualifications of intellectual or moral character which would make up for his defects of birth.[26]

So the five claimants descended from the eldest son of Saiyid 'Abd al-Fath were all rejected. The next closest claimant genealogically was Saiyid 'Alī Rasul, a descendant of Saiyid 'Abd al-Fath's youngest son 'Ataullāh.

The descendants of 'Ataullāh are admitted down to Masihullāh, and thereafter through his eldest son, Shāh 'Alī, to Saiyid Rājā Husain who died without issue. The claimant states that Masihullāh had three sons of whom the two younger, Fazl 'Alī and Kalbi 'Alī, went and settled at Dhulkot Gurgaon in the Panjab and that he is the great grandson of Fazl 'Alī by unblemished descent.[27]

[24] Ibid.   [25] Ibid.   [26] Ibid.   [27] Ibid.

This claim was backed up by an impressive array of documentary evidence and supported by witnesses of considerable standing (Khān Bahādur Pīrzāda Mahmūd Husain, a retired District and Sessions Judge and the Mīrzā Zafar 'Ali, High Court Judge of Lahore). Watson concluded:

The testimony of these gentlemen and the absence of any assertion to the contrary seems to me enough to establish that the candidate is morally fitted for the succession to which he aspires and that the marriages contracted by his male ancestors have not been unworthy of the position of Diwan.[28]

'Alī Rasul was duly appointed. The remaining twelve candidates' claims rested on lineal ties with the agnates and ancestors of Saiyid 'Abd al-Fath, so they could only succeed if none of his more direct descendants were able to prove they had the necessary qualifications for diwanship.

At Partition Diwan 'Ali Rasul and his family migrated to Pakistan. On 5 May 1947, the Chief Commissioner selected 'Ināyat Husain as the new Diwan.[29] This appointment has given rise to a controversy which still exercises the community attached to the dargāh. The opposition to 'Ināyat Husain believes that he was qualified neither on grounds of genealogy, nor on grounds of personal qualities.

In 1948 Saiyid 'Allām al-dīn brought a suit against 'Ināyat Husain alleging that the office of Diwan is a hereditary office and, according to the law of primogeniture, he himself was the nearest qualified male relation in the male line of the former Diwan, and was, therefore, entitled to succeed to the office.

---

[28] Ibid.
[29] The Chief Commissioner was entitled to make this appointment under his power vested in his office by Paragraphs 37 and 38 of the *Ajmer Regulations*:
'Para. 37. No person shall be deemed entitled to any exemption, total or partial, from the land-revenue assessment or to any assignment or land-revenue except under a *sanad* granting or recognising such exemption or assignment issued by or under the authority of the Chief Commissioner as hereinafter provided.
'Para. 38. It shall be in the discretion of the Chief Commissioner ... to grant or recognise ... any such exemption or assignment.' With this authority the Chief Commissioner was appointing 'Ināyat Husain to the *jāgīr* of Hokran, Kishenpure and Dilwara and therefore automatically making him Diwan as these villages were bequeathed to that office.

The appointment of 'Ināyat Husain was, he maintained, illegal. The defendant in the case, 'Ināyat Husain, contested the suit pleading that the office of Diwan was not hereditary but that succession thereto was determined by the Chief Commissioner or local representative of the government of the day. He also pleaded that the plaintiff was not in fact the nearest qualified relation through the male line of the former Diwan.

The case proceeded slowly as certain legal objections raised by the defendant as to the validity of the suit had to be cleared first. This led to a series of appeals from the court of the Additional Sub-Judge, to the District Judge, to the Judicial Commissioner and finally to the Supreme Court. When these preliminary objections were out of the way, the issues before the court were 1) Is the succession to the office of Diwan governed by the rule of primogeniture and, if so, is the plaintiff the nearest male relation through the male line of the former Diwan? 2) If the plaintiff is the nearest male relation, is he qualified to succeed to the office? 3) In 1955 the *Dargāh Khwāja Sahib Act* came into force. Section 13 of this Act gave the Dargāh Committee (the administrative body constituted under the Act to manage the affairs of the dargāh) the right to appoint the Diwan. Section 21 of the Act provided that:

The person holding the office of Sajjāda-Nishīn immediately before the commencement of this Act shall on and from such commencement continue to hold that office subject to the other provisions of this Act and the final decision in the suit relating to that office which is pending on such commencement and to which the said person is a party.[30]

'Ināyat Husain died while the case was still pending and before this act came into force. The court had to decide whether the assumption of office by his son, Saulat Husain, was not invalidated by the *Dargāh Khwāja Sahib Act*.

The High Court of Rajasthan decided that the Dargāh Act did not invalidate Saulat Husain's assumption of office. Section 21 of the Act provided that 'Ināyat Husain should continue to hold office subject to the final decision of the pending law suit.

[30] *Dargāh Khwāja Sahib Act*, No. 36 of 1955, Section 21.

It is argued on behalf of the defendants that the provisions of Section 13 were attracted on the death of Hakīm 'Ināyat Husain for the office of the Sajjāda-Nishīn which fell vacant after the commencement of the act and, consequently, appointment to the office of the Sajjāda-Nishīn can take place only in the manner provided in Section 13 of the Act. This argument has not impressed me at all. A careful reading of Section 13 would reveal that the intention of the legislature in enacting Section 13 was to determine the disputes as to the succession to the office of Sajjāda-Nishīn if the office of the Sajjāda-Nishīn fell vacant after the coming into force of the Act. As regards the dispute relating to the office of the Sajjāda-Nishīn which had already occurred before the coming into force of the Act and for which a suit was pending at the commencement of the Act, it was specifically enacted in Section 21 of the Act that the vacancy, though filled up by the appointment of Hakīm 'Ināyat Husain, shall be subject to the decision of the present suit. Even if Hakīm 'Ināyat Husain had survived till today his appointment as Sajjāda-Nishīn would have been subject to the result of this suit. If that is so it cannot be said that on the death of Hakīm 'Ināyat Husain the office of Sajjāda-Nishīn fell vacant so as to attract the provisions of Section 13 of the Act. The present suit relates to the vacancy caused by the migration of Saiyid 'Alī Rasul Khān and since that vacancy fell vacant admittedly before the commencement of the Act, Section 13 cannot be applied and the jurisdiction of the civil court to decide the suit was, in my opinion, saved by Section 21 of the Act.[31]

By this stage both parties in the suit were prepared to accept that succession to the office of Diwan should be governed by primogeniture. The problem was, therefore, first to decide who was the nearest male relation in the male line of 'Alī Rasul Khān when he migrated to Pakistan in 1947.

'Alī Rasul is descended in the male line from Saiyid 'Abd al-Fath. The plaintiff, 'Allām al-dīn, is descended in the male line from Saiyid Husām al-dīn, one of 'Abd al-Fath's brothers. The defendants, 'Ināyat and Saulat Husain, are in the male line from Saiyid 'Abd al-Fath's father's brother, Diwan Mu'īn al-dīn IV. While Imām al-dīn is therefore closer genealogically to 'Alī Rasul, Saulat Husain argued that he was not the closest relation at the time of the former Diwan's migration to Pakistan. If Haidar 'Alī was older than his brother Imām 'Ali, Bashīr al-dīn was the closer relation. The High Court Judge decided

[31] Judgement of the High Court of Judicature for Rajasthan at Jodhpur, 9 August 1974.

that Haidar 'Alī was older than Imām 'Ali, and that therefore Bashīr al-dīn was the rightful heir to Diwanship in 1947. However, Bashīr al-dīn never pressed his claim and died while the suit was still pending.[32] The Judge continued:

So far as nearness in propinquity [*sic*] to the last holder is concerned, undisputedly 'Abd al-'Azīz was nearer in degree than the plaintiff.[33]

However, 'Abd al-'Azīz had the disadvantage of being illiterate and has since died leaving no heir. But the Judge held that he would have been debarred from office anyway on the grounds of illiteracy.[34]

However, in 1947 none of the claimants to Diwanship had been disqualified from the office on grounds of the absence of the necessary personal qualities.

It therefore cannot be said that Hakīm 'Ināyat Husain was appointed to the office of Sajjāda-Nishīn in preference to the plaintiff because the latter was not qualified to [*sic*] the office of the Sajjāda-Nishīn. In the circumstances, it follows that the appointment of Hakīm 'Ināyat Husain was unjustified, improper and illegal and he had no right or title to succeed to the office of Sajjāda-Nishīn in the presence of the plaintiff who was the nearest male relation through the male line of the last Sajjāda-Nishīn.[35]

The question then arose as to whether 'Allām al-dīn was sufficiently qualified to succeed to the office. To evidence his competence Saiyid 'Allām al-dīn submitted his Certificate of Matriculation, Certificate of the Degree of Bachelor of Science, and Certificate of Deputy Rationing Officer. The Judge decided that these documents were not sufficient and therefore rejected his application.

'Allām al-dīn had succeeded in proving that he was the nearest male relation in the male line of the last Sajjāda-Nishīn, but failed to demonstrate that he was suitably qualified for the position. The Judge felt that this last issue was outside his jurisdiction.

In these circumstances, he ['Allām al-dīn] is entitled to a declaration that so far as nearness in propinquity [*sic*] to the last Sajjāda-Nishīn is concerned, he is the rightful person entitled to succeed and hold the

---

[32] Ibid.   [33] Ibid.   [34] Ibid.   [35] Ibid.

office of Sajjāda-Nishīn. Whether he is qualified or not for the office of Sajjāda-Nishīn it will be open to the appointing authority (now the Governor of Rajasthan) to determine the same.[36]

So the case was referred to the Governor of Rajasthan who, on 7 July 1975, decided in Saiyid 'Allām al-dīn's favour, and duly had Saulat Husain deposed and 'Allām al-dīn installed in his place. The turban-tying ceremony of appointment was performed just in time for the beginning of the 'urs which began in 1975 on 11 July.

Saulat Husain immediately launched an appeal against the Governor's decision. The outcome of this was not known at the time of writing.

8

The Administration of the Dargāh

Before the reign of Akbar the shrine had been managed by the *khuddām* community with a titular leader in the shape of a Sajjāda-Nishīn after the appearance of Shaykh Tāj al-dīn Bāyazīd. In the sixteenth century the office of *mutawallī* was created. A *mutawallī* is a secular administrator of a religious endowment.

The first such appointment was made when Akbar banished Shaykh Husain from Ajmer. The Emperor needed someone to look after the shrine and administer the endowment he had made in its favour in 1567. Hence the appointment of Muhammad Bukharī.[1]

The *Mir'āt al-Asrār* supports that this was the beginning of the office of *mutawallī* at the shrine.

Akbar had endowed certain villages in the *pargana* of Ajmer for the expenses of *langar* and other affairs so that a government *mutawallī* of the emperor could perform these services relating to the shrine, the poor and the needy. This system continues to the present day [1654].[2]

There is very little information about the early *mutawallīs*.

Badāyūnī mentions that Malik Mahmūd had the job at one time and implies that it was a position greatly sought after:

Malik Mahmūd exerted all the influence and employed all the interest which he possessed in preferring his request that he might be permitted to depart from the Court and undertake the guardianship of the holy man's tomb, employing himself in the circumambulation of its

---

[1] For the endowments of the dargāh see below, pp. 174–6 and for the appointment of Muhammad Bukharī see above, p. 154.

[2] Quoted Beg, *Persian, Urdu and English Documents*, Introduction, pp. ii–iii.

threshold, the dwelling-place of angels, and urged his request with an utter disregard of the emperor's wishes. Since he was thoroughly sincere in his intention and design, and was altogether free from any suspicion of hypocrisy or worldly designs, his prayer was naturally granted.[3]

Badāyūnī himself hoped to get the post of *mutawallī*:

His Majesty, who is near the sun in excellence, has, for some reason, without the intervention of any person whatsoever, taken the name of me, the humblest of his slaves, on his blessed tongue, expressing some intention of bestowing on me the trusteeship [*mutawallī*] of [the shrine in] the exalted region of Ajmer. Nevertheless I have not yet been installed in the office, and it is my earnest desire that the effects of this good fortune may soon emerge from the region of probabilities into that of accomplished facts.[4]

In the end Badāyūnī was considered too valuable at court as a translator, so he never achieved the office at Ajmer.

Nothing more is known of the *mutawallī* until 1636–7 when Shāh Jahān fixed a salary of 3010 *dāms* per annum on the post.[5] In 1661, on 20 May, the *mutawallī* 'was awarded a robe of honour, a female elephant and a present of one thousand rupees.'[6] In 1692, the *mutawallī* is known to have erected a mosque in the bazaar near the dargāh.[7]

There follows a considerable gap in the evidence relating to the post of *mutawallī*. In AH 1214/1799–1800 the Mahārājā Scindia issued the following *sanad*:

Mīr 'Azīz 'Alī, son of Mīr 'Azīmullāh, greetings from Daulat Rao Scindia! Be it known ... that to the *mutawallīship* of the *Dargāh Hazrat Khwāja Sahib* in Ajmer, Mīr 'Azīmullāh and his ancestors have been appointed, therefore, in view of this the office of *mutawallī* is now given to you, Mīr 'Azīz 'Alī, which has been held by your ancestors in the past, will now be held by you from father to son, generation to generation.[8]

---

[3] *Muntakhab al-Tawārīkh*, vol. 3, pp. 197–8.

[4] Ibid., vol. 2, pp. 400–1.

[5] Beg, *Persian, Urdu and English Documents*, Persian Document No. 2.

[6] Muhammad Kasim, *'Alamgīr Nāma*, quoted Tirmizi, 'Persian Inscriptions', 1959, p. 45.

[7] Tirmizi, 'Persian Inscriptions', 1959, pp. 42–4.

[8] Judgement of the Judicial Committee of the Privy Council, 1946, Privy Council Appeal No. 36 of 1945.

In fact, this office had not been held exclusively by the ancestors of 'Azīz 'Alī. His father stated in court that he had held the office by the grace of the secular rulers of the time and had been removed from office and reappointed more than once. He also observed that the son of the then Sajjāda-Nishīn had been appointed to the *mutawallīship* and that they were not of the same family. Further, the previous *mutawallī* had been Shyām Rāo, a Hindu.[9] So the office had little to do with either heredity or religious conviction. Scindia's edict was anomalous and doubtless the result of successful lobbying by 'Azīmullāh and 'Azīz 'Alī.

In 1802, the income of the village of Dantra was assigned to the *mutawallī* by Mahārājā Daulat Rao Scindia in lieu of the salary which had been fixed by Shāh Jahān. However, the village of Dantra had been bequeathed to the dargāh itself in 1718, so this move of Scindia's was a breach of the law of waqf.[10]

In 1827, after the advent of British rule in Ajmer, the Emperor, Akbar Shāh II, issued a *farmān* stating that the appointment and dismissal of the *mutawallī* 'had been done by us', but, as the management had been incompetent and 'Azīz 'Alī had appropriated most of the dargāh's money for himself, he directed that 'Azīz 'Alī should be removed from office and Mirzā Muhammad Timur Shāh, the grandson of the Emperor, should be appointed in his stead.[11]

The British Superintendent at Ajmer, H. Middleton, accepted the intervention of Akbar Shāh:

In matters of the dargāh like these, [British] government servants have not been authorised or appointed to interfere, and it was apparent that removal from and appointment to this office has always been done by His Majesty. Therefore it is necessary and binding that the order of His Majesty should be given effect to [*sic*].[12]

[9] Beg, *Persian, Urdu and English Documents*, Persian Document No. 22. See Persian Documents Nos. 10 and 18 for a list of the incumbents of the post of *mutawallī* at the dargāh; several other non-Muslim names occur in these lists.

[10] Waqf is money or property given as an endowment to a religious institution and no one is allowed to alter the terms of the bequest. The right of ownership passes to Allāh, and the purpose of the endowment must be a work pleasing to Him. See *Encyclopaedia of Islam*, vol. 4, pp. 1096–7.

[11] Privy Council Judgement, p. 8.   [12] Ibid.

This was not acceptable to 'Azīz 'Alī, who had been removed from office, and who now appealed to the Commissioner. The Commissioner directed him to file a suit in court, but the case was dismissed by the Assistant Commissioner of Ajmer.[13]

In 1837 'Azīz 'Alī died. In the meantime Mīrzā Timur Shāh was the nominal *mutawallī* from 1827 until 1834 when it appears, though the position is not clear, that his tenure of office was terminated by order of the British government. From 1834 to 1838 there was no regular *mutawallī*, the administration of the dargāh being carried on by the government, a task burdensome to itself and at variance with its consistent policy.[14]

In 1838 the government appointed a certain Najaf Husain as *mutawallī* and fixed a salary of Rs 150 per month on him. The village of Dantra was reunited with the rest of the dargāh's waqf property.

Meanwhile 'Azīmullāh succeeded in regaining the favour of the British administration and was restored to the office of *mutawallī* in 1842. He assumed that this was in recognition of his claim of his hereditary right to the office which Daulat Rao Scindia had sanctioned in the *sanad* of 1799–1800. So in 1848, on the day before his death, he applied to the Commissioner that his grandson, Mīr Hāfiz 'Alī, should be appointed *mutawallī*, and act in consultation with his brother, Mīr Wazīr 'Alī. Immediately after his death the Commissioner appointed Mīr Hāfiz 'Alī on these terms.[15]

However, the administration of the dargāh was beset by corruption and incompetence. The factions of the *mutawallī*, *khuddām* and Sajjāda-Nishīn all vied with each other for prestige, offerings and privileges.[16] There was no authority outside the dargāh which could control their excesses. The government's authority only extended to the appointment and dismissal of the *mutawallī*, and selection of the Sajjāda-Nishīn on an incumbent's death.

In 1863 the Religious Endowments Bill was enacted. Its purpose was to enable the government to rid itself of the responsibility of managing religious endowments and to ensure

[13] Ibid., p. 9.   [14] Ibid., p. 10.   [15] Ibid., p. 11.
[16] See below.

their efficient administration in the future. Section 3 of the Act required provision to be made for the appointment of a manager of the religious institution, and Section 7 required committees to be established to take ultimate responsibility for the administration of the institution. This meant, in the case of Ajmer, that the power of appointing the *mutawallī*, formerly vested in the government, was transferred to the newly-formed management committee.[17]

A report was prepared under the Secretary of the Board of Revenue to suggest how the provisions of the Act should be put into practice at the dargāh. Acting on the findings of this report a Management Committee was finally set up, consisting 'of five members, of whom one, who will also act as President, shall be an independent native gentleman professing the Mussulman religion, and the others shall be selected from the parties interested in the management in the proportion of one from the family of the Diwan, one from that of the *mutawallī*, and two from among the *khuddām*.'[18]

These provisions represented a singular naïvety on the part of the Lieutenant-Governor. The constitution of the management committee meant that every faction at the dargāh was now formally involved in the running of the shrine. It is difficult to see how peaceful and efficient administration could follow.

The committee of five, containing as it did representatives of class interests, could not possibly have brought about any improvement in the situation and a deadlock was inevitable. The committee under Section 7 was for life and it would have been a miracle if its few members had not indulged in a campaign for self-aggrandizement.[19]

The *mutawallī*, Hāfiz 'Alī, died in 1878. In his will he reasserted the old claim that the post was hereditary in his family: 'If I may die during this illness of mine, after me my elder son, Mīr Amīr 'Alī, will be the *mutawallī* of the *Dargāh Khwāja Sahib* in accordance with the usage of my family.'[20] The

---

[17] Section 13, *Bengal Regulations*, 1810, provided the government with authority to appoint and dismiss managers of religious institutions.
[18] *Government Gazette N.W.P.*, 1867, p. 396.
[19] 1949 Report, p. 74.   [20] Privy Council Judgement, p. 13.

Dargāh Committee did not accept this 'usage' unconditionally, but they agreed to appoint Mīr Amīr 'Alī *mutawallī* on probation for two years.[21] In 1880, after the probationary appointment expired, the President and another member of the Dargāh Committee, accused Amīr Alī of 'incompetence, dishonesty, negligence of duty and disobedience of orders.'[22] Since the appointment of Hāfiz 'Alī the dargāh debts and amount of unrecovered outstanding credits had been steadily increasing. By 1878 the dargāh's recoverable monies stood at Rs 20,000.[23]

The case came before the Assistant Commissioner who decided that Amīr 'Alī was not fit to occupy the position of *mutawallī*, yet directed that 'If at any time he satisfies the civil court of his fitness for office, he may be reinstated in his ancestral position.'[24] In the meantime the Assistant Commissioner directed that a substitute should be appointed. Amīr 'Alī, predictably, appealed to the Commissioner who agreed that 'this office is (subject to the fitness of the incumbent) hereditary', and granted Amīr 'Alī a further two probationary years as *mutawallī*.[25]

Nevertheless, Amīr 'Alī was still not regarded as fit for office after this period. He had still failed to collect the debts owed to the dargāh. Contrary to the ruling that the office is hereditary, one Bhura Mal was appointed *nā'ib mutawallī* to assist in extracting the arrears of rent from the dargāh's waqf properties. Amīr 'Alī appealed against this decision, urging that his brother, Nisār Ahmad, should be appointed in Bhura Mal's place. Amīr 'Alī won the case, on the grounds that:

although the probability of receiving the arrears would certainly be greater if Bhura Mal was appointed; he is a man who bears a good reputation and is one of the family of hereditary *qanungoes* and is well-versed in Land Revenue details ... considering the very strong feeling that exists as to the desirability of recognising the hereditary right of the family of the *mutawallī* if a fit representative could be obtained, and the fact that Nisār Ahmad has received a liberal education far superior to that received by the *mutawallī* and the fact that he

[21] Ibid.   [22] Ibid.
[23] Beg, *Persian, Urdu and English Documents*, Introduction, p. xix.
[24] Quoted Privy Council Judgement, p. 14.
[25] Ibid.

has already been giving his brother considerable assistance, this court considers there are not sufficient reasons for setting aside the nomination of the Dargāh Committee, who are really responsible for their co-religionists for receiving the income belonging to their shrine.[26]

However, maladministration of the dargāh continued. By the end of the year Nisār Ahmad had failed to improve the shrine's financial affairs and he had also contrived to alienate his nominees, the Dargāh Committee, by trying to assert his independence of them. He was therefore removed from office by court order in 1888[27] over two years after the end of his unsatisfactory probationary period.

A series of *nā'ib mutawallīs* were appointed until Amīr 'Alī's death in 1915. In his will he nominated Mīr Nisār Ahmad his successor, but before Amīr 'Alī's death, another member of the same family, Mīr Zaharul Husain, contested the claim. The Chief Commissioner ruled that genealogically Nisār Ahmad had a prior right to the office and that he was fit for office. Zahurul Husain lost his case.[28]

The controversy over this appointment did not end there. The Dargāh Committee decided to assert its rights given under the 1863 Act. It claimed that it was the only body with authority to nominate and appoint the *mutawallī*. The legal battle which followed continued until 1921 when the Commissioner, Colonel Patterson, ordered the final recognition of Nisār Ahmad as *mutawallī* of the dargāh.[29]

Nisār Ahmad continued as *mutawallī* until his death in 1940. His appointment was constantly being disputed by his opponents, but their appeals in the Court of the Sub-Judge of Ajmer in 1926 and in the Court of the Special Additional District Judge were both rejected.

On his father's death in 1940, Asrār Ahmad claimed the right to succeed him as *mutawallī* on grounds of heredity. The

[26] Judgement of the Court of the Commissioner and District Judge, Ajmer-Merwara, Civil Case No. 1 of 1885.

[27] Ibid., Appeal No. 9 of 1887.

[28] Court of the Chief Commissioner, Ajmer-Merwara, Civil, Second Appeal No. 35 of 1916.

[29] Memorandum No. 27941 of the Commissioner, Ajmer-Merwara, English Document No. 11.

Dargāh Committee (newly constituted under the Dargāh Act of 1936) opposed his claim.[30] The case finally came before the Judicial Committee of the Privy Council in 1945, which declared that the office of *mutawallī* was not hereditary. Misunderstandings on the subject originated from the *sanad* of 1799–1800 issued by the Mahārājā Scindia who then ruled Ajmer. British administrators who had agreed with the principle set out in this *sanad*—that the office was hereditary—had been misled and had contravened practice properly associated with the long-established office of *mutawallī*. The office of *mutawallī*, they judged, was rightly an appointment made by the government of the time until the Religious Endowments Act of 1863 which gave this responsibility to the Management Committee of the shrine. The situation in the dargāh had been made yet worse by the inability of the family that claimed hereditary *mutawallīship* to produce anyone capable of administering the shrine efficiently and honestly.[31]

An impression of the state of affairs may be gained from the District Magistrate's judgement in 1908, where he comments on 'the unbridled rapacity of its attendants', on Nisār Ahmad as 'a manager slovenly, careless and unbusiness-like to the last degree besides being by no means above suspicion in the matter of honesty' and 'the greedy hordes of his underlings'. He concludes that 'if the great one, to whom the shrine is dedicated, can still take cognisance of mundane matters he must contemplate with profound melancholy the degeneracy and incompetence of his modern representatives.'[32]

Disputes over succession to office, the status and rights of the *khuddām*, and the distribution of offerings could not be controlled by the Dargāh Committee consisting as it did of representatives of these rival groups. Action was clearly needed and there seemed to be 'a very considerable body of Muhammadan opinion which desires to have a really independent Dargāh Committee and to abolish the tyranny, wastefulness and dishonesty

[30] Privy Council Judgement, p. 17.
[31] Ibid., *passim*.
[32] District Magistrate's Court, Ajmer, Criminal Case No. 5. Quoted in 1949 Report of the Committee of Enquiry, p. 76.

which must inevitably characterise the administration of the dargāh's affairs by such a body as the existing Committee.'[33]

Sir Charles Watson, Political Secretary, endorsed this opinion of the need for the reform of the Dargāh Committee, and suggested that the notification of 1867 and Act XX of 1863 should be amended.[34]

A private Bill was introduced in 1936 and passed in the same year into law. The new Dargāh Committee was to consist of nine local members and sixteen from outside of Ajmer. The members' term of office was reduced from life to five years. It was hoped that these alterations would loosen the hold of vested interests and enable the government to keep out of the affairs of the shrine. There was a growing body of Muslim opinion which resented the government's interference in the management of their religious institutions.[35]

The new legislation, however, resulted in little improvement. The sixteen independent members of the newly constituted committee took no interest in the shrine and were prevented from vigilance by the distance which separated them from Ajmer. This enabled the remaining nine members to fully exploit the opportunity for furthering the vested interests of rival groups within the Committee and acting for their own profit.[36]

After the migration of many Muslims to Pakistan in 1947, administration of the dargāh fell into the hands of the only two members of the committee who remained behind. Both were *khuddām*. They immediately reappointed Asrār Ahmad as *mutawallī* and together they retained control of the shrine until legislation enacted in 1955.[37]

By 1949 the need for the reform of the administration of the dargāh was again recognized. The Dargāh Khwāja Sahib Committee of Enquiry was established to investigate thoroughly the affairs of the shrine and 'to recommend such measures as

---

[33] Quoted in *What Indian Musalmans and Provincial Governments in India Think of the Dargah Khwaja Sahib Bill*, ed. Mirza 'Abd al-Qadir Beg, 1936, pp. 9–10.
[34] Ibid., p. 8.   [35] Ibid., pp. 43–4.
[36] Report of the *Dargāh Khwāja Sahib Committee of Enquiry*, 1949, p. 78.
[37] Ibid., p. 82.

appear necessary to secure, by efficient management of the dargāh endowment, the conservation of the shrine in the interests of the devotees as a whole.'[38] The Enquiry Committee found that the Dargāh Act of 1936 had 'led to greater disputes in management and ... greater friction between the Sajjāda-Nishīn, the *mutawallī*, the *khuddām* as a community and the Dargāh Committee constituted under the Act.'[39]

The Enquiry Report concluded that the nine local members of the post-1936 Committee 'had brought the administration of the dargāh into disrepute.'[40]

The recommendations of this Enquiry Committee were partially put into effect by the *Dargāh Khwāja Sahib Act* of 1955. The title of this Act announces that it is

to make provisions for the proper administration of the dargāh and the endowment of the dargāh of Khwāja Muʿīn al-dīn Chishtī, generally known as the Dargāh Khwāja Sahib, Ajmer.[41]

Accordingly a newly constituted committee was appointed consisting of

not less than five and not more than nine members all of whom shall be Hanafi Muslims and shall be appointed by the Central Government ... A member of the committee shall hold office for a period of five years ... The Central Government may, in consultation with the committee, appoint a person to be Nāzim [manager] of the dargāh ... The committee shall exercise its powers of administration, control and management of the dargāh endowment through the nāzim; ...

The post of *mutawallī* was finally abolished.

However, this newly formed committee still lacks co-operation from the factions associated with life at the dargāh and the necessary executive powers to establish conditions in the shrine which could begin to accord with the ideals and standards of the Chishtī Sufis. The continuing disputes over the looting of the *degs*, the distribution of offerings made at the shrine and the succession to the office of the Diwan together with the rapacity of some of the *khuddām* are sad witnesses to the failure of the present administration.

[38] Ibid., p. 1.   [39] Ibid., p. 78.   [40] Ibid., p. 93.
[41] Act No. 36, 14 October, 1955.

9

The Endowments and Finances of the Dargāh

Records of the financial affairs of the dargāh are far from complete and thus, with a few exceptions, it is not possible to establish more than a general impression. A small number of documents survive from Mughal times, which provide some indication of the nature of the dargāh's resources in that period. More recently, information can be gleaned from the records of the many legal disputes, from Government Administration Records, and from the official enquiries. In addition, the dargāh's accounts since 1973 were examined. Early dargāh records were not made available.

Endowments

No property of any kind was endowed in favour of the dargāh until the reign of Akbar who, in 1567, granted it the revenue of eighteen villages, and a levy of 1 per cent on the sale of salt at Sambhar, to pay for the distribution of food from the shrine.[1] Another document (1574–5) from Akbar's reign shows that the emperor provided oil for the lamps within the mausoleum. The *pargana* of Sambhar was to provide one *maun* of oil annually for this purpose.[2]

Shāh Jahān issued a new *farmān* in 1637 in place of Akbar's, endowing the shrine with lands producing Rs 15,723 per annum in rent from seventeen villages, and Rs 10,057 in cash. The management was directed to use this to defray the cost of the

[1] *Ajmer Regulations*, vol. 2, p. 562.
[2] *Ajmer Documents*, p. 3. A *maun* of lamp-oil at wholesale prices cost 80 *dām* in the reign of Akbar (*A'īn-i Akbarī*, vol. 1, 65–8).

'urs, distribution of food, the lighting of the mausoleum, prayer carpets, flowers for the tomb, prayer leaders for the shrine's mosques, the *muezzin*, reciters of the Quran, servants for the shrine, and good works in general.[3] In 1717 Farūkh Siyar granted two more villages to the waqf of the dargāh, which added Rs 3,984 per annum to the income of the shrine.[4]

The next bequest came in 1850 when the Nizam of Hyderabad issued an order that the entire income from certain villages in the sūba of Berar should be assigned to the Ajmer dargāh. This estate was worth Rs 6,480 per annum.[5] When this part of the state of Hyderabad fell into British hands the Nizam issued a new *sanad* to give the dargāh another estate. This second grant, made on 23rd Shawwal, AH 1278/23 April 1862, was worth Rs 18,471 per annum.[6]

From 1893 onwards the Nizam gave Rs 12,000 per annum from the waqf income of the Hyderabad state to the dargāh, of which one share went to the *mutawallī* and was used for the expenses of the *langar*, scents, *sandal*, and other requirements for the tomb; one share went to the Diwan and the third to the *khuddām* .... The Nizam also granted 1200 rupees a year to the *Dargāh Muinia Usmania* school, and about 600 rupees a month for the new Naqqār-Khāna, etc.[7] In 1948, the Nizam set up a charitable trust to benefit the dargāh. This produces an income which appears to be decreasing. In 1973–4, it was Rs 5,095; in 1974–5, Rs 5,176; in 1975–6 it had fallen further to Rs 4,685, and by 1976–7 it was Rs 4,000.[8]

According to the Ajmer-Merwara Administration Report of

[3] *Ajmer Documents*, pp. 158–62. The income of the dargāh was supplemented by the practice of the *mutawallī* on behalf of the shrine taking over, on the death of the *khuddām*, half of the *madad-i ma'āsh* land granted to them. Shāh Jahan ended this arrangement and ordered that all the land should be distributed among the surviving *khādim* family on condition that they continued to perform their duties at the shrine (See *farmān*, dated 27th *Dhu'al Hijja*, 1047 AH, 11 May, AD 1638, *Ajmer Documents*, p. 189). So at that date lands given in *madad-i ma'āsh* grants became hereditary at Ajmer. This contradicts the statement of Irfan Habib that it was not until AD 1690 that *madad-i ma'āsh* holdings became hereditary (*Agrarian System*, p. 311).
[4] 1949 Enquiry Report, p. 26.   [5] *Ajmer Documents*, p. 338.
[6] Ibid., pp. 339–40.   [7] Sarda, *Ajmer*, p. 99.
[8] These figures are taken from the accounts of the shrine. Earlier accounts were not available for examination.

1872 the annual revenue of the dargāh was at that time Rs 21,604. In 1909 it was thought that, with good management, the dargāh estate should be able to produce an annual income of between Rs 50,000 and Rs 60,000. But in 1924 the income was only Rs 22,000, and by 1940 the dargāh was Rs 52,063 in debt, although it was due Rs 31,172 as unrecovered rents.[9] As the accounts of the shrine before 1973–4 were not available, only a general impression of the financial situation can be given.

Offerings to the Dargāh

A substantial proportion of the dargāh's revenue has always come from offerings made by devotees. The visits of the Emperor Akbar were always marked by his making generous gifts, which the *Akbarnāma* extols:

He encompassed all the attendants of the shrine with liberal favours ... [He] scattered coins in the skirts of the attendants.[10]
So liberal were his bounties that no single individual was excluded from the feast of good things.[11]
He divided a large sum of money among those who sat at the threshold of the shrine.[12]
Dirhams and *dinars* were showered down like rain-drops.[13]

In AH 988/1580–1, Akbar sent his son, Prince Dāniyāl, with Rs 25,000 to the Ajmer shrine.[14]

The *Tuzuk-i Jahāngīr* records the generosity of Akbar's successor on the occasion of his visits to Ajmer:

I bestowed on the darvīshes with my own hand and in my own presence 55,000 rupees and 190,000 *bīga* of land with 14 entire villages and 26 ploughs and 11 *karwār* [ass-loads] of rice.[15] On the night of Sunday (Rajab AH 1615), as it was the anniversary of the great khwāja, I went to his revered mausoleum and remained there till midnight. The attendants and Sufis exhibited ecstatic states, and I

---

[9] See the Administrative Reports for Ajmer-Merwara for the years 1872, 1924, and 1940. The estimate of Rs 50,000–60,000 per annum is quoted from a letter to the Governor-General of Rajputana in the 1949 Enquiry Report, p. 75.
[10] *Akbarnāma*, vol. 2, pp. 477, 496.
[11] Ibid., p. 516.   [12] Ibid., vol. 3, p. 233.
[13] *Muntakhab al-Tawārīkh*, vol. 2, p. 188.   [14] Ibid., p. 297.
[15] *Tuzuk-i Jahāngīr*, vol. 1, p. 279.

gave the faqīrs and attendants money with my own hand; altogether there were expended 6,000 rupees in cash, 100 *saub-kurta* [ankle-length robes], seventy rosaries of pearls, corals and amber.[16]

With such a wealth of offerings, and with so many *khuddām* attending the shrine in addition to the rival Sajjāda-Nishīn and *mutawallī*, there has always been controversy over the correct method of apportioning these offerings.

It will be remembered that the original arguments about the position of Shaykh Husain were occasioned by an offering from Akbar and attempts to distribute it to everyone's satisfaction. Akbar was also involved in further attempts to regulate the distribution of offerings at the shrine as is shown by a document dated 8 Shawwāl 988/16 November 1580. Shaykh Hāshim, son of Shaykh Fathullāh, had appealed to the Emperor for a judgement to prevent the various factions fighting over the offerings. In answer to this appeal, Qāzī Saiyid 'Imād al-dīn, on behalf of the Emperor, ordered the quarrelling to cease. However, we are given no details of how the problem was resolved, nor of the identities of the different factions within the dargāh community.[17]

These details are furnished by another imperial order issued four years later (1584). 'The servitors of the shrine contract to adhere to the following system: The offerings will be divided into 5½ shares of which 'Ālim 'Abd al-Karīm and his brothers would receive 1½ shares, Shaykh Hāshim, the son of the late Shaykh Fathullāh would receive half of one share, Shaykh Ibrāhīm and his family, 1 share, Shaykh Qutban and his people 1 share, Shaykh? (name illegible) 1 share, and half of one share for Shaykh Mansūr.'[18]

In the fifteenth year of Jahāngīr's reign (1619) a *farmān* was issued to modify this system. Now the offerings were to be divided into 6½ parts of which Shaykh Hāshim would get half of one share; 2 shares would go to the progeny of Bahlōl, half of one share to that of Ibrāhīm, 1½ to that of Mas'ūd, and 2 to that of Taikhā. The change in the distribution was caused by a complaint from Bahlōl's faction which numbered 109 compared

[16] Ibid., p. 297.   [17] *Ajmer Documents*, p. 14.
[18] Ibid., pp. 15–17.

to 64 of Mas'ūd and 12 of Ibrāhīm.[19] This method of settlement did not prevent further disputes, as other documents reveal.

During his reign, Shāh Jahān sent a gift of fifty *ashrafīs* to the attendants of the shrine. A *sanad* had to be issued to ensure that a certain Shaykh Khubullāh received his rightful share, and that the *mutawallī* followed the procedure established in Jahāngīr's reign.[20]

By the time of Muhammad Shāh (1719–20) the system had become more elaborate. By then there was an accepted custom whereby all offerings made at the tomb of Mu'īn al-dīn's daughter, Bībī Jamāl, which were made in rupees, *ashrafīs*, gold or silver, were divided among the *haft bārīdār*. An appeal was made to the court of Muhammad Shāh challenging the rectitude of this system of distribution when an offering of seventy *tolas* of silver was made. A *sanad* was issued certifying that the traditional method of settlement was valid, and should be adhered to.[21]

No other evidence concerning the distribution of offerings at the shrine could be found until a court case judgement in 1931. In 1929 the Sajjāda-Nishīn, 'Alī Rasul Khān, claimed that he was entitled to all the offerings made within the precincts of the dargāh. The issue was taken to court. The Judge decided as follows: The Diwan was entitled to a half share of any articles of gold or silver valued at over Rs 8, gold and silver coins of a value of over Rs 2, cloth of good quality, and jewellery provided that it was presented at the *takht* (foot of the tomb). He was also granted the right to a half-share of all animals presented at the steps of the dargāh. However, he had no right to offerings made outside the mausoleum but within the dargāh, nor to offerings made within the mausoleum but not at the *takht*, nor to any offerings made on the final day of the 'urs.

Inevitably this decision was accepted by neither *khuddām* nor Sajjāda-Nishīn. An appeal was made to the Judicial

---

[19] Ibid., p. 68.

[20] Ibid., p. 186. One *ashrafī* during the reign of Shāh Jahān ranged in value from Rs 12.5 to Rs 14. The exact date of this offering is not known. But for most of his reign the *ashrafī* was stable at Rs 14. (Irfan Habib, *Agrarian System*, pp. 384–7).

[21] *Ajmer Documents*, p. 301.

Commissioner, who ruled that all offerings of *ghilā* are the property of the Dargāh Committee; all offerings made outside the mausoleum are the property of the *khuddām* with the exception of animals offered at the steps of the dargāh which should be the property of the Diwan; and all offerings made within the mausoleum were to be divided between the *khuddām* and the Diwan.[22]

By 1949 the Diwan had leased his right over offerings made within the mausoleum to the *khuddām* for Rs 1,000 per annum.[23] When offerings were sent to the shrine without the specific name of the recipient being recorded, the following practice was observed by the Enquiry Committee of 1949: Money destined for 'Hazrat Khwāja Gharīb Nawāz' was divided between the Diwan and the *khuddām*. Money sent to '*dargāh sharīf, bārīdār, khuddām* or chief *khādim*' was appropriated by the *bārīdār* on duty that day.[24]

The *Dargāh Act of 1955* attempted further to regulate the situation. Sub-section 1 of Section 14 of the Act states:

No person other than the Nāzim (manager of the dargāh) or any person authorised by him in this behalf shall receive or be entitled to receive *nazars* or offerings on behalf of the dargāh.

Sub-section 2 states:

Whoever solicits or receives *nazars* or offerings in contravention of the provisions of Sub-section 1 shall be punishable with fines which may extend to one thousand rupees.

The legal position has not changed since 1955. However, the *khuddām* are still to be seen within the precincts of the dargāh soliciting offerings from pilgrims, while official notices exhort devotees to place their offerings in the green boxes provided for that purpose.

In spite of the *khuddām* intercepting offerings which by law should go to the Nāzim, the income of the dargāh from *nazar* is

---

[22] 1949 Enquiry Report, pp. 58–67.
[23] Ibid.
[24] Ibid., p. 42. The report further mentions that the *bārīdārs* would liaise with the postmen to delay delivery of money orders until it was their turn to be on duty at the shrine.

not inconsiderable. In 1973–4 it was Rs 109,371, and it rose gradually to Rs 125,000 by 1976–7.[25]

Donations are also made for specific purposes. For example, between 1973 and 1975 Rs 52,942 were given to fund the construction of a modern guest-house for visitors to the shrine, and in 1973, Rs 16,000 were given specifically for the improvement of drainage.

Income of the Sajjāda-Nishīn

The income of the Sajjāda-Nishīn is separate from the income of the dargāh itself. In addition to his share of the offerings made at the shrine, the Sajjāda-Nishīn has an official residence. This was formerly a splendid *havelī* of traditional design built around a courtyard. However, with constant litigation and consequent doubt over the tenure of office, the residence is now in an alarming state of disrepair. Members of former Diwans' families who believe they are the rightful incumbents of the post refuse to leave the *havelī* and still inhabit certain quarters. Other parts are let out as shops to supplement the Diwan's income. The whole is rapidly deteriorating because neither the Diwan nor the Dargāh Committee admit responsibility for its repair and maintenance.

The office of Sajjāda-Nishīn was endowed in 1770 by Shāh 'Ālam with the income from the villages of Hokran, Kishenpura and Dilwara. In addition to this, one-third of the Nizam of Hyderabad's endowment income went to the Sajjāda-Nishīn. In spite of this diversity of resources, by 1886 the Diwan is recorded as being heavily in debt. The government loaned him '45,000 rupees ... and 4,650 rupees subsequently. Towards the close of the year the Diwan's *jāgīr* villages in the district of Ajmer were vested, by virtue of a special enactment, in Her Majesty's Government and are now managed by the Assistant Commissioner of Ajmer on behalf of Government.'[26]

---

[25] The figures for 1976–7 were the dargāh's accountant's estimate; the final figures had not been prepared at the time field-work was carried out.

[26] *Report on the Administration of the Ajmer-Merwara District*, 1886–7, p. 5. The authority of the government to take over the management of the diwan's property was given by Para. 102 of the *Ajmer Land and Revenue Regulation*, II of 1877.

An indication of the level of the Diwan's income in the nineteenth century can be gained from the figures prepared when the government was overseeing his financial affairs (Table 9.1).

TABLE 9.1

The Diwan's Estate, 1886–1907 (in rupees)

Year	Income	Expenditure
1887–8	8024	9906
1888–9	7385	9103
1889–90	10,299	8208
1890–1	9974	8841
1891–2	6483	7838
1892–3	9531	8652
1893–4	9122	9527
1894–5	9150	8871
1895–6	8577	8809
1896–7	11,200	11,298
1897–8	8986	8485
1898–9	6994	6407
1899–1900	6994	6407
1904–5	8010	7727
1905–6	4045	7286
1906–7	9172	11,552
1907–8	6160	11,829[27]

It will be noted that expenditure often ran ahead of income. Comments on the Diwan's finances abound in the Annual Administration Reports. 'He was, and is, a reckless spendthrift.' 'Financial ability in the management of his estate is wanting.'

By 1924 the Diwan's income was reported to be Rs 11,500 per annum.[28] This would have been supplemented by his share of the offerings, and of the Nizam's bequest.

By 1949 the Diwan's annual income had fallen to Rs 3800. As a result of the legislation of 1955, his endowed land was confiscated and he received compensation.[29] No details are available of this compensation. It can, however, be assumed that the compensation money was in some way vested in the Dargāh

[27] The income figures do not include the loans which the Diwan received from the government. The expenditure figures do, however, include the necessary repayments of the debt.

[28] Sir Charles Bayley, *The Ruling Princes, Chiefs and Leading Personages in Rajputana and Ajmer*, p. 213.

[29] Ajmer Abolition of Intermediaries and Land Reforms Act, 1955 (Ajmer Act 3 of 1955).

Committee, and that the Committee is now responsible for
paying a salary to the Diwan. According to their accounts, the
committee paid the Diwan a salary of Rs 2400 in 1974. In
addition to this, he receives his share of the offerings. One may
conclude that his total income is still substantial, since competition for the job is intense; this is evident from the endless
litigation which threatens the incumbent.

Remuneration of Other Officials

Like the Diwan, other officers—who now receive a salary—
formerly obtained their income through land revenues. The
land was assigned from the waqf of the dargāh, and in cases of
special need this revenue was supplemented by an allowance of
commodities from the dargāh's stores. The essence of the
relevant documents is set out below:
1616–17	30 *bīga* of land from the dargāh waqf, together with a
daily allowance of 2 *seers* of wheat is assigned to two of the
shrine's qawwāls and their mother.[30]

Four *seers* of wheat from the Langar Khāna of the dargāh are
to be given daily to the sons of Abd al-Rahman who was killed
by lightning.[31]

Owing to the large numbers of dependants connected with
Shaykh Hashīm and his brother, Shaykh Ibrāhīm, ½ *maun* of
wheat from the dargāh's Langar Khāna, and 1 *seer* of oil from
the dargāh's waqf is to be given to them.[32]
1617–18	A document confirming the grant of 160 *bīga* of land
from the waqf of the dargāh in favour of Saiyid Mahmūd, son
of Saiyid 'Abd al-Samad, and Saiyid Chānd and his brothers.[33]
1623–4	Two *seers* of wheat from the Langar Khāna had been
assigned as a daily allowance to Fātimah, daughter of Shaykh
Qutub. Fātimah has died, and her sons are now to receive 1 *seer*
of wheat daily.[34]
1630–1	Two *tankas* are to be spent daily on flowers for the
tomb of Bībī Hāfiz Jamāl, the daughter of Mu'īn al-dīn. Saiyid

[30] *Ajmer Documents*, p. 147. 1 *seer* then equalled 1.359 lb.
[31] Ibid., p. 150.
[32] Ibid., p. 148. 1 *maun* during the reign of Jahāngīr equalled 66.38 lb.
[33] *Ajmer Documents*, p. 153.		[34] Ibid., p. 154.

Fath Muhammad, *khādim* of the shrine, is detailed to purchase and present the said flowers.[35]

1646–7   Two qawwāls who play in the *samā'* on Thursdays and during the 'urs are assigned 300 *bīga* of land and 5 *seers* of wheat per day from the waqf of the dargāh.[36]

1717   One rupee is assigned to Muhammad Saleh, son of Muhammad Daulat from the Waqf of the Dargāh. (It is not specified if this is a daily allowance.)[37]

Documentary evidence is severely limited, but it is legitimate to deduce that, besides providing for payments and expenses of the kind noted above, the income from the dargāh's waqf also had to provide for the institutions which operate within the dargāh, to which attention has already been drawn. These are not recent innovations; there is early evidence for the Naqqār Khāna, the distribution of *langar* and the performance of *samā'*. The cost of these, of the ceremonial performed daily within the shrine, and the subsistence of those who worked there had all to be met from the same sources.

The Expenditure of the Dargāh

The dargāh is responsible for several institutions all of which are run within its precincts and all require considerable funds. The Langar Khāna, Samā' Khāna, Naqqār Khāna, and the various mosques of the shrine have all been mentioned above. In addition to these, the dargāh runs its own dispensary (Shi fā Khāna) and theological college (Madrasa). For the year 1974–5 expenditure on these institutions was:

Langar Khāna	Rs 54,410	Dispensary	Rs 9,354
Madrasa	Rs 16,261	Samā' Khāna	Rs 6,670
Mosques	Rs 11,540	Naqqār Khāna	Rs 1,980

In addition to funding these enterprises, the dargāh spends a proportion of its income on poor relief and education for the less fortunate among the population of Ajmer. The total of this expenditure in recent years was Rs 24,217 in 1973–4, Rs 23,499 in 1974–5, Rs 24,920 in 1975–6, and Rs 31,952 in 1976–7.

---

[35] Ibid., p. 204.   [36] Ibid., pp. 183–4.   [37] Ibid., p. 280.

The salaries of the dargāh staff constitute a major part of the shrine's expenditure. The employees in 1975 were, amongst the administrative staff: Nāzim, Assistant nāzim, secretary/ personal assistant to nāzim, accountant, treasurer, 7 clerical workers, rent collector, store-keeper, and 6 peons. The dargāh staff consisted of the Diwan/Sajjāda-Nishīn, 8 qawwāls, 3 imāms, 3 *muezzins*, 6 musicians in the Naqqār Khāna, 1 *shehnai* player, 1 *gharyālī* (time-keeper), 1 *hāfiz*, 1 sweet-maker, 2 *chobdārs*, 8 *farrāshes* (carpet-spreaders), 4 teachers in the Madrasa, 9 employees in the Langar Khāna, and 3 water-carriers, 1 clock-mender, 1 flower-man (to prepare flowers for the tomb), 1 shoe-keeper at the gate, 3 employees in the dispensary (nurse, compounder, *hakīm*), 8 cleaners, and 7 peons. The salaries for these employees is given below for the period 1973–7 in rupees.

	Dargāh Office Staff	*Dargāh*
1973–4	35,640	43,255
1974–5	38,921	50,898
1975–6	41,341	55,300
1976–7	49,229	61,574

In addition to expenditure on salaries, the following figures are available for administrative expenses: 1973–4, Rs 33,729; 1974–5, Rs 40,578; 1975–6, Rs 54,946; and 1976–7, Rs 54,800. However, no details of the nature of these administrative costs are known. Income which is not used for the above purpose is either invested or spent on construction and improvement work on the shrine. The total expenditure of the shrine for the period 1973–7 was: 1973–4, Rs 458,952; 1974–5, Rs 448,666; 1975–6, Rs 526,137; and 1976–7, Rs 832,000.

The information presented above on the financial affairs of the dargāh and its attendant community is very far from complete. This is determined partly by the paucity of evidence available, and partly by the fact that this study examines the whole religious and historical context within which the dargāh has developed. There is clearly scope for considerably more research on the administration and finances of the shrine, as well as its internal politics.

10

Conclusion

The death of the Prophet Muhammad left a gulf between man and God. This gulf came in subsequent centuries to be filled by saints—intermediaries who could keep the lines of communication open between this world and the next. The development of saint-veneration in Islam was stimulated by pantheistic beliefs among converts to the Muslim faith. Moreover, as the lifetime of Muhammad became more remote from that of his followers, substitutes for him could be found in the form of saints who were closer to their devotees both in time and space.

Mu'īn al-dīn is one such intermediary, and one of the most widely revered saints of Islam in the Indo-Pakistan subcontinent. Hundreds of thousands of pilgrims visit his shrine every year. His cult was fostered by the patronage of ruling families—the Khiljis, the Mughals, as well as local Rajput mahārājās. The shrine has become elaborate and wealthy as successive generations of devotees have commemorated their attachment to the saint by bequests, the construction of new buildings and the embellishment of old ones. The cult has been important enough politically for rulers to take pains to gain the favour of its participants and to take a hand in the internal affairs of those who attend and administer the shrine. Mu'īn al-dīn is believed to have been Allāh's appointed evangelist in Hindustan, to have been instrumental in the victory of the Muslim armies in their final invasion of India, to have had authority over Mughal emperors, to have performed countless miracles, embodied the values of Islam, to communicate readily with God and man, and to watch constantly over the welfare of his devotees.

However, this faith in Mu'īn al-dīn rests on assumptions about his life and about the origins of the cult which subsequently developed that have only very limited historical justification. Similarly the belief that Mu'īn al-dīn's earthly representative, the Diwan, is directly linked to him through ties of patrilineal descent and genealogical succession is seen to be based on meagre evidence. Furthermore, the shrine itself, held in especial reverence by the devotees, has often been the scene of exclusively material preoccupations. Rather than a spiritual elite, the dargāh community appears to the observer to be more of a privileged class intent on accumulating and safeguarding its privileges and property, characterized less by devotional enthusiasm than by its ceaseless involvement in corruption and material dispute.

At first glance, therefore, it would appear that the application of scholarly and objective standards of judgement to the subject of the life and cult of Mu'īn al-dīn results in something purely destructive, likely to cause affront to those who venerate Mu'īn al-dīn. But the question is less clear-cut.

The fact that attendants of the shrine appear to be more interested in material rather than spiritual matters has not deterred devotees of Mu'īn al-dīn from making the pilgrimage to Ajmer; rather, they come in increasing numbers. This can perhaps be explained in terms of the motives given by the devotees themselves. The majority of pilgrims go to Ajmer to petition the saint for help, or to thank him for favours that they have received. Their prayers can be seen as a form of bargaining— divine help, inspired by the intercession of Mu'īn al-dīn, in return for offerings at the shrine. The relationship between dead saint and living pilgrim is characterized by contractual obligations which are not dissimilar to those between individuals in their everyday life. If the vision of the next world is patterned on the hierarchical structure of this world, then the 'worldliness' of the shrine's community is not inappropriate. As Mu'īn al-dīn is powerful and influential in the heavenly hierarchy, then his representatives and attendants in this world should also be high in the earthly hierarchy. If they were not, this would be evidence of Mu'īn al-dīn's insignificance and lack of divine favour. The wealth and splendour of the shrine— however much such prosperity may contradict the principles of the Sufi order of which the interred saint was a member—are therefore an inevitable adjunct of a flourishing saint-cult.

Before the significance of individuals of religious importance can be understood in a way which is consistent with contemporary standards of historiography, legendary accretions must be stripped away from biographical fact. It is not unusual in the study of religious cults to find that only very few of the traditions relating to the founder himself are historically reliable.[1] Mu'īn al-dīn proves to be no exception to this.

One may conclude that it is not simply the career of an individual that creates a religious cult. The evolution of a cult only becomes intelligible if the religious attitudes which the founder is known to have personified, the ideas which his followers believe him to have embodied, and the aspirations which were current among them are considered against the historical, social and political circumstances in which these sets of ideas interacted to produce the cult.

[1] See, among other things, W. H. McLeod, *Guru Nanak and the Sikh Religion*; T. Andrae, *Muhammad, The Man and His Faith*; P. Worsley, *The Trumpet Shall Sound, A Study of Cargo-Cults in Melanesia*; and recent essays in New Testament Studies and Christology, e.g. J. Hick (ed.), *The Myth of God Incarnate*, and G. Bornkamm, *Jesus of Nazareth*.

Appendix I

The English texts to inscriptions of importance in the Ajmer Dargāh[1]

(a) An inscription in golden *nasta'līq* lettering inside the dome of the mausoleum of Muʿīn al-dīn Chishtī:[2]

(1) Lord of lords, Muʿīn al-dīn, most eminent of all the saints of the world, [is the]

(2) sun of the sphere of universe, king of the throne of the dominion of Faith.

(3) What room is there for doubt as regards his beauty and perfection? ... [there is a faulty reading of the inscription here].

(4) I have composed [another] *matlaʿ* in his praise, which, in its style is like a precious pearl:

(5) O ye, whose door is an altar for the faithful; [even] the sun and moon rub their forehead at thine threshold.

(6) It is at thine door that their foreheads are rubbed by [a] hundred thousands of kings [each as mighty] as the emperor of China.

(7) The attendants of thine shrine are all [like] Rizwān [the keeper of paradise], [while] in sanctity thine shrine is like the sublime heaven.

(8) A particle of its dust is like ambergris in nature; a drop of its water is like limpid [pure] water.

(9) The locum-tenens [Sajjāda-Nishīn] of Muʿīn Khwāja Husain, for the embellishment said this

(10) that 'the old may assume fresh hue anew, the dome of Khwāja Muʿīn al-dīn'.

(11) O Lord! As long as the sun and moon endure, may the lamp of the Chishtīs possess light!

(b) The text of the inscription over the frieze of the facade of Shāh Jahān's mosque in the Ajmer dargāh. The inscription is inlaid with black marble

---

[1] The texts of these inscriptions are all taken from A. Tirmizi's two articles on 'The Persian Inscriptions at Ajmer', *Epigraphia Indica, Arabic and Persian Supplement*, 1957–8, pp. 43–70, and 1959–60, pp. 41–56. These are included here for the sake of completeness. There is no pretence to original work in this field at Ajmer by the present author. Instead, there is a considerable debt to Tirmizi's pioneering epigraphical research—a debt acknowledged in this appendix by lengthy quotation from his articles.

[2] 'Persian Inscriptions', pp. 49–51.

occupying 66 horizontal panels; each panel contains a hemistich flanked by various attributes of God. The whole runs into 33 verses of high quality. The inscription is in masnawi form and the metre employed is a variation of the *mutāqarib*. The style of writing is *Naskh* of a very high order.[3]

(1) I have heard from the elite of happy omen that prior to [his] eternity-bound accession,

(2) Faith-cherishing refuge of the religion, of heavenly dignity, Shāh Jahān, the king,

(3) asylum of nations, lord of throne and crown, in whose reign the Divine Law prevails,

(4) after scoring victory over the Rānā, pitched up his tent at Ajmer with great dignity, pomp and felicity,

(5) for paying a visit to the shrine of the truthful Mu'īn [helper] of the world, Khwāja of the age.

(6) the refuge of truths, the receptacle of divine knowledge to whom the heaven has awarded the title of *Qutb-i 'Ālam* [pole-star of the world].

(7) [As] there was no mosque in [the enclosure of] that holy mausoleum, a desire for [constructing] a mosque arose in his heart.[4]

(8) Between the lord [Shāh Jahān] and God it was ratified that there should be a mosque in memory of him.

(9) Many revolutions of the sphere were not over when that altar of monarchs and angels

(10) occupied the seat of emperorship and sovereignty, through divine favour,

(11) girded up his loins and went ahead, not by way of formality, but through sincere intention [to put his desire into reality].

(12) By the grace of God, the work was done as desired. He laid the foundation of this mosque and it was completed.

(13) How excellent is the mosque of the king of the world which bears the stamp of the Bait al-Muqaddas [the name given to the mosque in Jerusalem]!

(14) How happy is the dignity of this house that on account of its sanctity is the companion of the Holy *Ka'ba*.

(15) It is a sacred shrine like the sanctuary of Abraham; the tongue is dedicated to honourable mention for its description.

(16) It is considered a twin of the *Ka'ba*; who has beheld a mosque with such splendour and grandeur?

(17) The sun makes a broom from its rays in order that he might receive the honorofic of 'sweeper' at this place.

(18) The *Ka'ba* is visible therein at the time of prayer, having opened the door of the niche towards the Holy Sanctuary.

---

[3] Ibid., p. 62; and for the text see pp. 64–6.
[4] This either is an unintentional inaccuracy or poetic licence; for Akbar had already built his mosque in the dargāh.

(19) When you rub your fortunate face on its floor, your book of deeds becomes as white as marble [i.e. your sins are washed away].

(20) The indigent seeker has his heart attached therein; its *guldasta* is the spring-time of prayers.

(21) When the King of the World [*Shāh-i Jahān*] turned the face of supplication towards its niche, at the time of prayer,

(22) through divine favour, the niche was honoured on both sides; it had its back to one *qibla* [the Ka'ba] and its face to another [the mausoleum, or perhaps Shāh Jahān].

(23) There are two pupils that sit in the eye of the world; one is the house of Ka'ba and the other is this [the mosque].

(24) The emperor of the faith sits in the mosque as if the Ka'ba occupies the mosque for ever.

(25) In the mosque prayer is favoured with response; so happy is the one who offers prayers here!

(26) The soul can be burned as incense at its pulpit from which the name of the King of the World [*Shāh-i Jahān*] is raised.

(27) To the throng of people who come to offer prayers its gate is always open as is the gate of penitence.

(28) In order that the sermon of the king may be worthy of it, it is befitting that its pulpit should be made out of the wings of angels.

(29) Its reservoir is full to the brim with the water of Zam Zam; through its niche it is door to door with the Ka'ba.

(30) Its limpid water has drawn a sword of waves to sever relations [with everything mundane].

(31) The joints of the stone have been so finely set together that you may say it was carved of a single piece.[5]

(32) Since at the behest of the Shadow of God [i.e., the king], destiny raised this edifice,

(33) Men of faith recorded for its chronogram the words: 'the edifice of the emperor of the surface of the world 1047 [AH].'

(c) The inscription recording the construction of the Sola Khamba, the burial place of Shaykh 'Allā al-dīn.[6]

(1) Khwāja Mu'īn al-dīn, the asylum of Community and Faith,

(2) Whose sublime mausoleum is a second Mecca;

(3) in the vicinity of the sepulchre of that royal falcon whose seat is the Lord's throne,

(4) and under whose royal feather lies the egg of Islam,

(5) The foundation of the mausoleum was laid by Shaykh 'Allā al-dīn,

(6) May his end be good!

[5] Tirmizi misreads the inscription here. The editor's reading and translation of this verse is therefore preferred.

[6] Tirmizi, 'Persian Inscriptions', 1959–60, p. 41.

(7) When Reason sought for the year of its completion,

(8) Wisdom said, 'Count with ease [the words] "adorned mausoleum". '

(9) 1070 [AH] [AD 1659].

(d) Inscription on the Karnātakī Dālān in the Dargāh of Mu'īn al-dīn[7]

(1) He is the Helper.

(2) In the court of the lord of both the worlds—that Mu'īn al-dīn, King of Emperors,

(3) When that Amīr al-Hind, mine of justice and equity, ocean of generosity and heaven of devotion,

(4) namely, that nawāb of elevated rank whose name is Wālā Jāh, having high station,

(5) Who is a successful ruler of the dominion of Karnātak and who is undoubtedly a favourite servant of God,

(6) With sincerity of intention and chaste truthfulness laid the foundation of a charming edifice,

(7) With a view to people reposing therein and thus it may certainly be the cause of blessings;

(8) In the reign of Shāh 'Ālam [II] the King, this abode was constructed with glory and splendour;

(9) I sought from the heart the year of its construction; it became enraptured and opened its lips,

(10) Saying, 'Since it is an edifice of Wālā Jāh, [and as] its foundation is dedicated to God,

(11) Seek the year of its construction in this benediction: 'May this blessed building endure for ever!' 1207 [AH]

(12) Seek thirty-five from the year of the king's succession, [and] it was completed in the holy month of Rajab.

(13) The devoted servants of Wālā Jāh, Muhammad Ja'far Khān, Qādir Yar Khān and 'Alī Muhammad Khān had the good fortune of supervising its construction.

---

[7] Ibid., pp. 51–2.

Appendix II

Phonetic transliteration of terms used in the text

'Abd al-'Azīz
'Abd al-Ghanī
'Abd al-Ḥaqq
'Abd al-Khair
'Abd al-Khāliq
'Abd al-Raḥman
'Abd al-Ṣamad
Abu 'l-Faẓl
Aghāṣ (pl. of ghawṣ)
Aḥādīṣ
Aḥmad
'Ālam-i Ṣaḥv
'Alī al-Mukhatib Āṣif Khān
Amīr Ḥasan Sijzī
Anīs al-Arwāḥ
Anṣārī
Aqtāb
Arḥat-i Nūr
'Arsh-i A'ẓam
'Aṣā
Awḥad al-dīn
A'ẓam
'Azīmullāh
'Azīz
Barī Sawāniḥ-i 'Umrī
Bayāẓ
Bhishtī (or Bahiṣhtī)
Bībī Aṣmat
Bībī Ḥāfiẓa Jamāl
Bīgah (or Bīga)
Dewan (= Dīwān)
Dhikr
Fatḥ Muḥammad
Fātiḥa
Futūḥ

Futūḥ al-Salāṭīn
Fuẓalā'
Gharī
Ghariyālī
Ghiyāṣ al-din Khiljī
Ghulām Murtaẓā
Gwalior (Gwāliyūr)
Ḥabīb
Ḥabibullāh
Ḥabullāh
Ḥadīṣ
Ḥajj
Ḥāfiẓa Jamāl
Ḥāfiẓ
Ḥaidar 'Alī Khān
Ḥajar al-aswad
Ḥakīm
Ḥalāl
Ḥalqa
Ḥamīd al-dīn Qalandar
Ḥamīd al-dīn Savālī
al-Ḥaqq
Ḥarām (= unlawful)
Ḥaram (= precinct)
Ḥasan
Ḥāṣilāt
Ḥavelī
Ḥayāt
Ḥaydār 'Alī
Ḥaẓrat
Ḥuffāẓ (pl. of Ḥāfiz)
Ḥujra
al-Ḥujwīrī
Ḥur al-nisā'
Ḥusain

Iḥrām-i Ziyārat
Jāmiʿ al-Ḥikāyāt
Kashf al-Maḥjūb
Lakh (or Lākh)
Maḥfil Khāna
Mahādeva
Mahārāja
Maḥbūb Subḥān
Maḥmūd
Malfūẓāt
Manṣūr
Maṣnawi
Miftāḥ al-ʿĀshiqīn
Miḥrab
Miṣāl
Miṣqāl
Muḥarram
Muḥammad Ghawṣī Shaṭṭārī
Muḥibullāh
Muḥsin
Muṣallā
Mutaṣadī
Muṭawwif
Nafaḥāt al-Uns
Najm al-dīn Ṣughrā
Naṣīrī
Nāṣir al-dīn
Nawāb (or Nawwāb)
Nazar (Anglo-Indian for Naḍhr)
Naẓar ilā ʾl-murd
Nāẓim
Niṣār Aḥmad
Niẓām
Niẓām al-dīn Awliyāʾ
Piṭhaurā
Qāẓī
Quʾrān
Quṭb
Quṭban ʿAlī
Quṭb al-dīn BakhtyārKākī Ūshī

Rabīʿ al-Ṣānī
Radwan (correctlyRiẓwān)
Raḥmatullāh
Ramaẓan
Riyāẓ Aḥmad
Sabāḥ al-dīn
Ṣādiq
Ṣadr al-dīn
Ṣadr al-Ṣudūr
Ṣafar (month)
Saḥib Maqām
Ṣandal Khāna
Ṣaub-kurta
Ṣaulat
Scindia (correctly Shinde)
Shīʿa
Shīʿite
Shīʿism
Siyar al-Aqṭāb
Ṣubadar
Ṣūbah
Subḥān Allāh
Sufi (= Ṣūfī)
Sūra Fātiḥa
Sūra al-Ḥamd
Sūra Ikhlāṣ
Surūr al-Ṣudūr
Tabaqāt-i Nāṣirī
Tāj al-Maʾāṣir
Ṭarīqa
Ṭarīqat
Tazkira
Ṭawāf
Ṭola
Tuḥfa-i Muʿīniyya
Wazīr-i Aʿẓam
Ẓafar Khān
Zamin-i Iḥyā
Zikr (= Dhikr)
Ẓiyāʾ al-dīn

Appendix III

Documents of offerings made to *khuddām*

2nd Sha'bān, AH *1084/12 November 1673*
20 *bīga* of land were given to Saiyid Dān, the *wakīl* of the donor, to finance his *khānqāh*.[1]

1st Sha'bān, AH *1087/9 October 1676*
A *khādim*, named Habullāh, establishes that he is the rightful recipient of a regular gift to the dargāh from money raised by a levy on every cart-load of copper in the *kotri* of Darabachinpur in the *sarkār* of Chittor. Formerly this money was given to the faqīrs of the dargāh; now it is for the exclusive use of Saiyid Habullāh, who is instructed to busy himself in praying for the well-being and longevity of the Emperor.[2]

AH *1094/1682–3*
Raja Amroda Singh of Bundi bestows the village of Chanigapur on his *wakīl*, Saiyid Ja'far.[3]

2nd Regnal Year of Farūkh Siyar (1714)
Muhammad Murād is the *wakīl* of Ja'far Khān Nāsirī and has received an elephant, a horse, and some gold trinkets from him. These were offerings to the dargāh made through his *wakīl*. Evidently there has been some dispute over the right of Muhammad Murād to keep them for himself. In this document he is appealing to the court of Farūkh Siyar to uphold what he believes are his rights.[4]

Jumādā I, 7th Regnal Year of Farūkh Siyar (1719)
Muhammad Namdar Khān and Qalandar 'Alī Khān, both *jāgīrdārs*, grant 15 *bīga* of land from the area of Chandina to Saiyid Jahāngīr and his sons, Saiyid Rāj, Muhammad and Saiyid Ghulām Murtazā.[5]

3rd Jumādā I, 3rd Regnal Year of Muhammad Shāh (1 April 1721)
Azīm Khān, *jāgīrdār* of Ajmer, gives 700 rupees as an offering to the shrine of his *wakīl*, Saiyid Sharīfullāh, son of Habībullāh.[6]

19th Rajab, 8th Regnal Year of Muhammad Shāh (23 March 1726)
A letter from a devotee to his *wakīl* enclosing a gift of Rs 96 in return for

---

[1] *Ajmer Documents*, p. 246. [2] Ibid., p. 248. [3] Ibid., p. 250.
[4] Ibid., p. 288. [5] Ibid., p. 281. [6] Ibid., p. 297.

which he expects prayers to be said for him in the dargāh on his behalf and some *tabarruk* to be sent to him.[7]

3rd Shawwāl, 9th Regnal Year of Muhammad Shāh (24 May 1727)
Azīm Khān sends Rs 3000 to his *wakīl*, Saiyid Sharifullāh.[8]

Reign of 'Ālamgīr II (1754–9)
Mahārājā Sawā'ī Madhū Singh writes to his *wakīl*, Saiyid Mas'ūd. The Mahārājā acknowledges receipt of some *tabarruk* and sends a money offering in return. He expresses a wish that his *wakīl* will continue to pray for him at the shrine.[9]

Reign of Shāh 'Ālam II, AH 1173/1759–60
Another letter from Mahārājā Sawā'ī Madhū Singh to his *wakīl*, Saiyid Mas'ūd, thanking him for some more *tabarruk* that he has received and sending in return some money as an offering for the shrine.[10]

13th Shawwāl, AH 1177/ 14 April 1764
A document from the Court of Manh Singh, Mahārājā of the State of Kishengarh, in answer to an appeal from his *wakīls*, Saiyid Rajab 'Alī and Muhammad 'Alī, son of Rahmatullāh, son of 'Ināyatullāh. The *wakīls* claimed that a former Mahārājā of Kishengarh had bestowed 129 *bīga* of land on their grandfather, 'Ināyatullāh, but that their family had subsequently lost the original *sanad* which legitimized the bequest and wanted another copy. Their claim was accepted by Manh Singh who issued another document granting the same land to their family in perpetuity on condition that they continued to pray for the well-being of the Mahārājās of Kishengarh at the shrine.[11]

2nd Safar, AH 1204/22 October 1789
Allāh Bakhsh and Husain Bakhsh grant 10 *bīga* of their landholding near Shahjahanabad, Rampur, to their *wakīl*, Mīyān Qalandar Bakhsh, son of Saiyid Taj Muhammad.[12]

Reign of Akbar Shāh II, AH 1231/1815–16
The Nawāb of Lohārū grants Rs 450 annually to his *wakīls*, Saiyid Sadar 'Alī and Saiyid Bayātullāh.[13]

---

[7] Ibid., p. 299.   [8] Ibid., p. 300.   [9] Ibid., p. 320.   [10] Ibid., p. 323.
[11] Ibid. There is additional evidence for the connection between the Kishengarh Court and the Ajmer Dargāh in the form of a miniature by Amar Chand, dated c. A.D. 1760–66. The painting depicts Mīr 'Umar, *mutawalli* of the shrine, attending a moonlight singing party presided over by Sardar Singh at his palace at Rupnagar, see E. Dickenson and K. Khandalawala, *Kishengarh Painting*, p. 38.
[12] Ibid., p. 326.   [13] Ibid., p. 331.

26th Dhu al-Qaʿda, AH *1230/29 October 1815*
Shāh Muhammad Khwāja Bakhsh Ahmadī grants 5 *bīga* of land from his holding in the Saharanpur district to his *wakīl*, Mīyān Qalandar Bakhsh. He mentions that the ancestors of Shaykh Qalandar Bakhsh have been the *wakīls* of his family for many past generations.[14]

15th Rabīʿ II, AH *1240/7 December 1824*
The Nawāb of Thonk, Bahādur Mīr Khān, grants Rs 100 per annum to his *wakīl*, Mīr Qazim ʿAlī, son of Saiyid Muhammad Hayāt.[15]

26th Jumādā II, AH *1251/ 19 October 1835*
The Nawāb of Bahāwalpūr, Muhammad Khān Abhāsī, gives one maun of sesamum oil to his *wakīl*, Saiyid Kamar ʿAlī Shāh.[16]

[14] Ibid., p. 333.   [15] Ibid., p. 334.   [16] Ibid., p. 335.

Appendix IV

A digest of Mughal *madad i ma'ash* documents

AH *967 / 8 February 1560.*
A previous grant of 20 *bīga* of land including two wells, in favour of Shaykh Qutban 'Alī is confirmed.[1]

AH *984 / 28 May 1576.*
Akbar grants 6890 *bīga* to Shaykh Fathullāh and his brothers. The land consisted of 4200 *bīga* of cultivated land and 2690 *bīga* of uncultivated wasteland. The revenue of 1000 *bīga* of this land was to be assigned to the expenses of the 'urs, while the remainder was for the maintenance of the grantees.[2]

AH *995 / 1586–7.* Akbar grants 240 *bīga* of land to a *khādim* named Shaykh Ismā'īl.[3]

AH *1023 / 1614–15.* Jahāngīr grants 400 *bīga* to Saiyid Khubullāh, Saiyid Karamullāh, and Muhammad Raza.[4]

AH *1026–30 / 1617–21.* Between these years several *farmāns* were issued, all of which were concerned with a prolonged controversy over Jahāngīr's grants of land to the *khādim* community, which, at that time, numbered 229. He bestowed a total of 27,310 *bīga* on the *khuddām*. However, when Jahāngīr visited Ajmer, only 198 *khuddām* presented themselves to him at court. The 31 *khuddām* who failed to go to the imperial court had all their land (1866 *bīga*) confiscated and the remaining 198 *khuddām* had their land grants

---

[1] *Ajmer Documents*, p. 11.
[2] Ibid., pp. 5–6. The difficulties of computing the actual value of these land grants are legion, but it is possible to obtain a very approximate idea. The *Ā'īn-i Akbarī* records that the revenue demand for the Ajmer area averaged out at 11 *dām* per *bīga* (vol. II, p. 272). The grantee was allowed to collect and keep the land-revenue. So the value of Shaykh Fathullāh's grant was 11 multiplied by 6890 *dām* per *bīga* per annum = 75,790 *dām* per annum, of which 11,000 *dām* were to be set aside for the expenses of the 'urs. This left Shaykh Fathullāh and his brothers with 64,790 *dām* per annum. 40 *dām* was equal to one rupee. So their annual income was approximately Rs 1618. This method of computation has no claim to great accuracy. It leaves out of account such factors as the quality of the land, the proportion cultivated and uncultivated and the relative values of the crops grown. An income of 1618 Akbarī rupees per annum—approximately Rs 135 per month—compares, for example, with Rs 7–8 per month for a cavalry private, or 1½ rupees per month for a camel-driver. (W. H. Moreland, *India at the Death of Akbar*, pp. 75, 191–2.)
[3] Ibid., p. 19.   [4] Ibid., p. 40.

reduced from a total of 25,450 *bīga* to 5161 *bīga*. (The discrepancy here of 6 *bīga* can perhaps be explained by a clerical error.) The whole *khādim* community was far from satisfied by this treatment and followed Jahāngīr to Malwa and Mandu where he stayed for the next eight months. The *khuddām* continually petitioned the Emperor and eventually succeeded in obtaining a new set of *farmāns*. These still did not benefit the thirty-one who had not presented themselves to Jahāngīr on his arrival at Ajmer, but half the original quota of land of the remaining *khuddām* was returned to them (i.e., a total of 12,725 *bīga*). All this land was situated in and around two villages, Bhir and Konkinawas, in the area surrounding Ajmer.[5]

4th Ramadan, AH *1020/10 November 1611.* A previous grant of 140 *bīga* in favour of Shaykh Chandan is confirmed.[6]

AH *1024/1615–16.* Jahāngīr grants 36 *bīga* of land to Hajjī Muhammad.[7]

AH *1024/1615–16.* 230 *bīga* of land is redistributed in favour of Bibi Jan and other *khādim* widows.[8]

23rd Jumāda II, AH *1092/10 July 1681.* The Emperor Aurangzēb grants 30 *bīga* of cultivated land to Shaykh Bayāzīd, who is said to be a very old man with no other source of income.[9]

AH *1092/1681–2.* 30 *bīga* are granted in favour of Saiyid Ayyūb[10]
4th Rabī‘ II, AH *1092/7 April 1681.* 30 *bīga* are granted to Saiyid A‘zam, son of Saiyid Sulaimān, who is said to be destitute with many dependants.[11]

14th Rajab, AH *1094/9th July 1683.* 45 *bīga* are granted to Saiyid Bāqir Muhammad and colleagues (an unspecified number), all of whom were scholars of Islam and had no other source of income.[12]

Reign of Shāh ‘Ālam Bahādur Shāh, 1707–12. Saiyid Muhammad ‘Āqil is granted 100 *bīga* of land.[13]

Reign of Shāh ‘Ālam Bahādur Shāh, 1707–12. Shaykh Muhammad Mumrīz, son of Shaykh Nūr Muhammad and his sons are granted 100 *bīga*.[14]

---

[5] Ibid., pp. 51–116. There were precedents for this confiscation of land grants. In the reign of Akbar, between the 40th and 48th regnal years, the Emperor issued orders which reduced by half all the land grants in the province of Gujerat See W. H. Moreland, *India at the Death of Akbar,* p. 99. Badāyūnī's grant of 100 *bīga* was made on condition that he attended the Court. After a prolonged absence, half his land was confiscated. See *Muntakhab al-Tawārīkh,* vol. 2, p. 283.

[6] *Ajmer Documents,* p. 148.   [7] Ibid., pp. 146–7.   [8] Ibid., p. 42.
[9] Ibid., pp. 229–30.   [10] Ibid., pp. 233–4.   [11] Ibid., pp. 237–8.
[12] Ibid., pp. 240–1.   [13] Ibid., p. 261.   [14] Ibid., p. 267.

29th Rabī' II, AH *1126/14 May 1714*. The Emperor Farūkh Siyar grants the village of Geegul, which had an annual revenue of Rs 949, to all the *khuddām*.[15]

27th Dhu 'l-Hijja, AH *1137/5 September 1725*. 28,000 *dām* per annum, the revenue from the village of Banuri in the environs of Ajmer are granted to the *khānqāh* run by Muhammad Saleh, *khādim* of the dargāh of Mu'īn al-dīn.[16]

[15] Ibid., p. 279.	[16] Ibid., p. 291.

Bibliography

'Abd al-Haqq Dihlawī, *Akhbār al-Akhyār*, translated into Urdu by Muhammad Latif Malik (Lahore, 1962) (AH 1641)).

Abu'l-Fazl al- 'Allāmī, *Ā'īn-i-Akbarī*, vol. 1, tr. H. Blochman, Biblio Indica (Calcutta, 1873); vols. 2 & 3, tr. H. S. Jarret, 1893–6, ed. Jadunath Sarkar (Calcutta, 1948).

—— *Akbarnāma*, tr. H. Beveridge, Biblio Indica (Calcutta, 1907–39).

Abun-Nasr, J., *The Tijaniyya* (London, O.U.P., 1965).

Afifi, Abu al-Ala, *The Mystical Philosophy of Ibn al-'Arabī* (Cambridge, C.U.P., 1939).

Ahmad, A., *An Intellectual History of Islam in India* (Edinburgh, University Press, 1969).

—— *Studies in Islamic Culture in the Indian Environment* (Oxford, Clarendon Press, 1964).

—— 'The Sufis and Sultans in pre-Mughal India', *Der Islam*, 38, 1–2 (1968), pp. 142–53.

Ahmad, A. S., *Millenium and Charisma among the Pathans. A Critical Essay in Social Anthropology* (London, Routledge and Kegan Paul, 1976).

Ajmer Documents, See Ma'nī.

Allāh Diyā, *Siyar al-Aqtāb* (Lucknow, 1877 (AH 1647)).

Alland, A., 'Possession in a Revivalist Negro Church', *Journal for the Scientific Study of Religion*, vol. 1 (1961), pp. 204–13.

Allen, N., 'The Ritual Journey, a Pattern Underlying Certain Nepalese Rituals', *Contributions to the Anthropology of Nepal*, ed. C. von Fürer-Haimendorf (Warminster Aris and Phillips, 1974).

Amīr Khurd, *Siyar al-Awliyā'*, Urdu tr. (Lahore, 1914 (AH 1388)).

Amīr Hasan Sijzī, *Fawā'id al-Fu'ād* (Delhi, 1865).

Anawarti, G. D. and Gardet, L., *La Mystique Musulmane* (Paris, J. Vris, 1961).

Andrae, Tor Muhammad, *The Man and His Faith*, tr. Menzil, T. (London, Allen and Unwin, 1956 (1932).

Ansari, G., 'Muslim Caste in India', *Eastern Anthropologist*, vol. 9 (1955–6), pp. 104–11.

Arnold, T., *The Preaching of Islam* (London, Constable, 1913).

—— 'Saints and Martyrs (Muhammadan India)', *Encyclopaedia of Religion and Ethics*, vol. 2 (Edinburgh, 1920), pp. 68–73.

—— 'Survivals of Hinduism among the Muhammadans of India', *Transactions of the Third International Congress of the History of Religion*, vol. 1 (1908), pp. 312–20.

Bābur, *Bāburnāma, Memoirs of Bābur*, tr. A. S. Beveridge (London, Luzac & Co., 1921).

Badāyūnī, 'Abd al-Qādir, *Muntakhab al-Tawārīkh*, vol. 1, tr. G. S. A. Ranking; vol. 2, tr. W. H. Lowe; vol. 3, tr. Sir W. Haig (Calcutta, 1898).

Baranī, Diyā' al-dīn, *Ta'rīkh-i-Fīrūzshāhi*, Biblio Indica (Calcutta, 1890).

Barth, F., *Political Leadership among the Swat Pathans* (London, Athlone Press, 1959).

Battacharjee, P. N., 'Folk-Custom and Folklore of the Sylhet District', *Man in India*, vols. 9–10 (1929–30), pp. 116–49, 244–70.

Bayley, Sir Charles S., *The Ruling Princes, Chiefs and Leading Personages in Rajputana and Ajmer* (Calcutta, 1924 (1984)).

Beg, 'Abd al-Qādir, *Collection of Persian, Urdu and English Documents Relating to the Office of the Mutawallī, Dargāh Hazrat Khwāja Muʿīn al-dīn Chishtī, Ajmer* (Ajmer, Job Press, 1941).

Begg, W. D., *The Holy Biography of Hazrat Khwāja Muʿīn al-dīn Chishtī* (Ajmer, 1960).

Berger, M., *Islam in Egypt Today* (Cambridge, C.U.P., 1970).

Bhajan, S. V., 'The Chishtī Sufis of India' (Hartford Seminary M.A. Thesis, 1959).

Bharati, A., 'Pilgrimage in the Indian Tradition', *History of Religion*, vol. 3 (1963–4), pp. 135–67.

Bhardwaj, S. M., *Hindu Places of Pilgrimage in India. A Study in Cultural Geography* (Berkeley, Los Angeles, London, University of California Press, 1973).

Bhatnagar, I. C., 'Mystic Monasticism during the Mughal Period', *Islamic Culture*, vol. XV (1941), pp. 79–90.

Birge, J. K., *The Bektashi Order of Dervishes* (London, Luzac & Co., 1937).

Bornkamm, G., *Jesus of Nazareth* (London, Hodder and Stoughton, 1960).

Broughton, T. D., *Letters from a Mahratta Camp*, Constable's Oriental Miscellany, vol. 4 (London, 1892).

Brown, J. P., *The Darweshes, or Oriental Spiritualism* (reprint, London, Frank Cass, 1968).

Brown, P., 'The Rise and Function of the Holy Man in Late Antiquity', *Journal of Roman Studies*, vol. LXI (1971), pp. 80–101.

al-Bukharī, *Les Traditions Islamiques*, tr. O. Houdas, W. Marcais, 3 vols. (Paris, Imprimerie Nationale, 1903–14).

Burridge, K. O. L., *New Heaven, New Earth: A Study of Millenarian Activities* (Oxford, Basil Blackwell, 1971).

Burton, Sir R. F., *Sindh and the Races that Inhabit the Valley of the Indus* (reprint, Karachi, O.U.P., 1972).

Carter, G. E. L., 'Religion in Sind', *Indian Antiquary*, XLVI (1917), pp. 205–8; XLVII (1918), pp. 197–208.

Cohn, B. S. and Marriott, M., 'Networks and Centres in the Integration of

Indian Civilization', *Journal of Social Research*, vol. 1 (1958), pp. 1–9.

Coryat, Thomas, *Observations of Thomas Coryat, Haklyutus Posthumus, or Purchas His Pilgrimes*, ed. S. Purchas (Glasgow, James MacLehose).

Crapanzano, V., *The Hamadsha. A Study in Moroccan Ethno-psychiatry* (Berkeley, Los Angeles, London, University of California Press, 1973).

Crooke, W., 'Notes on Saints and Shrines in U.P.', *Indian Antiquary* (1924), pp. 97–9.

——— 'Panchpiriya', *Encyclopaedia of Religion and Ethics*, vol. 9, pp. 600–1.

——— 'Pilgrimage', *Encyclopaedia of Religion and Ethics*, vol. 10, pp. 24–8.

——— *Popular Religion and Folklore of North India* (London, Constable, 1896).

Darling, M. L., *Rusticus Loquitur. The Old Light and the New in the Punjabi Village* (London, O.U.P., 1930).

Davidson, F. M., 'Shrines on the North-West Frontier', *Muslim World*, vol. 36 (1946), pp. 170–2.

Delehaye, H., *The Legends of the Saints*, tr. D. Attwater (London, Geoffrey Chapman, 1962 (1905)).

Depont, O. and Coppolani, X., *Les Confréries Religieuses Musulmanes* (Algiers, Adolphe Jourdan, 1897).

Dickenson, E. and Khandalawala, K., *Kishengarh Painting* (New Delhi, Lalit Kala Akademi, 1959).

Diehl, C. G., *Instrument and Purpose in South Indian Ritual* (London, Gleerup Lund, 1956).

Digby, S., ' 'Abd al-Quddus Gangoh. The Personality and Attitudes of a Medieval Indian Sufi', *Medieval India. A Miscellany*, vol. 3 (1975), pp. 1–66.

——— 'Crosscurrents in the Religious Life of the Delhi Sultanate.' Vol. I: 'The Rise of the Chishtī Shaykhs in Delhi and Attempts to Displace Them'. Vol. II: 'Tabarrukat and Succession in the Chishtī Silsila'. (Unpublished).

——— 'Early Pilgrimages to the Tomb of Mu'īn al-dīn Sijzī, and Other Indian Chishtī Shaykhs'. (Unpublished).

——— 'Encounters with Jogis in Indian Sufi Hagiography' (Unpublished paper delivered to S.O.A.S. Seminar on Aspects of Religion in South Asia, 1970).

——— 'Qalandars and Related Groups: Elements of Social Deviance in the Religious Life of the Delhi Sultanate of the Thirteenth and Fourteenth Centuries A.D.' (Unpublished paper delivered to Conference on Islam in S. Asia, S.E. Asia and China at University of Jerusalem, April 1977).

—— 'Sufis and Travellers in the Early Delhi Sultanate: The Evidence of the Fawā'id al-Fu'ād', *Socio-Cultural Impact of Islam in India*, ed. Altar Singh (Chandigarh, 1976), pp. 171–7.

Dixon, Lt.Col. C. G., *Report on Ajmeer and Mairwara Illustrating the Settlement of the Land Revenue and the Revenue Administration of those Districts* (Agra, 1853).

Dorn, B., *History of the Afghans* (London, J. Murray, 1829).

Douglas, Mary, *Natural Symbols. Explorations in Cosmology* (Harmondsworth, Penguin Books, 1973 (1970)).

—— *Purity and Danger. An Analysis of Concepts of Pollution and Taboo* (Harmondsworth, Penguin Books, 1970 (1966)).

Dumont, L., *Homo Hierarchicus*, tr. M. Sainsbury (London, Weidenfeld and Nicolson, 1970).

Eaton, R. M., 'The Court and the Dargāh in the Seventeenth Century Deccan', *Indian Economic and Social History Review*, vol. X (1973), pp. 50–63.

Eglar, Z., *A Punjabi Village in Pakistan* (New York, Columbia University Press, 1960).

Eickelman, D. F., *Moroccan Islam. Tradition and Society in a Pilgrimage Centre* (Austin and London, University of Texas Press, 1976).

Eliade, M., *Myths, Dreams and Mysteries*, tr. P. Mairet (London and Glasgow, Collins, 1972 (1957)).

Elliott, Sir H. M., and Dowson, J., *The History of India as Told by its Own Historians* (London, Trubner and Co., 1967–77).

Evans-Pritchard, E. E., *The Sanusi of Cyrenaica* (Oxford, O.U.P., 1949).

Farīd al-dīn Mahmūd, 'Surūr al-Sudūr', MS at Dargāh of Hamīd al-dīn Savālī, Nāgaur.

Firishta, Abu'l-Qāsim, *Ta'rīkh-i Firishta*, tr. J. Briggs as *History of the Rise of Muhammadan Power in India* (London, 1829).

Foster, W. (ed.), *Early Travels in India* (Oxford, O.U.P., 1921).

Frank, J. D., *Persuasion and Healing, A Comparative Study of Psychotherapy* (Baltimore, Johns Hopkins Press, 1961).

Friedlander, I., 'Khidr', *Encyclopaedia of Religion and Ethics*, vol. 7, pp. 693–5.

Garcin de Tassy, J. H., *Mémoire sur les Particularités de la Religion Musulmane dans l'Inde* (Paris, Adolphe Labitte, 1869).

Gardet, L., *Dieu et la Destinée de l'Homme* (Paris, J. Vrin, 1967).

Geertz, C., *Islam Observed. Religious Development in Morocco and Indonesia* (Chicago and London, 1971) University of Chicago Press, 1968).

Gellner, E., *Saints of the High Atlas* (London, Weidenfeld and Nicolson, 1969).

Gesūdarāz, Muhammad, *Jawāmiʿ al-Kilm* (Hyderabad, Intizami Press, n.d.).

Ghulām, Ahmad Khān, *Majmūʿa-i Malfūzāt-i-Khwājagān-i Chisht* (Lucknow, 1892–3).

Gibb, E .J. W., *A History of Ottoman Poetry* (London, Luzac and Co., 1958 (1950)).

Gill, M. M. and Brennan, M., *Hypnosis and Related States: Psychoanalytic Studies in Regression* (New York, John Wiley & Sons, 1966).

Gilsenan, M., *Saint and Sufi in Modern Egypt* (Oxford, Clarendon Press, 1973).

Goldziher, I., *Muslim Studies*, tr. S. M. Stern and C. R. Barber (London, Allen and Unwin, 1967–71).

Goswamy, B. N. and Grewal, J. S., *The Mughals and the Jogis of Jakhbar* (Simla, Indian Institute of Advanced Study, 1967).

—— *The Mughal and Sikh Rulers and the Vaishnavas of Pindori* (Simla, Indian Institute of Advanced Study, 1969).

Government Publications: *All-India Law Reports.*

—— *Annual Administration Reports of the Ajmer-Merwara District.*

—— *Ajmer Regulations.*

—— *Bengal Code* (1905).

—— *Census Reports of the Province of Ajmer-Merwara* (Decennial).

—— *Gazetteer of the Dera Ghazi Khan District* (1883–4).

—— *Gazetteer of the Rajputana District* (1904).

—— *Gazette of India.*

—— *Government Gazette. North West Provinces.*

—— *Report of the Dargāh Khwāja Sahib Committee of Enquiry, 1949.*

Habib, Irfan, *The Agrarian System of the Mughal Empire* (Bombay, Asia Publishing House, 1963).

Habib, Muhammad, 'Shaykh Nāsir al-dīn Chiragh of Delhi', in *Collected Works*, vol. 1, *Politics and Society during the Early Medieval Period*, ed. K. A. Nizami (New Delhi, People's Publishing House, 1974).

—— 'Chishtī Mystic Records of the Sultanate Period', *Medieval India Quarterly*, vol. 3 (1950), pp. 1–42.

—— *Hazrat Amīr Khusrau of Delhi* (Bombay, Taraporevala Sons, 1927).

—— 'Shaykh Nāsir al-dīn Mahmud Chiragh-i-Delhi as a Great Historical Personality', *Islamic Culture*, vol. XX (1946), pp. 129–53.

Habib, M. and Nizami, K. A., *A Comprehensive History of India*, vol. 5: *The Delhi Sultanate* (Delhi, People's Publishing House, 1970).

Hamid Qalandar, *Khair al-Majālis*, ed. K. A. Nizami (Aligarh, 1959).

Haq, E., 'Sufi Movements in India', *Indo-Iranica*, No. 1 (July 1948), pp. 1–12.

Haq, S., 'Samā' and Raqs of the Darwishes', *Islamic Culture*, vol. 18 (1944), pp. 111–30.

Hasan, N., 'Chishtī and Suhrawardī Movements in Medieval India' (D. Phil. thesis, Oxford University, 1948).

Hasluck, F. W., *Christianity and Islam under the Sultans* (Oxford, Clarendon Press, 1929).

Heber, Bishop R., *Narrative of a Journey through the Upper Provinces of India* (London, John Murray, 1849).

Hick, J., *The Myth of God Incarnate* (London, S.C.M. Press, 1977).

Hughes, T. P., *A Dictionary of Islam* (reprint, London, W. H. Allen, 1935).

al-Hujwīrī, 'Alī 'Usmān, *Kashf al-Mahjūb*, tr. R. A. Nicholson (reprint, London, Luzac & Co., 1976).

Husain, Y., *L'Inde Mystique an Moyen Age* (Paris, Adrien Maisonneuve, 1929).

―――― 'Sufism in India', *Islamic Culture*, vol. XXX (July 1956), pp. 239–62.

Ibbetson, Sir D., *Outlines of Panjab Ethnography being Extracts of the Panjab Census Report, 1881, Treating of Religion, Language and Caste* (Calcutta, Government Press, 1883).

Ibn Battuta, *The Rehla of Ibn Battuta*, tr. Mahdi Husain (Baroda, Oriental Institute, 1953).

Ibn Hasan, *The Central Structure of the Mughal Empire* (reprint, Karachi, O.U.P., 1976).

Ikram, M., *Muslim Civilization in India* (New York and London, Columbia University Press, 1964).

Irvine, R. H., *Some Account of the General and Medical Topography of Ajmeer* (Calcutta, W. Thacker, 1841).

Irving, M., 'The Shrine of Bābā Farīd Shakarganj in Pakpattan', *Journal of the Panjab Historical Society*, vol. 1 (1911), pp. 70–7.

Isamī, *Futūh al-Salātīn*, ed. Usha (Madras, 1948).

Islam, R., 'A Survey in Outline of the Mystic Literature of the Sultanate Period', *Journal of the Pakistan Historical Society*, vol. 3 (1955), pp. 201–8.

Izutsu, T., *Ethico-Religious Concepts in the Koran* (Montreal, McGill University Press, 1966).

―――― *God and Man in the Koran* (Tokyo, Kèio Institute of Cultural and Linguistic Studies, 1964).

Jahān, Muhammad Akbar, *Ta'rīkh-i-Khwāja-i Ajmer* (Ajmer, 1903).

Jahāngīr, *Tuzuk-i Jahāngīr*, tr. A. Rogers, ed. H. Beveridge (London, Luzac and Co., 1909–14).

Jamālī, *Siyar al-'Ārifīn* (Delhi, 1893 (AH 1530–36)).

Jāmī, 'Abd al-Rahman, *Nafahāt-al-Uns* (1476–79).

Jameson, A. S., 'Gangaguru. The Public and Private Life of a Brahmin Community of North India' (D. Phil. thesis, Oxford University, 1976).

Karim, A. K. N., 'Some Aspects of Popular Belief among the Muslims of Bengal', *Eastern Anthropologist*, vol. 9 (1955–6), pp. 29–46.

Khān, Amīn al-dīn, *Kitab al-Tahqiq* (Ajmer, 1946).

Khān, Ghāzī, *The Khadims of the Khwaja Sahib of Ajmer and the Baneful Effects of the Dargah Khwaja Sahib Bill on their Rights* (Ajmer, 1936).

Lammens, H., *Islam, Beliefs and Institutions*, tr. E. Denison Ross (London, Methuen and Co., 1929).

Lane, E. W., *Manners and Customs of the Modern Egyptians* (London, Everyman, 1836 (1908)).

Le Chatelier, A., *Les Confréries Musulmanes du Hedjaz* (Paris, Bibliothèque Orientale Elzevirienne, 1887).

LeStrange, G., *The Lands of the Eastern Caliphate* (Cambridge, C.U.P., 1095).

Lévi-Strauss, C., *Structural Anthropology*, tr. Claire Jacobson and Brooke Grundfest Schoepf (London, Allen Lane, 1963).

Lewis, I. M., 'Sufism in Somaliland. A Study in Tribal Islam', *Journal of the British School of Oriental Studies*, vol. 17 (1955), pp. 581–602; and vol. 18 (1956), pp. 145–60.

Lings, M., *A Sufi Saint of the Twentieth Century* (London, Allen and Unwin, 1971 (1961)).

Macdonald, D. B., 'Emotional Religion in Islam as Affected by Music and Singing', *Journal of the Royal Asiatic Society* (1901), pp. 195–252, 705–48; (1902), pp. 1–28.

McLeod, W. H., *Guru Nanak and the Sikh Religion* (Oxford, Clarendon Press, 1968).

Malinowski, B., *Magic, Science and Religion*, ed. R. Redfield (New York, Doubleday, 1954 (1926)).

Mandelbaum, D. G., *Society in India* (Berkeley, Los Angeles and London, University of California Press, 1970).

Ma'nī, *A Collection of Persian and Urdu Documents Relating to the Ajmer Dargāh* (Bombay, 1952).

Manucci, N., *Memoirs of the Mughal Court*, ed. M. Edwardes (London Folio Society, 1957).

Marriott, McKim, 'Little Communities in an Indigenous Civilisation', in *Village India*, ed. McKim Marriott (Chicago, University of Chicago Press, 1955).

Massignon, L., *Essai sur les Origines du Lexique Technique de la Mystique Musulmane* (Paris, Paul Geuthner, 1954 (1922)).

Mayer, A. C., 'Pirs and Murids in West Pakistan', *Middle Eastern Studies*, vol. 3 (1966–7), pp. 160–9.

Mrs Meer Hasan Ali, *Observations on the Mussulmauns of India*, ed. W. Crooke (reprint, London, New York and Delhi, O.U.P., 1974).

Minhāj al-Sirāj Jūzjānī, *Tabaqāt-i Nāsirī*, tr. H. G. Raverty (London, Asiatic Society of Bengal, 1881).

Misra, S. C., *Muslim Communities in Gujerat* (London, Asia Publishing House, 1964).

Moreland, W. H., 'The Agricultural Statistics of Akbar's Empire', *Journal of the United Provinces Historical Society*, Lucknow, vol. 2, part 1 (June 1919), pp. 1–39.

—— *The Agrarian System of Muslim India* (Cambridge, Heffers, 1922).

—— 'Akbar's Land Revenue System as Described in the *Ā'īn-i Akbarī*',

Journal of the Royal Asiatic Society, London (January 1918), pp. 1–43.

——— *From Akbar to Aurangzeb. A Study in Indian Economic History* (London, Macmillan and Co., 1923).

——— *India at the Death of Akbar* (London, Macmillan and Co., 1920).

——— 'Prices and Wages under Akbar', *Journal of the Royal Asiatic Society*, London (October 1917), pp. 815–25.

——— 'The Value of Money at the Court of Akbar', *Journal of the Royal Asiatic Society*, London (1918), pp. 375–85.

Morton, A. H., 'The Ardabil Shrine in the Reign of Shah Tahmasp I', *Iran. Journal of the British Institute of Persian Studies*, vol. 12 (1974), pp. 31–64; vol. 13 (1975), pp. 39–58.

Mu'īn al-dīn Chishtī, '*Anis al-Arwāh*, Discourses of Khwāja 'Usmān Hārwanī', tr. into Urdu by Ghulām Ahmad Khān in *Majmū'a-i Malfūzāt-i Khwājagān-i Chisht*, 1892–3.

——— *Ganj al-Asrār*, tr. into Urdu by Muhammad Yūsuf 'Alī Shāh, 1890.

——— 'Letters Addressed to Khwāja Qutb al-dīn Bakhtyār Kākī', MS. India Office Library.

Mundy, Peter, *The Travels of Peter Mundy* (London, Hakluyt Society, 1914).

Mujeeb, M., *The Indian Muslims* (London, Allen and Unwin, 1967).

Nasr, S. H., *The Ideals and Realities of Islam* (New York, Praeger, 1967).

——— 'The Influence of Sufism on Traditional Persian Music', *Islamic Culture*, vol. 45 (1971), pp. 176–9.

——— *Sufi Essays* (London, Allen and Unwin, 1972).

National Archives of India, *A Calendar of Persian Correspondence* (New Delhi, 1949).

Nicholson, R. A., *The Mystics of Islam* (London and Boston, Routledge and Kegan Paul, 1975 (1914)).

——— *Studies in Islamic Mysticism* (Cambridge, C.U.P., 1921).

Nizami, K. A., 'Some Aspects of Khānqāh Life in Medieval India', *Studia Islamica*, vol. 8 (1957), pp. 51–69.

——— *Some Aspects of Religion and Politics in Thirteenth Century India* (Bombay, Asia Publishing House, 1961).

——— 'Chishtiyya', *Encyclopaedia of Islam* (New Edition), vol. 2, pp. 50–6.

——— 'Early Indo-Muslim Mystics and their Attitude towards the State', *Islamic Culture*, vol. 22 (1948), pp. 387–98; vol. 23, pp. 13–21, 162–70, 312–21; vol. 24, pp. 60–71.

——— 'Iltutmish the Mystic', *Islamic Culture*, vol. 20 (1946), pp. 165–80.

——— 'Khwāja Mu'īn al-dīn Hasan Chishtī', *Encyclopaedia of Islam* (New Edition), vol. 2, pp. 49–50.

——— *The Life and Times of Shaykh Farīd Ganj-i Shakar* (Delhi, Idarah-i-Adabiyat, 1955).

—— *Studies in Medieval Indian History and Culture* (Allahabad, Kitab Mahal, 1966).

O'Brien, Major A. J., 'The Muhammadan Saints of the Western Panjab', *Journal of the Royal Anthropological Institute*, vol. 41 (1911), pp. 509–20.

O'Brien, D. B. Cruise, *The Mourides of Senegal* (Oxford, Clarendon Press, 1971).

Oppler, M. E., 'The Extensions of an Indian Village', *Journal of Asian Studies*, vol. 16 (1956), pp. 497–505.

Patton, W. M., 'Saints and Martyrs (Muhammadan)', *Encyclopaedia of Religion and Ethics*, vol. 2, pp. 63–8.

Pelsaert, F., *Jahāngīr's India. The Remonstratie of Francisco Pelsaert*, tr. W. H. Moreland and P. Geyl (Cambridge, W. Heffer, 1925).

Prince of Wales Museum, Bombay, *Indian Art*, 1964.

Qanungo, K. R., *Sher Shah* (Calcutta, Kar, Majumder, 1921).

Quddusī, Rukn al-dīn, *Lata'if-i Quddusī* (Delhi, Mujitabai Press, 1894).

Qurban 'Alī, *Hasht Bahisht* (Aligarh, Matba Institute, n.d.).

Qutb al-dīn Bakhtyār Kākī, 'Dalil al-'Ārifin', Discourses of Mu'īn al-dīn Chishtī, tr. into Urdu by Ghulām Ahmad Khān in *Majmū'a-i Malfūzāt-i Khwājagān-i Chisht*, 1892–3.

Rahaman, Saiyid Sabāh al-dīn, 'A Critical Study of the Dates of Birth and Death of Hazrat Khwāja Mu'īn al-dīn Chishtī of Ajmer', *Indo-Iranica*, vol. 17 (1964), pp. 29–32.

Rashid, A., *Society and Culture in Medieval India* (Calcutta, Firma K. L. Mukhopadhyay, 1969).

Rizvi, S. A. A., *Muslim Revivalist Movements in Northern India in the Sixteenth and Seventeenth Centuries* (Agra, Agra University Press, 1965).

—— *Religion and Intellectual History of the Muslims in Akbar's Reign* (New Delhi, Munshiram Manoharlal, 1975).

Robson, T., *Tracts on Listening to Music* (London, Royal Asiatic Society, 1938).

Rose, H., *A Glossary of the Tribes and Castes of the Panjab* (Lahore, 1911–19).

—— 'Shrines in the Panjab', *Journal of the Panjab Historical Society*, vol. 3 (1914–15), pp. 194–6.

Rose, H. and Elliott, Major A. C., 'The Chuhas, or Rat Children of the Panjab and Shah Daula', *Indian Antiquary*, vol. 38, pp. 27–32.

Sadler, A. W., 'A Visit to a Chishtī Qawwāli', *Muslim World*, vol. 53 (1963), pp. 287–92.

Salim, M., 'Reappraisal of the Sources on Mu'īn al-dīn', *Journal of the Pakistan Historical Society*, vol. 16 (1968), pp. 145–52.

Sarda, H., *Ajmer, Historical and Descriptive* (Ajmer, Fine Art Printing Press, 1941).

Sargant, W., *Battle for the Mind* (London, Heinemann, 1957).

Sarkar, Sir J., *Anecdotes of Aurangzeb and Historical Essays* (Calcutta, M. C. Sarkar and Sons, 1912).

—— *History of Aurangzeb* (Calcutta, M. C. Sarkar and Sons, 1912–24).

Schimmel, A., *Mystical Dimensions of Islam* (Chapel Hill, University of North Carolina Press, 1975).

Sell, E., *The Religious Orders of Islam* (Madras, 1908).

Sen, S. R. (editor), *Indian Travels of Thevenot and Coreri* (Delhi, National Archives of India, 1949).

Shackle, C., 'Some Problems of Islamic Sociology in S.E. Asia' (B. Litt. Thesis, Oxford University, 1966).

Sharib, Z. H., *Khwaja Gharib Nawaz* (Lahore, Muhammad Ashraf, 1961).

Sharif, Ja'far, *Islam in India, or Qanun-i-Islam*, tr. G. A. Herklots, ed. W. Crooke (London and Dublin, Curzon Press, 1972).

Sharma, D., *Early Chauhan Dynasties* (Delhi, S. Chand and Co., 1959).

—— *Social Life in Medieval Rajasthan* (Agra, Lakshmi Narain Agarwal, 1968).

Shattārī, Muhammad Ghausī, *Gulzār-i Abrār* (Agra, 1908 (1605–13)).

Sleeman, Major-General Sir W. H., *Rambles and Recollections of an Indian Official* (London, Hatchard and Sons, 1844).

Smith, M., *Readings from the Mystics of Islam* (London, Luzac and Co., 1972 (1950)).

Smith, W. C., *Modern Islam in India* (London, Victor Gollancz, 1946).

Spencer-Trimingham, J., *The Sufi Orders in Islam* (London, Oxford and New York, 1973 (1971)).

Storey, C. A., *Persian Literature: A Bio-Bibliographical Survey*, vol. 1, Part 2 (London, Luzac and Co., 1953).

Subhan, J. A., *Sufism. Its Saints and Shrines* (New York, Samuel Weiser, 1970 (1938)).

Suhrawardī, Shihāb al-dīn Umar, *Awārif al-Ma'ārif*, tr. H. Wilberforce Clarke (Calcutta, 1891).

Sumption, J., *Pilgrimage. An Image of Medieval Religion* (London, Faber, 1975).

Swan, G., 'Saintship in Islam', *Muslim World*, vol. 5 (1915), pp. 229–39; vol. 8 (1918), pp. 259–62.

al-Tabatabai, Muhammad Husain, *Shi'ite Islam*, tr. and ed. S. H. Nasr (London, Allen and Unwin, 1975).

Tambiah, S. J., 'The Ideology of Merit and the Social Correlates of Buddhism in a Thai Village', in *Dialectic in Practical Religion*, ed. E. Leach, pp. 41–121 (Cambridge, C.U.P., 1968).

Tara Chand, *Influence of Islam on Indian Culture* (reprint, Allahabad, The Indian Press, 1976 (1922)).

Temple, Sir R. C., 'A General View of the Indian Muslim Saints' (MS, British School of Oriental and Africn Studies).

—— *Legends of the Panjab* (Bombay, Education Society's Press, 1884–5).

Tirmizi, A. A., 'Persian Inscriptions at Ajmer', *Epigraphia Inica, Arabic and Persian Supplement* (1957–8), pp. 43–70; (1959–60), pp. 41–56.

Titus, M., *Indian Islam* (London, O.U.P., 1930).

—— *Islam in India and Pakistan* (Calcutta, Y.M.C.A. Press, 1959).

Tod, J., *Annals and Antiquities of Rajasthan or The Central and Western Rajput States of India*, ed. W. Crooke (reprint, London, O.U.P., 1920).

Turner, B. S., *Weber and Islam* (London, Routledge and Kegan Paul, 1975).

Turner, V., *The Ritual Process. Structure and Anti-Structure* (London, Routledge and Kegan Paul, 1969).

—— 'The Centre Out There: Pilgrim's Goal', *History of Religions*, vol. 12 (1973), pp. 191–230.

—— *Dramas, Fields and Metaphors* (Cornell, Cornell University Press, 1975).

Van Gennep, A., *Les Rites de Passage*, tr. M. B. Vizedom and G. L. Caffee (reprint, London, Routledge and Kegan Paul, 1960 (1909)).

Vidyarthi, L. P., *The Sacred Complex in Hindu Gaya* (London, Asia Publishing House, 1961).

von Grunebaum, G. E., *Muhammadan Festivals* (London, Curzon Press, 1976 (1951)).

Watt, W. M., *Islam and the Integration of Society* (London, Routledge and Kegan Paul, 1961).

Wensinck, A. J., 'Ka'ba', *Encyclopaedia of Islam* (New Edition), vol. 4, p. 320.

Westermarck, E., *Pagan Survivals in Muhammadan Civilisation* (London, Macmillan and Co., 1933).

—— *Ritual and Belief in Morocco* (London, Macmillan and Co., 1962).

Westphal-Hellbusch, S. and Westphal, H., *The Jat of Pakistan* (Berlin, Duncker and Humbolt, 1964).

Wilber, D. N., *Pakistan* (New Haven, H.R.A.F. Press, 1964).

Wilson, B. R., *Magic and the Millenium* (London, Heinemann, 1973).

Wiser, W. H., *The Hindu Jajmani System* (Lucknow, Lucknow Publishing Co., 1936).

Wise, J. 'The Muhammadans of Eastern Bengal', *Journal of the Asiatic Society of Bengal*, vol. 63 (1894), pp. 28–63.

Worsley, P., *The Trumpet Shall Sound. A Study of 'Cargo' Cults in Melanesia* (London, MacGibbon and Kee Ltd, 1957).

Yasin, Muhammad, *A Social History of Islamic India* (Delhi, Munshiram Manoharlal, 1974 (1958)).

Yazdani, G., *Mandu: The City of Joy* (Oxford, O.U.P., 1929).

Index

People

214   *Index*